Eros and Androgyny

Eros and Androgyny

The Legacy of Rose Macaulay

Jeanette N. Passty

Rutherford ● Madison ● Teaneck
Fairleigh Dickinson University Press
London and Toronto: Associated University Presses

© 1988 by Associated University Presses, Inc.

Associated University Presses
440 Forsgate Drive
Cranbury, NJ 08512

Associated University Presses
25 Sicilian Avenue
London WC1A 2QH, England

Associated University Presses
P.O. Box 488, Port Credit
Mississauga, Ontario
Canada L5G 4M2

The paper used in this publication meets the requirements
of the American National Standard for Permanence of Paper
for Printed Library Materials Z39.48-1984.

Library of Congress Cataloging-in-Publication Data

Passty, Jeanette N.
  Eros and androgyny.

  Bibliography: p.
  Includes index.
  1. Macaulay, Rose, Dame—Criticism and interpretation.
2. Sex in literature.   3. Sex role in literature.
4. Women in literature.   5. Feminism in literature.
6. Androgyny (Psychology) in literature.   I. Title.
PR6025.A16Z86   1988   823′.912   85-46027
ISBN 0-8386-3284-X (alk. paper)

Printed in the United States of America

For
Professors James H. Durbin, Jr., and Gregory B. Passty
"And gladly wolde he lerne and gladly teche."

In point of fact, those who establish the virtues of writers are the writers themselves, however intelligently posterity may write essays on them.

—Rose Macaulay

Contents

Acknowledgments

A SCHOLARLY BOOK is a composite of the efforts of a multitude of individuals of varying talents, of great industry, and of even greater good will. The contributions of many of these individuals are rigorously detailed in the notes to the text, but I wish to enumerate them here with heartfelt gratitude. This book owes its inception to Professor James H. Durbin, Jr., Department of English, University of Southern California. In the ten years since he first recommended I should write on Rose Macaulay, I have benefited greatly from Professor Durbin's wisdom, wit, and erudition, and from his meticulous emendations to my text. John Halperin, Centennial Professor, Department of English, Vanderbilt University, critiqued my manuscript, chapter by chapter, and offered innumerable suggestions for its enrichment. Professor Jane Marcus, formerly my colleague at The University of Texas at Austin, now at CUNY Graduate School and The City College of New York, provided me with courage, counsel, and countless reprints and references crucial to my work. Professor Nancy Topping Bazin, Chair, Department of English, Old Dominion University, generously shared her perceptions of androgyny in general, and of Rose Macaulay in particular. Professor Azizah al-Hibri, Department of Philosophy, Washington University, St. Louis, Missouri, provided pre-prints of her own research and enthusiastically encouraged mine. Brother Eldridge Pendleton, Ph.D., Assistant Archivist for the Society of Saint John the Evangelist in Cambridge, Massachusetts, supplied a wealth of newly catalogued material that included two Rose Macaulay letters heretofore unexamined by any scholar. In the best tradition of academic spouses, my husband, Professor Gregory B. Passty, Department of Mathematics, Southwest Texas State University, shared manfully in the child care, the housework, the typing of a preliminary draft of this manuscript, and in several years' worth of minutiae essential to its completion in final form. Credit for the initial realization of the source for *Trebizond* is his.

For personal reminiscences concerning Rose Macaulay and/or her readership, I am greatly indebted to the following: the late Professor Alan Gabriel Barnsley (Gabriel Fielding), Lord Bonham-Carter, Professor Donald Johnson Greene, Naomi Haldane Mitchison (Lady Mitchison).

The following libraries and archives provided research materials and a multitude of invaluable reference services: the Doheny Memorial and College Libraries, University of Southern California; the Harry Ransom Hu manities Research Center and the Perry-Castañeda Library, The University of Texas at Austin; the Blumberg Memorial Library and the Center for Women Studies, Texas Lutheran College; the San Marcos Public Library; the Southwest Texas State University Library; the Suzzallo Library, University of Washington at Seattle; the National Library of Canada; the Society of St. John the Evangelist, Cambridge, Massachusetts.

For research assistance, scholarly insights, emotional support, and a multitude of other, indispensable services, I wish also to thank the following individuals: Kay Banning, Helen Barber, Professor Alice R. Bensen, Professor Ronald E. Bruck, Dorothy Esther Cady, Yolanda Cavazos, John Chalmers, Ellen Clark, Crystal Collins, Ken Craven, Professor Richard John Dunn, Professor Dennis R. Estes, Patrice S. Fox, Professor Barbara Gibbs, Professor Gloria S. Gross, Father Frederick C. Gross, S.S.J.E., Margo Gutierrez, Ofelia Guzman, Cathy Henderson, Professor Angela Ingram, Professor Harry Keyishian, John Kirkpatrick, Frances A. Koopmann, Stephanie Langenkamp, May E. Macnamara, Dr. Juanita Mantovani, Carol McClung, Cathy Mear, Mollie Nyda, Benjamin W. B. Passty, Heather Erika Passty, Diane Pilcher, Jeanne Rector, Nancy Revelette, Brother John Paul Roberts, S.S.J.E., Adelle ("Fritzi") Robinson, Danielle Robinson, Shelley Rode, David Rosso, Tammy Rosso, Denise Scales, Father Superior M. Thomas Shaw, S.S.J.E., Mel Simoneau, Father Robert C. Smith, S.S.J.E., Susan Smith, Cathe Thomas, Kathy Walton, Professor Thomas G. Wilkens, Stephen Wilkison, Peggy O'Neal Abel, M.D., Roy Flukinger, Dr. James Halseth, Theresa Holloway, Barbara McCandless, Kathryn Pinto, Deborah J. Well, Brenda Wisian, Julien Yoseloff, Professor Stephen H. Statham.

I wish also to express my sincere appreciation to Krista Wittman, who typed this manuscript with assistance from Susanne Fawcett and Nancy Till, and who creatively and capably assisted with the "Abbot Daniel" transcription. Finally, I want to thank Beth Gianfagna, my editor, for years of empathy and encouragement, above and beyond the call of duty; Jill Kushner, who copy edited the manuscript; and Professor W. Preston Reeves for his photoreproduction of "The New Woman—Wash Day" (© 1901 by R. Y. Young) from the files of the Center for Women Studies, Texas Lutheran College.

Grateful acknowledgment is made to the following for permission to quote from the correspondence and other published and unpublished writings of Dame Rose Macaulay and Father Hamilton Johnson, S.S.J.E.: Constance Babington Smith, M.B.E., F.R.S.L., for the Rose Macaulay Estate; Father Superior M. Thomas Shaw and the Society of Saint John the Evangelist; Ms. Cathy Henderson, Research Librarian, on behalf of the Harry Ransom Humanities Research Center, The University of Texas at Austin.

All Rose Macaulay quotations are reprinted by permission of A D Peters & Co Ltd.

Introduction
"Dear Mr. Adcock, . . ."

IN THE FILES of the Humanities Research Center at The University of Texas at Austin, there is a letter from author Rose Macaulay to Mr. Arthur St. John Adcock of the Bookman Literary Circle:

29th January 1929

Dear Mr. Adcock,
  Thank you for your letter. I am afraid I should not know how even to start an article on whether women feel amusement or not. It would be as difficult as to start producing evidence as to whether they can feel grief, or annoyance, or any other of the ordinary human emotions. Will the world never tire of these fatuities?[1]

Virtually every novel by Rose Macaulay seeks to articulate the common humanity of women with men, to give voice to the needs of men for gentleness and beauty, to give vent to the anger of women deprived of autonomy and achievement. Here, then, is the social legacy that she has left us: the steadfast belief that a human being finds true fulfillment by following the vocation and avocations most congenial to the heart and mind; the firm faith in what Sandra Gilbert has called "a gender-free reality."[2]

Gilbert's division of male and female modernists into two camps can aid us in "placing" Rose Macaulay. For the one camp—represented by Joyce, Lawrence, Yeats, and Eliot—"the hierarchical order of society is and should be a pattern based upon gender distinctions."[3] For the other camp—represented by Woolf, H. D., and Barnes and anticipated by Brontë, Dickinson, Nightingale, and Schreiner—"an ultimate reality exists only if one journeys beyond gender" to "an ontological essence so pure, so free that 'it' can 'inhabit' any self, any costume."[4] Rose Macaulay's novels, and various of her other writings, place her quite securely in the latter camp. They constitute a deliberate act of rebellion against the cultural myths that pin both men and women to Procrustean standards of masculinity and femininity, without regard to individual needs and natures. They examine—with extraordinary sociological accuracy—the positive and negative aspects of issues still relevant in our day—celibacy, sexuality, matrimony, child-bearing, child-rearing, sex roles, and sexual stereotypes.

This book-length study—the first treatise on Macaulay's writings to be published in eighteen years—examines those writings for what they have to say to us today about sex roles and sexuality, as well as the social forces that encourage or inhibit both. It postulates as factors common to her novels Macaulay's erogenous and androgynous sensibilities and feminist outlook. Harvey Curtis Webster asserts, and Maria Jane Marrocco reiterates, that Rose Macaulay is

> among those writers of this century who "do not deserve the neglect they have received since it has become convenient to think of Joyce, Virginia Woolf, Dorothy Richardson, D. H. Lawrence, and E. M. Forster as the only modern novelists worth taking seriously."[5]

The author of the present biocritical analysis takes Rose Macaulay very seriously indeed, believing that *Potterism* (1920), *Dangerous Ages* (1921), *Told by an Idiot* (1923), *Orphan Island* (1924), *Crewe Train* (1926), *They Were Defeated* (1932), and *The World My Wilderness* (1950)—save for their largely infelicitous titles[6]—are exquisitely crafted novels that will prove richly revealing to critics of this generation. I believe also that *The Towers of Trebizond* is surpassed in this century only by *Orlando*, as an expression of what Herbert Marder, Nancy Topping Bazin (and Samuel Taylor Coleridge before them) hail as "the androgynous mind."[7]

Before entering empathetically into that mind, as it manifested itself in the writings of Rose Macaulay, it will be useful to remember who she was, what she wrote, and what sort of criticism she has evoked thus far.

Dame Rose Macaulay (b. 1881) was a cousin of Lord Thomas Babington Macaulay and a distinguished literary figure in her own right. In the fifty years from 1906 to 1956, she published twenty-three novels, thirteen nonfiction books, and a "formidable"[8] quantity of journalism. Widely known to readers in the British Commonwealth and on the European Continent, Macaulay was involved in an unhappy love entanglement with Rupert Brooke, hobnobbed with Virginia and Leonard Woolf, and became a beloved friend of E. M. Forster. References to her work appear in such unlikely places as the murder mysteries of Agatha Christie and Dorothy L. Sayers. Her novels *Potterism* (1920) and *The Towers of Trebizond* (1956) were bestsellers in both England and America. Honors which accrued to her included the Femina-Vie Heureuse prize (1922) and the James Tait Black Memorial prize (1957). Hailed by her contemporaries as "one of the most brilliant of living women writers,"[9] Rose Macaulay was awarded an Honorary Doctorate of Letters by Cambridge University (1951), and was created a Dame of the British Empire by Queen Elizabeth II, whose sister, Princess Margaret, contracted the habit of reading aloud passages from *Trebizond* to her friends.

Rose Macaulay died in 1958, but her enormous contribution to English letters was obvious in her lifetime and has been reaffirmed with regularity in the three decades since her death. To understand the extraordinary enthusiasm with which American and British readers embraced *Potterism*, Macaulay's satire in the cause of responsible journalism, it should be noted that, from September 1920 to March 1921, this book was *printed* by its American publisher, Boni and Liveright, at least *thirty-one* times.[10] Other editions appeared in 1950 and 1971. A survey of *Books In Print* for 1986 yields some eleven separate titles by Macaulay from twelve different publishers in sixteen separate editions. Her scholarship explicating *Some Religious Elements in English Literature* (1931) was reprinted in 1972. Her studies, [John] *Milton* (1934) and *The Writings of E. M. Forster* (1938), were both reprinted in 1974. Her collection of essays, *Personal Pleasures* (1935) is currently available from three separate publishers. *The Pleasure of Ruins*, which commemorates with impeccable scholarship architecture's greatest triumphs through the millenia, is perpetually reborn with new illustrations. The latest in a distinguished series since the first in 1953 is the 1984 edition.

But it is Rose Macaulay's fiction that constitutes her greatest legacy to English Letters. Other novels besides *Potterism* were heralded in their own time and remain enduringly popular. *They Were Defeated* (American title, *The Shadow Flies*) recreates seventeenth century Devonshire and Cambridge with such fidelity that not a single word is used in it that was not current when Cromwell took a kingdom from Charles I. John Milton, Robert Herrick, Henry More live and breathe in its pages. The book jacket of the 1960 edition wears the plaudits of the literati like medals of honor. On it, Richard Church writes: "Rose Macaulay was a literary artist. . . . It throws a light into every corner of that period of English history." Raymond Mortimer concurs: "Rose Macaulay has here brought off an astonishing feat." John Connell agrees: "A just book, a wise book, a compassionate and a brave book. An astonishingly moving experience. [In the years since its original publication in 1932,] It has lost not a whit of its freshness, but it has acquired new depths of truth and meaning, and a soft glowing beauty." And *The Times Literary Supplement* rejoices: "What an achievement it is! The thought, the allusions, the mental furniture of educated and uneducated are wholly of their time. *They Were Defeated* will convince and hearten its readers; may they be many, as the book deserves."

Subsequent reprints of Rose Macaulay's fiction met with similar appreciation from readers who felt she still had much to teach them about the barbarous aftermath of war, in *The World My Wilderness* (1950; reprint. 1983); about marital harmony and marital discord, in *Crewe Train* (1926; reprint. 1986); about woman's striving for selfhood and suffrage and man's struggle to retain the status quo, in *Told by an Idiot* (1923; reprint. 1983). Of this latter novel, an engaging narrative of several generations of the same family, but also "a splendidly animated précis of [England in] the years 1879–

1923," Professor Robert Morss Lovett declared that, save for the sardonic allusion to *Macbeth* in its title, "it might be used as a textbook in modern social history as taught in our colleges."[11]

Paradoxically, while the obvious literary merit and rich thematic and aesthetic content of books *by* Macaulay has caused them to be reprinted at an ever-accelerating rate, books *about* her have utterly vanished, save for the present one. Scholarly articles of merit have been few and far between. We shall now consider—sometimes with appreciation, sometimes with disappointment—some past efforts.

Macaulay's pre–World War II popularity with a German press and a European readership is substantiated by archival materials at The University of Texas at Austin[12] and was duly reflected by the scholarship of that era. Margarete Kluge's lengthy analysis of women characters in the novels, "Die Stellung Rose Macaulays Zur Frau" (1928) quite appropriately, as we shall see in the course of this study, describes Macaulay as "the English woman's author par excellence." Kluge's attempt to classify Macaulay's women characters into "types,"[13] and her mention of the subordinate status of men in many of the novels make her study a worthy precursor to this one. Subsequent to the appearance of Kluge's article, two of her countrywomen's dissertations on Macaulay were published. These are Margot Brussow's *Zeitbedingtes in den Werken Rose Macaulays* (1934) and Irmgard Wahl's *Gesellschaftskritik und Skeptizismus bei Rose Macaulay* (1936).

Not until 1959 did an American dissertation appear in the field, Philip Louis Rizzo's extremely useful "Rose Macaulay: A Critical Survey" (1959). Rizzo's bibliography of primary and secondary sources is invaluable. Two issues raised by his study upon which I have elaborated are those of Laurie Rennel's castration in *The Valley Captives* and of E. M. Forster's influence on the entire Macaulay corpus. Also of interest is Robert Earl Kuehn's "The Pleasures of Rose Macaulay: An Introduction to Her Novels" (1962). Kuehn's dissertation augments Rizzo's original bibliography, and, as Alice R. Bensen notes, provides a "perceptive"—if considerably derivative— "discussion of the novels."[14]

Professor Bensen's own volume in the Twayne English Authors Series, *Rose Macaulay* (1969) is the only book-length study of that author's total output—fiction and nonfiction—ever published. Wonderfully concise, comprehensive, and informative, it is currently out of print, but it shouldn't be.

The scholarly articles dealing with Macaulay's fiction have too often ranged from the sublimely ridiculous to the ridiculously sublime. Two cases in point: In *Some Goddesses of the Pen* (1927), Patrick Braybrooke, a Fellow of the Royal Society of Literature, charges Rose Macaulay "with an obvious pandering to the disgusting license that certain women novelists take such a pernicious delight in exhibiting."[15] Macaulay, it seemed, had displayed excessive earthiness in her portrayal of the pregnant heroine of *Crewe Train*

(1926) with this sentence: "Denham felt, and often was, sick in the mornings" (*C.T.*, p. 169).[16] By contrast, some years later, William J. Lockwood etherealizes the same Rose Macaulay into the limbo of *Minor British Novelists* (1967) by noting:

> She is limited in her ability to deal with the disturbing, personal repercussions of the world she represents. . . . Ultimately, as I think we shall see, Rose Macaulay's real kinship is with a [spiritual] world beyond human relationships.[17]

That the critical misreadings of the 1920s were perpetuated into the 1960s is nowhere better exemplified than in Reginald Brimley Johnson's *Some Contemporary Novelists (Women)*. Handsomely rebound in red, blue, and gold, the 1967 edition is, nevertheless, page for page and word for word the identical twin of the 1920 edition. In the chapter titled "Rose Macaulay," Johnson first stresses the overwhelming importance of that author's "individual characters" (as opposed to content or style).[18] He then sprints so heedlessly through nine of the novels that he calls *Laurence* Juke by the name "Phillip" (when writing about *Potterism*), confuses Daphne Sandomir with The Rev. C.M.V. West (when discussing *Non-Combatants*), and twice refers to *Tommy* Crevequer as "Tony" (when considering *The Furnace*).[19]

There are superb—if sometimes hostile—exceptions to criticism of this sort. A 1912 review by Rebecca West brilliantly and mercilessly parodies the story and style of *Views and Vagabonds*. West concedes that the novel is "exquisitely written"; however, she is adamant that its quiet presentation of Louie Bunter, a passive working class wife, constitutes an act of "treachery" towards women and the poor.[20] Fifty-four years later, Alice R. Bensen writes with equal brilliance in her article, "The Ironic Aesthete and the Sponsoring of Causes," that the character of Louie Bunter constitutes irrefutable evidence of Rose Macaulay's "impassioned involvement" in the plight of the socially and economically deprived, despite the innately "ironic cast" of the author's mind.[21] Dame Cicely Wedgwood's beautifully crafted introduction to the 1960 edition of *They Were Defeated*, Alan Pryce-Jones's affectionate reminiscences in the 1961 edition of *Orphan Island*, Constance Babington Smith's 1973 Stopes Memorial Lecture, "Rose Macaulay in Her Writings"[22]—all offer insights of inestimable value.

Lamenting in her 1984 anthology, *Time and Tide Wait for No Man*, that Smith's biography of Macaulay "makes little of her feminism," Dale Spender calls for additional "biographical work and literary criticism"[23] from scholars of the 1980s. Nevertheless, Smith's authorized biography (1972; reprint. 1973), and her editions of the *Letters* (1961) and *Last Letters* (1962) to Father Hamilton Johnson provide a wealth of information.

In the late 1970s and the 1980s, as in the late 1920s and the 1930s, Rose

Macaulay's fiction has sparked useful critical commentary, especially from scholars on the European Continent and in the British Commonwealth. Marie-José Codaccioni's stimulating comparative study of novels by Macaulay and Muriel Spark, "L'échange dans *The Towers of Trebizond* et *The Mandelbaum Gate*," was read at the Strasbourg meeting of the prestigious Société des Anglicistes and handsomely printed in the proceedings (1982).[24] Australian Jane Novak became the first researcher to examine the Macaulay papers at The University of Texas for the purpose of incorporating them into her study, "Literary Life in London" (1978).[25] In "Women's Novels of the First World War: Rose Macaulay's *Non-Combatants and Others* and *What Not* and Rebecca West's *The Return of the Soldier*," another Australian, Sue Thomas, demonstrates that "each writer regards her analysis of the [complex] relationship between the individual and war as a constructive contribution to . . . [human] understanding."[26] A previous study, Maria Jane Marrocco's "The Novels of Rose Macaulay—A Literary Pilgrimage" (Ph.D. diss., University of Toronto, 1977), is even more explicit and emphatic concerning Rose Macaulay's "keen perception of" the "futility of . . . four years of slaughter."[27] Both Thomas's paper and Marrocco's dissertation seem to challenge implicitly Sandra Gilbert's terse assumption of "the apparently naive envy of male combatants [in the First World War] expressed by women like Macaulay."[28]

By far the finest work on Macaulay in recent years is Marrocco's, which is outstanding for its exegesis, extrapolation, and command of the biography and criticism. With much emphasis on Macaulay's early novels, on *The World My Wilderness* (1950), and on *Trebizond*, Marrocco sees beyond the popular conception of Macaulay as a satirist, as "a mere wit or iconoclast," to the profound seriousness of her personal spiritual "quest for salvation." Significantly, more than a chapter is devoted to "Macaulay's own preoccupation with the limitations of the role of women," both in her own life and work and as manifested by various of her "masculine," or "sexless," women characters.[29] Because Marrocco's study emphasizes spirituality, but deals briefly with androgyny, and because the present study reverses these emphases, the two are complementary. They will, I hope, be read together.

The profound *spiritual* influence of Father Hamilton Johnson on Rose Macaulay has been a matter of record for twenty-six years. Using archival materials from The University of Texas at Austin and from the Monastery of The Society of St. John the Evangelist in Cambridge, Massachusetts, this study will be the first to reveal that Father Johnson's influence was profoundly *literary*, as well. To him, Macaulay—and we—owe the source of her most famous—and most androgynous—novel: *The Towers of Trebizond*. To him, also, Macaulay may very well have owed the inspiration for *The*

Shadow Flies, as revealed by newly discovered correspondence between the two, dating from the 1920s.

The present study explores in depth the inherent androgyny, not only of Macaulay herself, but of her total fictional output. In keeping with her credo that a human being is best fulfilled by pursuing a way of life that will let him or her be true to the Inner Self, most of Macaulay's major characters are androgynous. The dilemmas of males who want to be artists and poets, or of females who should have been sailors, statesmen, or physicians, are sensitively delineated in her fiction. The "feminine" men were generated by a variety of life experiences particular to Macaulay. These included her thwarted passion for Rupert Brooke; her searing conflicts with her father; her guilt, grief, and anger over a long-term involvement with a married man; her intimate friendship with E. M. Forster, and her awareness of Forster's enduring devotion to Robert Buckingham.

Another category of androgynous characters, "masculine" women, was inspired not by particular circumstances, but by the persistence of Macaulay's "boyish" body and androgynous mind. The verisimilitude of these characters was congenial to other celebrated women writers of the time: Virginia Woolf, Agatha Christie, and Dorothy L. Sayers were among the many who paid homage to Rose Macaulay in writings of their own. Frequently paired with a slightly inferior male "twin" who serves as a foil, Macaulay's masculine women are true to themselves only when they dress, act, play, work, think, or dream in a way that others in their social milieu. choose to regard as more appropriate to men. Such characters represent not only autobiographical yearnings, but a feminist striving to expand the parameters of behavior for *all* women, secular and religious, so that they may become, as eighteen-year-old Stanley Garden[30] so earnestly hopes, "doctors, lawyers, human beings, everything. . . ."

Eros and Androgyny

1

"Concerning the Abbot Daniel" and a Certain British Novelist

IN THE SIXTH-CENTURY tale "Concerning the Abbot Daniel and a Certain Religious Woman" (appendix A), a revered Father of the Byzantine Church in Egypt loses the emblems of his priestly function to a female outcast, while, in other ways as well, traditional sex roles as one experiences them in literature are turned topsy-turvy. This is all the more remarkable because the story has been preserved and transmitted across fourteen centuries by a succession of monks: first, the Abbot Daniel's own "Disciple," a nameless Byzantine monk of the latter half of the sixth century, wrote it down in Greek. Then, Johannes Monachus, a Western European monk of the tenth and eleventh centuries, translated it into medieval Latin as one of the forty-two stories preserved in his *Liber de Miraculis*. Eventually, P. Michael Huber, a Benedictine monk, reproduced variants of the Latin text in a scholarly edition printed in Heidelberg in 1913. Finally, Hamilton Johnson,[1] an Anglo-Catholic monk of the twentieth century living in Cambridge, Massachusetts, laboriously converted it into English sometime around February or March of 1951. He sent it across the ocean to his cousin, Rose Macaulay, a celebrated literary figure living in London. Along with it he included an extensive commentary explaining why and how

> Anyone who is trying to live a religious life, ought to plan for the reading, or recitation, of some sort of *daily Office;* especially anyone who is not able to take part daily in the public services of the Church.[2]

On March 21, 1951, his cousin Rose wrote back:

> Yesterday afternoon came your air letter of 17th [*sic*]—a particularly good one—and the big envelope with the Abbot Daniel story and your notes and letter inside. The story is delightful; I like the Abbot's exquisite courtesy in thanking the Abbess for his unsatisfying meal—and how hungry he and his disciple must have been by that time! The inebriate *must* be related from life; indeed, the whole nunnery

21

must. . . . The Byzantine period, in all its aspects, is so fascinating. I have read all your notes, with great attention and interest. They suggest all kinds of good ideas to me. . . .[3]

Rose Macaulay mentions two of these "good ideas" to Father Johnson immediately: First of all, she will purchase the prayer book cited by him in the notes to his translation; secondly, she will "make an arrangement of Morning and Evening Prayer to say," as these same notes set forth in some detail.[4] But there is a third "good idea" that Father Johnson's small, holographic, heavily annotated and handbound pamphlet suggests to her, which she *never* acknowledges in what has survived of their correspondence, but which should be obvious to anyone who has ever read Macaulay's last, most celebrated, and most androgynous novel. In its Byzantine setting, but even more especially, in its portrayal of the "Hebriosa," a sinful woman transformed—outwardly at least—into a saintly man, Father Johnson's rendering into English of "De Abbate Daniele et Quadam Sanctimoniali" is the immediate progenitor of *The Towers of Trebizond* (1956).[5]

The "feminist slant"[6] and "androgynous vision"[7] characteristic of Rose Macaulay and manifested in her fiction would have rendered her particularly receptive to a tale which takes the Byzantine Abbot Daniel on a journey up the Nile to a Thebaid monastery where he is greeted fearfully, tearfully, and reverently by a community of five thousand "fathers"[8] of the Church. Before these monks the old man remains completely silent. To the plea of their Archimandrite that the multitude assembled before him in the desert "might hear some word from his mouth," Abbot Daniel's only response is to dictate a single sentence to his disciple who hands it to another monk so that it can be "interpret[ed] . . . to the brethren in the Egyptian language." The sentence is, "If you desire to be saved, follow along the way of poverty and silence; for it is upon these two virtues that the entire life of monks depends." After hearing this, the five thousand monks weep and humbly depart, "For not one of them had the boldness to suggest to him that they should make a love-meal."[9]

Abbot Daniel then journeys back down the Nile to a "monastery of women" which is called by the name of St. Jeremiah, in a city suggestively named "Hermopolis."[10] There, his reception is far less deferential. He and his young disciple are kept waiting outside while "the sister who kept the door" refuses to summon the Abbess until the disciple establishes his status as a monk. Even when the Abbess comes, she at first refuses permission for them to take shelter there that night, implying that they are in far more danger of being "devoured" (sexually harassed) by the nuns than of being eaten by the wild desert beasts.[11] Only when the disciple informs her, "It is the Abbot Daniel of Scithis," does the holy man receive from the three hundred sisters of the monastery the ritual reverence and emotional ceremony that are his due. But the supper in the Refectory which follows serves to counterbalance these; it is an affirmation of the power, wealth, and status of the nuns, and a negation of that of the monks. Sitting down with the Abbess and her Assistant, in a place set apart, "the old man" does as she requests: "Give a blessing, Father, to thy hand-maids, that they may taste a little food in thy presence." But it is only the Abbot Daniel and his disciple who taste a *little* food, and that of the very simplest variety: "And those who waited upon them set before the old man a little bowl of bean broth, uncooked vegetables, dates and some water. Before the disciple they set boiled lentils, a little bread, and wine mixed with water." Meanwhile, "the sisters" feast on "various sorts of helpings;—fish, and wine, as much as they wanted; and they made a very good meal."[12] Constrained by that very same rule of silence which he had enjoined upon the five thousand monks,[13] Abbot Daniel is helpless to protest until *after* dinner, and there, too, the Abbess is able to argue far more subtly than he, and thus to retain her ascendancy:

> You are a monk and I had a monk's food set before you. Your disciple, on the other hand, is a monk's disciple, and before him I set a disciple's food. We, however, are novices, and we eat the food of novices. ("A.D.", Text, p. 14)

Hearing this, the Abbot Daniel is helpless and can only respond with what Rose Macaulay describes as "exquisite courtesy . . . [although] how hungry he and his disciple must have been by that time!"[14] A temporary reversal in the story's female ascendancy occurs when Abbot Daniel's intuitive spirituality enables him to reveal that a ragged "drinking woman" the nuns have sheltered but shunned for her apparent sinfulness is, in reality, a "hidden servant" of God. Because the sisters, even the Abbess, lament the many "unkind things" they "have done" to this woman, they must make confession to, and seek absolution from, the elderly hermit; but having exercised this priestly function, he departs from Hermopolis, "with his disciple, back to his own cell."[15]

Thus, the nuns are left as they were when the story began. In the words of Father Johnson's commentary, they are "unshepherded," without a male "chaplain to minister to them the Sacraments, or to instruct and guide them, in religious or in practical matters."[16] Moreover, their lives are not at all centered around Christ and His "Sacrifice," and are thus not Christian, not New Testament, however much they are monastic.[17] Still, despite his many objections to the cultural context and other content of "De Abbate Daniele," Father Johnson took pains to translate it with absolute precision and with obvious delight.[18] He was an avid and perceptive reader of his cousin's works; and, even more so, of her unconventional and guilt-ridden soul. In those works he accurately read the implicit feminism and obvious androgyny. In that soul he read a deep religious yearning and a profound repentance for over two decades of adultery. And so he knew she would be able to see herself in the story of the nuns of "St. Jeremiah" (coincidentally her lover's baptismal name!)[19] and the alleged "Drinking Woman," the "Hebriosa,"[20] the "irregular Religious"[21] with a secret, tormented, but special relationship to God; a female mystic far more capable than any of the "statue"-like sisters of the convent of repentance, tears, and reverence, but only when she thought herself alone and unobserved. "And the old man [Abbot Daniel] said, 'It was on her account that I came hither [to this Monastery]; for inebriates of that sort are dear to God.' "[22] That "inebriates of that sort" are also often androgynous, the tale likewise makes abundantly clear. Having been, in a sense, baptized by the disciple at Abbot Daniel's command, the Hebriosa, sprawled on the floor of the Monastery hall, awakes "as if out of a drunken state."[23] A few hours later, realizing that the sisters have seen her at prayer and are trying to find out more about her,

> the woman . . . went off quietly to the place where the old man had been lying down, stole his walking stick and his headcovering, opened the monastery door, and, having written a note on the bar with which the door had been bolted saying: "Pray for me, and forgive me for everything wherein I have done you wrong," went out and was seen no more.[24]

And thus she escapes into the wider world "looking," in Father Johnson's words, "like a monk of the desert."[25]

The "Abbot Daniel" manuscript proves irrefutably that Laurie, the androgynous heroine of *The Towers of Trebizond* (1956), recapitulates not only Rose Macaulay, as scholars have long been aware,[26] but an anonymous, androgynous religious mystic in a sixth-century tale. Torn, like the Hebriosa, by spiritual conflicts that no one else can fully understand, frequently drunk, drugged, dreamy, and drowsy; Laurie, too, has a "desert" to cross that is as much metaphysical as physical. Macaulay's literary debt to Father Johnson is partially acknowledged in *Trebizond* by an allusion to "the Cowley Fathers in America" and their "Monastery" "in Cambridge, Mass."[27]

How this fragile, onionskin manuscript, bound to its worn blue paper cover quite literally by a thread, survived the posthumous and deliberate destruction of every single letter written to Rose Macaulay by Hamilton Johnson may never be known.[28] But her letters to him survive in a printed version. Here is one of them, dated "16th May, 1952":

> Virginia Woolf—yes, I was devoted to her and am a great admirer. *Orlando* is nonsense, of course, but rather lovely and fascinating non-

sense, don't you think? Orlando him-her-self was taken from Vita Sackville-West, who is coming to see me in a day or two; I am v. fond of her, she is v. beautiful and nice (Mrs. Harold Nicolson).[29]

This passage, apparently written in reply to a question from Father Johnson, is uncharacteristic. During the almost eight years of their correspondence,[30] Rose Macaulay's letters to her cousin and "confessor," the "dear Father" who sent her "absolution from across the sea" and brought about her reentry into the Anglican communion,[31] dealt predominantly with religion and religious literature, with etymology—usually as it illuminated religion or philosophy—with the ordinary events of her daily life, with history, and with morality. When, in the letters to Father Johnson, she discusses fiction—infrequently—she is primarily concerned that her spiritual mentor should perceive it as edifying in a religious and/or moral sense. Her comments to him concerning the novel *Howards End* by her good friend E. M. Forster *are* typical:

> I *think* you'd like it; the characters are so real, the style so excellent, the humour so delightful, the problems so serious.[32]

One must acknowledge that Virginia Woolf's mock epic *Orlando*,[33] however "lovely" and "fascinating" Rose Macaulay may have found it, is far from "serious" in nature. There can be found in the letters no other instance of Macaulay commending any comparable "nonsense" to Father Johnson, an erudite and elderly Ango-Catholic ascetic of didactic literary preferences, for whom she felt the highest esteem and affection.

Why, then, does the reference to Woolf and *Orlando* occur at all? Since a great number of the letters in Rose Macaulay's possession at the time of her death—including all of those written to her by Father Johnson—were, as I have noted, posthumously burned at her request,[34] the question is a difficult one. It is rendered still more difficult in that the published letters from Macaulay to Father Johnson have appeared with numerous tantalizing ellipses, including one immediately preceding the passage on Woolf and *Orlando*.[35] Therefore, like archaeologists reconstructing an entire civilization from a few shards of pottery, or like anthropologists resurrecting a whole person from a few pieces of bone, one must rely here on evidence that is fragmentary but highly suggestive—the internal evidence of the letter itself. Apparently, Father Johnson has asked a question, to which Rose Macaulay's remark is a direct reply: "Virginia Woolf—yes. . . ." It is difficult to determine whether Father Johnson asked generally about Woolf or specifically about a novel Woolf published twenty-four years previously. What *is* ascertainable, however, is the *tone* of Macaulay's reply. There is an attempt at flippancy—"Orlando is nonsense, of course"—followed by an immediate attempt to justify her liking of the same—"but rather lovely and fascinating nonsense, don't you think?" A direct statement of the bisexual theme of the novel follows: "Orlando him-her-self was taken from Vita Sackville-West." Then Macaulay admits to having great affection for this very same individual—"who is coming to see me in a day or two"—and proceeds to express open admiration for Sackville-West's physical attractiveness. The passage is a surprising one, since praise for physical beauty cannot be said to be commonplace in Rose Macaulay's letters, while, in her fiction, personal beauty is usually linked with assorted negative attributes.[36] Finally, Macaulay appends a parenthetical reminder—almost as if she fears she has revealed perhaps a little too much and is attempting to reassure Father Johnson—that, after all, Vita Sackville-West *is* a respectable married lady, "*Mrs.* Harold Nicolson."

There is some evidence elsewhere in the letters[37] that the bisexual "Mrs." Nicolson[38] seemed to hold a particular fascination for "Miss" Rose Macaulay, and this can best be understood in the light of facts culled from Macaulay's biography. For, Emilie Rose Macaulay—like her friends Virginia Woolf and Victoria Sackville-West—had been preoccupied with the question of gender for many years. Frank Swinnerton writes that, at the time of Rose's birth

> Her mother, having already borne one daughter, had wanted her to be a boy, *so that from [her] earliest years Rose tried to behave as much as possible as a boy would have done.*[39]

Swinnerton's assessment of Macaulay's masculine orientation is confirmed by the juxtaposition of various passages from Constance B. Smith's biography of her cousin. One concerns Macaulay's earlier years:

> *Emilie Rose Macaulay* was born on the first of August 1881 at Rugby. . . . She was a second daughter, which to her mother, who had been hoping ardently for a son, was a sad disappointment. . . . as a girl 'Rosie' was very much a tomboy, and for years she believed that she would one day grow up 'to be a man'. [*sic*] Later too, in her novels Rose often gave names to her heroines which could equally well have been the names of men.[40]

As an adolescent, Macaulay persisted in her masculine longings:

> Rose, at twelve, was reaching her tomboyish stage. . . . And she not only behaved like a boy but boasted of what she would do when she was a man. She was determined that she was going to join the Navy.[41]

Today, when women are only beginning to make inroads into traditionally male fields of opportunity,[42] Macaulay's hankering after service in the navy would make her a popular subject for the national news media.[43] In the

traditional late Victorian milieu in which she was raised, it must have made
her a considerable oddity. Moreover, "in physical respects," so her sister
Jean Macaulay remembers, Rose was "an exceptionally late developer."[44]
Her Cambridge contemporaries have described her as being in appearance
"when she came up . . . like an unfledged bird, 'shy and vulnerable,' and
. . . she was rather slovenly in her ways." At the time she also exhibited a
considerable fondness for hockey, for boating, and for climbing trees and
roofs.[45] After she left college, her desire to engage in "mannish" pursuits
persisted:

> Rose in her early twenties was still exceedingly young for her age. It was
> only when [her younger brother] Aulay first appeared in Army uniform
> . . . that she was jolted out of the cherished dream that she herself
> would one day be able to join the Navy.[46]

In this and the preceding passages, Constance Smith seems to be implying
that Macaulay's aberrant behavior—in terms of the accepted sex roles of her
time—can be attributed to the fact that she was, physically and emotionally,
what Jean euphemistically termed a "late developer." If this was the case,
evidence provided by Smith's own book indicates that Rose Macaulay's
development must have been very late, indeed, since no slightest indication
of a sudden onslaught of femininity, physical or otherwise, can be elicited
from the accounts of those who knew Macaulay as she approached forty:

> The memories of her at this time that have remained with her friends are
> of a woman almost boyish in her youthfulness. It suited her to have her
> hair cut short in the new fashion. . . . Her wiry figure and coltish
> movements also had a certain charm.[47]

It is questionable whether bobbed hair, a "wiry figure," and a clumsy,
"coltish" gait will suffice to render a woman of forty "charming." While
such attributes will not necessarily confer masculinity on such a woman,
neither will they serve to establish her as feminine in character. Whether Rose
Macaulay at *any* stage in her development was *either* overwhelmingly male
or overwhelmingly female in the commonly accepted contemporary senses
of these words remains a matter for speculation. The accounts of those who
knew her only substantiate the ambiguity of her gender orientation. For
instance, her lover of twenty-four years, Gerald O'Donovan, professed
himself "particularly attracted" because Rose "had a brain like a man's."[48]
The man whom Constance Smith describes as Rose's "shrewd and perci-
pient" critic, Frank Swinnerton, stoutly proclaimed Miss Macaulay to be,
"despite" the "boyish traits" which she exhibited well into her seventies, "a
lady. . . . a remarkable woman, distinguished by great integrity and beautiful modesty."[49] Perhaps the most accurate description of the physical

essence of Rose Macaulay was published by her friend Rosamond Lehmann in a tribute written five months after Macaulay's death. This tribute included a description of the novelist as she appeared in her old age:

> One of the links between Rose and myself was the shared passion for swimming. . . . I still see her figure indomitably poised [on the diving board]: *androgynous tall figure*, flat as a shape cut out in white paper and blacked in to knees and shoulders; gaunt, comical, adorable— *heroically topped with an antique martial casque.*[50]

Not only is the term "androgynous"[51] applicable to Macaulay's "late developing" body throughout its seventy-seven years, but it portrays as well the quality of her mind throughout those same years. It was the sort of mind which, at age forty-nine, could fancy itself belonging to "a shipwrecked sailor . . . 'scanning the horizon for a sail,' " and it was contained in a figure which, also at age forty-nine, looked like that of "a lanky curly-haired boy."[52]

Rose Macaulay's inherent androgyny was apparent not only in her looks and in her life, but in almost every novel she wrote and even, occasionally, in her nonfiction. For example, in 1934, six years after the publication of Woolf's *Orlando*, Rose Macaulay produced an anthology entitled *The Minor Pleasures of Life*.[53] The book, headed by an epigraph from Leigh Hunt which recommends that "There should be a joyous set of elegant extracts—a *Literatura Hilaris* or *Gaudens*," contains hundreds of selections. Dating from classical to contemporary times, these passages deal—often in a whimsical way—with pleasures under headings arranged alphabetically, from "Agreeable Encounters" to "Xenophobia." The book is, as Macaulay herself confesses, predominantly English in orientation, and "disproportionately 17th century" in content (*M.P.L.*, p. 7); however, it includes an ample number of extracts from the eighteenth and nineteenth centuries, as well as a lesser number from other centuries and nationalities. Of these latter the major portion are from the "great translators' " renderings of Greek, Roman, and French originals.

The Minor Pleasures is, as its editor comments in the Preface, "slimmed . . . of much that I hoped it would contain" (*M.P.L.*, p. 7). Nevertheless, it is seven hundred fifty-one pages in length and contains nine hundred forty-one separate entries.[54] Only sixteen entries are from twentieth century writings.[55] Three of these are of great interest, not so much for what they reveal about the era which produced them as for what they indicate about the individual who felt it necessary to incorporate them into her book.

The very first item in *The Minor Pleasures of Life* listed under the general heading of "Female Pleasures" is a twentieth century poem written in seventeenth century style and entitled "Huntin' ":

Thro' the green Oake-wood on a lucent Morn
Turn'd the sweet mazes of a silver Horn:
A Stag raced past, and hallowing hard behind,
Dian's young Nymphs ran fleeting down the Wind.
A light-foot Host, green-kirtl'd all they came,
And leapt, and rollickt, as some mountain Streame
Sings cold and ruffling thro' the Forrest Glades;
So ran, so sang, so hoyted the Moone's Maids.
Light as young Lev'retts skip their buskin'd feet,
Spurning th'enamell'd Sward as they did fleet.
The Wind that buss'd their cheekes was all the Kiss
Was suffer'd by the Girles of *Artemis,*
Whose traffique was in Woods, whom the wing'd Boy
Leaguer'd in vain, whom Man would ne're injoy,
Whose Bed greene Moss beneath the forrest Tree,
Whose jolly Pleasure all in Liberty,
To sport with fellow Maids in maiden cheere,
To swim the Brook, and hollo after Deer.
Thus, the winds wantoning their flying Curles,
So rac'd, so chas'd, those most Delightfull Girles.

ANON
The Chase (c. 1675)
(*M.P.L.*, p. 211)

This poem, which is vastly superior to the bulk of the poetry published under its author's own name,[56] is actually a piece of "pseudo-period verse" written, says Constance Smith, by Macaulay herself.[57] It is significant for at least three reasons, the latter two having relevance to this study:

1. The imagery of wood, water, moon, morning, and music reverberates through fifty years of Macaulay's fiction, both before and after *Minor Pleasures*, and through both volumes of her poetry (q.v.), as well.
2. The young females, "whose traffique was in woods; whom the wing'd Boy/Leaguer'd. . . ," are archetypal Macaulay heroines, absorbed in what are characteristically masculine pursuits (in this case, running, roistering, leaping, swimming, hunting, and camping out).
3. These "seventeenth century" maids "whom Man would ne're injoy," and "whose jolly pleasure" is to be found "all in Liberty," and in each other, are depicted attractively and sympathetically by an authoress who ranked their uninhibited activities paramount among the "Female Pleasures" and who chose to remain anonymous until

Ten years later, in 1944, this poem proved an embarrassment to Rose, for when the eminent bibliophile John Hayward was preparing a collection of seventeenth-century verse, he asked her to specify its source. . . . 'The fact is that I wanted a poem about women hunting [she replied] and couldn't lay my hands on one at the moment, so I thought I would write one myself, and it amused me to put it into 17th century garb. . . . it is, as perhaps you know yourself, a rather entertaining pastime. One can take some modern poem and rewrite it in the style of each century. . . . It might be a good parlor game for those whom it amuses.'[58]

Shakespeare's "thane of Cawdor" had "studied . . . /To throw away the dearest thing he ow'd,/As 'twere a careless trifle."[59] This is a "study" in which Macaulay, too, excels, as evidenced not only by her letter to Father Johnson about Virginia Woolf and *Orlando*, but by other of her writings in which she may be observed making light of those things which, in fact, she holds quite dear.[60] The truth of this assertion is amply demonstrated by a scrutiny of the remaining selections sardonically categorized as "Female Pleasures." Undoubtedly Macaulay reveals far too much of herself here, so that "wit" must be used to camouflage the real depths of her feeling. This section of *The Minor Pleasures of Life* expresses her views on female-male relationships through the ages by the simple device of quoting misogynist men.[61] The irony readily apparent in these passages is deliberately engendered. Macaulay's "most Delightfull Girles" degenerate on the very next page, while gripped in the rude clutches of Joseph Addison, to unwomanly women who require a scathing denunciation:

> I have very frequently the opportunity of seeing a rural *Andromache*. . . . She talks of Hounds and Horses, and makes nothing of leaping over a Six-bar Gate. If a man tells her a waggish story, she gives him a push with her Hand in jest, and calls him an impudent Dog. (*M.P.L.*, p. 212)

When, in Addison's view, a woman tries to act "like a man," she is absurd.[62] Nor, if we may believe Napoleon, should a woman attempt to change the course of history, as *he* did, since

> Il faut que les femmes tricotent. (*M.P.L.*, p. 212)

With sexist hyperbole, Byron asserts that women should at all times be ornamental:

> A woman should never be seen eating or drinking, unless it be *lobster salad* and *champagne*, the only truly feminine viands. (*M.P.L.*, p. 213)

A woman should not, as Charles Lamb points out, participate actively in the world's drama:[63]

Mary had not been here four and twenty hours before she saw a thief. She sits at the window working; and casually throwing out her eyes, she sees a concourse of people . . . with a constable to conduct the solemnity. These little incidents agreeably diversify a female life. (*M.P.L.*, p. 213)

Nor is a woman well suited to mingle in even the world's more mundane affairs, since it is well known, as Boswell reminds, that

A woman who gets the command of money for the first time upon her marriage, has such gust in spending it, that she throws it away with great profusion. (*M.P.L.*, p. 217)

Women are intellectually deficient, or rather, as Richard Burton's thoughtful planning for their "needs" makes evident, they haven't any intellects at all:

Now for women instead of laborious studies, they have curious needleworkes, cutworkes, spinning, bone-lace, and many pretty devices of their own making. . . . This they have to busie themselves about, household offices, &c. neate gardens. . . . Their merry meetings and frequent visitations . . . which are so much in use, gossipping among the meaner sort, &c. (*M.P.L.*, p. 224)

Women are "things" existing but

. . . for shew
And pleasure, created to beare children,
And play at shuttle-cocke.

(*M.P.L.*, p. 222)

Women are sex-starved and crave one thing only:

PRUE: 'Tis true, Miss, two poor young creatures as we are!

HIPPOLITA: . . . Not suffer'd to go to Church, because the men are sometimes there! Little did I think I should ever have longed to go to Church!

(*M.P.L.*, pp. 216–17)

Women are saints worthy of veneration:

There is . . . piety peculiar to the Sex, which naturally renders them Subjects more pliable, to the Divine Grace, than men commonly are. . . . (*M.P.L.*, pp. 215–16)

Women must not compromise themselves:

> MRS. FORESIGHT: I own it, I think there's no Happiness like conversing with an agreeable Man . . . but . . . to be seen with a man in a Hackney Coach is scandalous.
>
> (*M.P.L.*, p. 221)

Women make their entire existences center around trifles:

> Ladies . . . were they not used with Ceremony, with Complements and Addresses, with Legs, and Kissing of Hands, they were the pittyfullest Creatures in the World. (*M.P.L.*, p. 218)

And famed diarist Samuel Pepys, in a generous mood, feels men should allow women their little toys:

> This evening my wife did with great pleasure shew me her stock of jewels, encreased by the ring she hath made lately as my Valentine's gift this year . . . and with this and what she had, she reckons that she hath above £150 worth of jewels . . . and I am glad of it, for it is fit the wretch should have something to content herself with. (*M.P.L.*, p. 222)

There are, in all, twenty-seven of these "female pleasures" listed: twenty-four are from the writings of men; two are labelled "anonymous"—the Macaulay "Huntin'" poem discussed above, and an excerpt from the January 1825 *Edinburgh Review:*

> It is generally remarked, that when the odious and corrupting propensity of gambling takes possession of the female mind, its ravages are still more unsparing than upon the characters and feelings of men. (*M.P.L.*, p. 214)

To one lone selection is appended the name of a woman: Elizabeth Barrett Browning. Macaulay has provided the bitterly ironic superscription, "Accomplishments," to but two lines from *Aurora Leigh*. They epitomize just how much waste there is in the "wasted lives" portrayed in Mrs. Browning's book-length poem:

> I danced the polka and Cellarius,
> Spun glass, stuffed birds, and modelled flowers in wax.[64]

This is the precise passage to which Virginia Woolf had alluded at least two years previously when she wrote, in an essay entitled "Aurora Leigh":

> At her [Aunt's] hand Aurora suffered the education that was thought proper for women. She learnt a little French, a little algebra; the internal laws of the Burmese empire; what navigable river joins itself to Lara;

what census of the year five was taken at Klagenfurt; also how to draw
nereids neatly draped, to spin glass, to stuff birds, and model flowers in
wax. For the Aunt liked a woman to be womanly . . . Under this
torture of women's education, the passionate Aurora exclaimed, certain
women have died; others pine. . . .[65]

Surely, it was with malice aforethought that Macaulay began her section of
sentiments on the "nature" of women with a poem of her own composition
in praise of active females who are forever independent of men and untram-
melled by sexist stereotypes, and who race "Light as young Lev'retts"
through life. It is a premeditated juxtaposition which makes all too obvious
the monumental contrast between what Macaulay *knew* she was, and what a
male-dominated society *said* every "woman" should be. To accept unexamined her statement to John Hayward that she was merely playing a
"parlor game" when she composed "Huntin' " and included it in her anthology would be to fall prey to the Intentional Fallacy of which serious
literary critics are justly wary. It would be as illogical as accepting, at face
value, Macaulay's tentative assertion to Father Johnson that Orlando was, "of
course," mere "nonsense. . . , but rather fascinating and lovely nonsense,
don't you think?"

A second item in *Minor Pleasures* significant for what it reveals is the only
entry under the heading "Sororal," a poem entitled "After the Party" by an
individual named E. J. Scovell who had, perhaps, more than a little hostility
toward the male sex, as the opening lines of the first stanza demonstrate:

A girl said to her sister, late, when their friends had gone:
"I wish there were no men on earth, but we alone."[66]

Unfortunately, men *do* visit and stay "late." The speaker, who has been
carefully watching her sister during the visit, jealously reveals her awareness
that a male friend (or friends) arouses an intense erotic response in her
sibling.

It is obvious that the bare essentials alone of Scovell's "After the Party"
suffice to establish that the poem is laden with lesbian suggestion: A girl
openly admires her sister's face and body (ll. 3, 8); remarks that her own
body is likewise beautiful (l. 8); feels that there is a special, non-verbal
communication between the two of them (ll. 9–14); insists "We should be
gay together" (l. 21); resents all men and all normal biological drives that
come between them (ll. 2–6, 17–18, 25–29); and sits beside her sister all night
with the lights off (ll. 24, 28), wishing "there was [*sic*] no love on earth but
ours alone" (l. 29).

Moreover, the careful reader should not balk at ascribing to various images
in the poem—the men's signal "flags" (l. 11), the girl's "eyes" (l. 27),[67] the
piercing and boasting "flames" induced by a masculine presence (ll. 4–5), the

"grass" (ll. 10, 14), the "reeds . . . in river mists" (ll. 6–7), the "thicket" (l. 22), the "low, crouched bramble" (l. 19), the "drenched upland fields" (l. 10), and the "chill pool" (l. 22)—some probable Freudian equivalents.[68] It is noteworthy that the poem equates Summer, noon, light, heat, and fire or flame with mature, heterosexual love (ll. 4, 7, 25–27); while Spring, dawn, dimness, coolness, and wetness represent the less mature "sisterly love" (ll. 7, 15–16, 18, 22, 24, 28). Perhaps, too, the desire of the girl that both she and her sister should remain "reed like" (ll. 3, 6–7) can be seen as a manifestation of her resistance to the curvaceousness of feminine physical maturation. Since she is as yet not quite fully sexually matured, she sees—and cannot help but *feel*—the necessity of men; simultaneously, she hates them because of the demands their existence makes on her and resists being drawn by them towards adult heterosexuality.[69]

It is readily apparent that "After the Party" by "Miss E. J. Scovell"—we learn the author's sex only by consulting the "Acknowledgements" (p. 733) at the conclusion of the anthology—is a poorly written poem. What can— only with charity!—be termed its "rhyme scheme" follows no discernible pattern. It is metrically deficient and imagistically inferior. It exhibits extremely infelicitous choices of diction and phrasing, has little to recommend it in the way of sonorities of language, and contains at least two glaring grammatical errors.[70] This undistinguished poem stands out from the majority of the 941 selections in Macaulay's largely exquisite collection of "elegant extracts" with an inferiority that is almost flagrant. Why, then, did Macaulay include it in *The Minor Pleasures* when, as she herself laments in the Preface, the volume has perforce been "slimmed . . . of much that I hoped it would contain" (*M.P.L.* p. 7)?

Surely "Sororal" feelings—the purported theme of the section of *The Minor Pleasures* including but the one item—Scovell's poem—*must* have been more effectively expressed by *someone* in the more than 2600 years and several lands spanned by this compilation. And most certainly Rose Macaulay—the Oxford-educated daughter of a Cambridge Lecturer in English who had translated Herodotus and edited Gower[71]—could have found *something* in her many months of research in the British Museum toward preparation of her book that would have been more to the point. She did! Elegantly poised beneath the label "Fraternal" occurring earlier in Macaulay's own anthology are three selections—one from Boswell, and one apiece from Macaulay's own cousins, Thomas Babington and Margaret Macaulay, giving eloquent testimony to the rewards and pleasures of sisterly and brotherly love (*M.P.L.*, pp. 225–28).[72]

Although, in compiling *The Minor Pleasures*, Rose Macaulay lacked the space to include all that she had so enthusiastically wished to include, she yet took two entire and very precious pages to reproduce what is, in essence, a manifestly inferior poem about lesbian love. Almost certainly, "After the

Party" was included in this anthology only because the editor let an over-whelming emotional preference for the poem's content overcome her usually more sensible critical perspective.

The third of the sixteen selections from the twentieth century incorpo-rated by Macaulay into *The Minor Pleasures* is a very lovely excerpt from the novel *Orlando* by Virginia Woolf. This passage of over 300 words, which Rose has labeled "Carnival," is reprinted in a section dealing with the pleasures of "Ice." It reads in part:

> London enjoyed a carnival of the utmost brilliancy. . . . Frozen roses fell in showers when the Queen and her ladies walked abroad. Col-oured balloons hovered motionless in the air. Here and there burnt vast bonfires of cedar and oak wood, lavishly salted, so that the flames were of green, orange, and purple fire. But however fiercely they burnt, the heat was not enough to melt the ice which, though of singular trans-parency, was yet of the hardness of steel. (*M.P.L.*, pp. 323–24)[73]

This scene is from the first chapter of *Orlando* in which "ice"—its cold-ness, its hardness, the feasting and other festivities held on it, its "melting" in the fires of sexual passion and its transformation into rain and river flood, emblematic of tears and despair—plays a very prominent metaphorical role.[74] Macaulay also made what may be a direct allusion to Chapter One of *Orlando* in her thumbnail history, *Life Among the English* (1942).[75] This rather slim volume chronicles the history of Britain from pre–Roman antiq-uity to World War II in forty-eight pages. In the section entitled "Feudal," the author writes:

> London life [after the Conquest] was a round of gaiety—football, cockfights, tournaments, ice sports *(for, as we know, it froze long and hard every winter in past centuries)*, fairs, performing animals, every kind of pleasure. . . . Social life was largely conducted round the well-spread board. (*L.A.E.*, p. 12; emphasis added)

Whether or not Rose Macaulay had the first chapter of Woolf's *Orlando* consciously in mind when she wrote these words in 1942, it is impossible to say. What can be demonstrated is that Macaulay knew and liked the novel sufficiently to utilize a lengthy quote from it in her anthology of 1934, and that the passage she then chose to quote—aside from its intrinsic literary beauties, which are many—is of interest because of the *position* it occupies in the work literary critic Herbert Marder calls Virginia Woolf's "hymn to androgyny."[76] Immediately following the section excerpted by Macaulay is the "Sasha episode" in which the youthful Orlando falls ecstatically in love with a person of indeterminate sex:

> He beheld . . . a figure which, whether boy's or woman's filled him
> with the highest curiosity. . . . extraordinary seductiveness . . . issued
> from the whole person. . . . When the boy, for alas, a boy it must be—
> no woman could skate with such speed and vigour—swept almost on
> tiptoe past him, Orlando was ready to tear his hair with vexation that
> the person was of his own sex, and thus all embraces were out of the
> question. But the skater came closer. Legs, hands, carriage, were a
> boy's, but no boy ever had a mouth like that; no boy had those breasts;
> no boy had those eyes which looked as if they had been fished from the
> bottom of the sea. . . . She was not a handsbreadth off. She was a
> woman. (*Orlando*, pp. 37–38)

Moreover, Orlando is also, from the first sentence of the book, of questionable sex, despite the narrator's ironic disclaimer:

> He—for there could be no doubt of his sex, though the fashion of the
> time did something to disguise it—was in the act of slicing at the head of
> a Moor which swung from the rafters. (*Orlando*, p. 13)

But the head is a relic from a bygone war fought by Orlando's father or grandfather,[77] and Orlando, alone in an attic at sixteen, playing at being a hero, is said to be "too young" to ride to battle. Further details of Orlando's "youthful beauty" fail to resolve the ambiguity of "his" gender. We read that he possessed

> . . . shapely legs. . . . [a] handsome body . . . well-set shoulders. . . .
> The red of the cheeks was covered with peach down. . . . he had eyes
> like drenched violets. . . . Sights disturbed him, like that of his mother,
> a very beautiful lady in green walking out to feed the peacocks . . .
> sights exalted him. . . . Orlando . . . sat down at the table. . . . took
> out a writing book labelled "Æthelbert: A Tragedy in Five Acts,"
> and . . . Soon he had covered ten pages and more with poetry. (*Orlando*, pp. 14–16)

The somewhat feminine character of the young Orlando cannot have been uncongenial to Rose Macaulay. In 1935, a year after her publication of *The Minor Pleasures*, Macaulay produced a biocritical volume on John Milton. There are some striking similarities between the effeminate, temperamental, and talented adolescent Orlando as Woolf conceived him in her first chapter, and the youthful Milton as Macaulay perceived him in her first chapter.[78] When Milton was but a boy

> Music . . . could dissolve him into ecstacies. He wrote poetry at
> ten. . . . We see him at the age of ten in Janssen's portrait . . . his

mother was not . . . too Puritan to set off her child's beauty with elegant dress. (*Milton*, p. 3)[79]

A few pages later, Macaulay writes that Milton was heckled by his contemporaries at Cambridge for his ladylike mannerisms:

> Let us picture, then, the undergraduate of sixteen and a half . . . so delicately beautiful of face and form, so elegantly nice in demeanour and habit as to be nicknamed in Cambridge, "the Lady," eager for learning, and, feeling himself dedicated and set apart for great things. (*Milton*, p. 9)

A few pages later, Macaulay again feels compelled to bring up the subject of her hero's less than masculine image at Cambridge by means of a spirited discussion of Milton's

> . . . protest against the nickname of "Lady," which [his biographer John] Aubrey says was given him for being "so fair and clear" [of complexion], but for which, as Milton suggested, there may have been other reasons. Was it he petulantly enquired, because he could not drink heavily, or because his hands were not hard with plowing, or because he did not prove his manhood by debauchery? But, he added, ever happy to compare himself with the classical great (with Ovid in rustication, with Pindar "when the assault was intended on the city," with Tiresias in blindness), Demosthenes himself was called by his enemies not enough of a man. (*Milton*, pp. 15–16)[80]

Both Macaulay's version of the historic Milton, and Virginia Woolf's portrayal of the fictional Orlando, should be considered with reference to Woolf's theory of the "androgynous mind." It was Woolf's expressed belief that a man must be in touch with the feminine qualities in himself and a woman must be in touch with the masculine qualities in herself if the wonderful possibilities life holds out to human beings are to be fully realized. In her feminist tract *A Room of One's Own*, Woolf voices her theory that "If one is a man, still the woman part of the brain must have effect; and a woman also must have intercourse with the man in her." She conjectures that "Coleridge perhaps meant this when he said that a great mind is androgynous."[81] Without the bisexual perspective, both the human individual in general, and the artist in particular, will be lacking the essential freedom to create—the one, a rich and meaningful life; the other, a rich and meaningful work. Woolf went so far as to say, "It is fatal for anyone who writes to think of their sex. It is fatal to be a man or woman pure and simple; one must be woman-manly or man-womanly."[82] She even admits the possibility that "a mind which is purely masculine cannot create, any more than a mind that is purely feminine."[83]

Literary critic Herbert Marder characterizes *A Room of One's Own* as a kind of lecture by Woolf "on freedom," while in *Orlando* he sees Woolf as indulging herself in that same freedom. "It is especially interesting," he comments, "that Orlando's first, and most spectacular, change of sex [from "man" to "woman"] is ushered in by an elaborate ritual of liberation."[84] Even the form of the novel is a liberated one. *Orlando*, like *Trebizond*, is a mixed-breed work that does not belong to any of the "established" literary genres, partaking, as it does, of qualities attributable to several:

> Fantasy, novel, biography, poem, history—all of these terms may be applied to the book, but no single one describes it adequately. It seems fitting that this book about the intermingling of the sexes should be a hybrid of several literary types.[85]

Likewise, the characters in this protean setting continually oscillate between maleness and femaleness. As Virginia Woolf observes in *Orlando*,

> Different though the sexes are, they intermix. In every human being a vacillation from one sex to the other takes place, and often it is only the clothes that keep the male or female likeness, while underneath the sex is the very opposite of what it is above.[86]

Using this passage as his point of departure, Herbert Marder discusses the various characters in Woolf's novel with reference to their continually shifting sexes:

> This intermixing of sexes, and the consequent ambiguity is observable in several characters. Sasha, the Russian Princess, at first appears to be a boy and later dresses as a man. The Archduchess Harriet reveals that she has only been masquerading as a woman. But she is not androgynous at all in the ideal sense, because the masculine element has always predominated in her, even before her dropping of the feminine disguise [and revelation of her true character as the "masculine," heavy-handed Archduke] brought inner and outer sexes into conformity with each other. . . . Orlando, and her husband Shelmardine, on the other hand, are truly androgynous, the two sexes within them almost evenly balanced. It is because of the fineness of this balance that Orlando must constantly be shifting back and forth, that is, conforming her outer sex to changes in the inner weather.[87]

A letter written by Rose Macaulay to Virginia Woolf in October 1940, five months before the latter's suicide, establishes that Woolf, and Woolf's an-

drogynous ideal, as expressed in her October 26th review of E. L. Griggs'
Biography of Sara Coleridge,[88] were at the time very much on Macaulay's
mind. The letter—reprinted with ellipses just where one would wish they
were not—includes the following:

> How I wish that I could see you! It's one of the sad things about this
> war, seeing people has become so much more difficult, at the same time
> more important. I like it so much when I do see you...I would like to
> talk about...Coleridge...some time, as I have long had in mind a novel
> about a girl who would be his descendant (great great grandchild, the
> fruit of mild and rural sin) and would take after him. I suppose she
> would be a very odd girl, wouldn't she—opium, metaphysics, flow of
> talk, cadging on friends, even poetry, but it needn't be as good as his.[89]

Constance Smith avers that "Rose's idea for a novel about a descendant of
Coleridge never came to anything though she told Daniel George that she
wanted to give it priority" over another work she planned to write, which
was then being researched for her by George.[90] Macaulay, at this time on
active wartime service as an ambulance driver in London, and continually
under devastating enemy bombardment, is obliged to deal, as she writes to
Woolf, with "victims beneath the ruins . . . [who] do make agonizing
conversation often."[91] Although her life at this time was not at all devoid of
excitement and adventure, still Rose Macaulay escaped into fantasies about a
girl who reincarnates a famous man, Coleridge; and who is—like the subject
of Woolf's review—his lineal descendant, doing everything that *he* did,
though she cannot do it quite so well. This girl can even indulge in "poetry,
but it needn't be as good as his."[92]

While Macaulay never did succeed in reincarnating Coleridge in female
form, she did manage to propagate a feminine version of one of his more
virile contemporaries. In *Going Abroad* (1934), six years before Macaulay
wrote the letter to Woolf discussing the possibility of a girl Coleridge, she
had already produced a comparable heroine in the person of "Hero Buckley," an avid swimmer in dangerous seas, an ardent flirt, a moody romantic
philosophizer, and—by coincidence!—a girl who bears a strong physical
likeness to Lord Byron, "for this peer was her great-great-great-grandfather,
it were indiscreet to explain how."[93] The fact that Macaulay was still obsessed with the idea of such an individual six years after making her a
principal character in a novel exceeding three hundred pages in length will
perhaps serve as an indicator of the tenacity of the obsession. Small wonder
that Macaulay would have so strong a desire to "talk to" Woolf concerning
her hero/heroine. Surely she would find a kindred spirit in the author of
Orlando. It was likewise small wonder that, on November 12, 1952, Rose
Macaulay delivered a lecture at Oxford on how an author's own sex, and his/

her expectations of the opposite sex, can affect the creation of characters. In a letter dated "24th October, 1952," she announces her topic to Father Johnson:

> I have to go to Oxford on Nov. 12th to address the University Literary Society on Men's women and Women's men, in literature. Not an unfruitful subject.[94]

At the conclusion of the "Abbot Daniel" tale, a man, heretofore active, peripatetic, and revered by the multitudes, quietly and prayerfully enters his solitary cell. Concurrently, a woman, heretofore immobilized, reclusive, and scorned by the many, steals the man's hood and staff and escapes into the wider world. The sex role reversal of this fourteen-hundred-year-old tale serves as a paradigm for most of Macaulay's own fictional men and women. "She attacks authority in literature," writes Virginia Woolf about her friend, "R.M."[95] The obvious androgyny of "R.M.'s" characters is, in virtually every one of her novels, the most salient feature of that attack.

2

"A Long White Building Facing South"

IN *MYSTERY AT GENEVA* (1922) Rose Macaulay observes that intellection may or may not be gender-biased, depending on the individual:

> It may be observed that there are in this world mental females, mental males, and mental neutrals. You may know them by their conversation. The mental females, or womanly women, are apt to talk about clothes, children, domestics, the prices of household commodities, love affairs, or personal gossip. . . . Mental males, or manly men, talk about sport, finance, business, animals, crops, or how things are made. . . . In between these is the No-Man's Land, filled with mental neutrals of both sexes. They talk about all the other things, such as books, jokes, politics, love (as distinct from love affairs), people, places, religion, . . . plays, music, current fads and scandals, public persons and events, newspapers, life and anything else which turns up. (*M.G.*, pp. 144–45)[1]

With tongue in cheek, Macaulay is arrogating to the exclusive province of the "Mental-Neutrals" far more than is theirs alone. Still, the underlying message is plain: One's mental set might or might not be a function of one's biological sex. A careful reading of Macaulay's novels demonstrates that she felt this was likewise true of an individual's appearance, mannerisms, psychological and social functioning, chosen vocation and chosen avocations. All of these might be masculine and/or feminine in varying degrees without regard to the nominal sex of the individual possessing or pursuing them.[2] Many masculine-seeming women and an assortment of feminine-seeming men appear in Rose Macaulay's fiction. Representative of the former is "John" (Joanna) Vallon of *The Valley Captives* (1911), who is sturdy, square-jawed, laconic, calm, unimaginative, aggressive and brave when confronted with danger. Her chief interests center around "practical farming." Representative of the latter is John's brother "Teddy" (Tudor) Vallon in the same novel. He is slight, frail, weak, verbal, creative, high-strung, nervous,

41

artistically inclined, fearful, and cowardly in the face of real or imagined peril. His most passionate desire is to be an artist.

Feminine men in Macaulay's fiction were generated by a variety of fantasies and experiences particular to her. Their cognates, masculine women, were inspired not by particular life experiences, but by a persistent state of Rose Macaulay's "boyish" body and androgynous mind. Often, in the novels, the two sorts of characters function in tandem as "twins"—i.e., as sisters and brothers or cousins with strong physical and/or mental affinities to one another.

The feminine men had three origins: first, and most especially in the early novels, they were fantasy projections of Macaulay's self. Second, they constituted an attempt to deal with a complex of emotions surrounding specific men with whom Macaulay was involved in meaningful relationships. Third, they were real men about whom Macaulay read or with whom she came into contact as she began to circulate freely in literary London.

The authority for the first of these—that some of Macaulay's young male characters were fantasy projections of herself—gains plausibility from descriptions of her most obviously autobiographical character, Imogen Carrington of *Told by an Idiot* (1923). Imogen, debarred by her youth and more especially by her sex from the adventures she craves, creates numerous male fantasy projections of herself and writes novels about them. Most especially, Imogen enjoys imagining herself as "lieutenant-commander" "Denis Carton," sailor and popular metaphysical poet.[3]

Most notable of Rose Macaulay's own projections along this line is Michael Travis, the onanistic mystic poet/protagonist of *The Secret River* (1909).[4] Michael is, beyond doubt, the most unreservedly sensual of all Rose Macaulay's characters.[5] Parts 1 and 2 of *The Secret River*[6] in which, as a prelude to a homosexual titillation and a heterosexual consummation, Michael swims nude down a woodland waterway—are the most intensely sensuous and the most unrestrainedly erotic writings Macaulay ever published. Regrettably, the remainder of the novel, which depicts Michael's mental, marital, and other problems and untimely death, fails to fulfill the promise of its first two parts and the only nominally masculine hero is of interest chiefly because he appears to be a surrogate for Macaulay herself. For this reason, both Michael and the very juvenile *Secret River* must be subjected to a closer scrutiny.

As the novel opens, Michael is observing his twentieth birthday. Physically he is "frail-bodied" (*S.R.*, p. 12), and exceedingly—perhaps excessively—sensitive, with a "face . . . like pale and shifting waters, . . . [which] took motion and hue from every passing image without, every stirring wind within" (*S.R.*, p. 13). Michael is a poet whose rapturous delight in the sensual and supersensual apprehensions he experiences lends a rare beauty to his poetry. He is frustrated by his awareness of the impossibility of attempting to translate his visions of the ineffable "in plain English . . . in black and white" (*S.R.*, p. 4). He knows, even as he writes, the utter futility of such an attempt.[7]

Michael Travis loves two people with all the intensity of his poetic nature. Mentioned in part 1 is Michael's suntanned, tall, strong, and handsome friend Jim. Michael's delight in Jim's lithe body and beautiful face has in it a strong suggestion of the homoerotic.[8] Mentioned in part 2 is Michael's fiancée Cecilia, a physically attractive but prosaic young woman, with whom he has absolutely nothing in common. Although Cecilia is beautiful to look at and to listen to, and Michael is profoundly affected by the sound of her voice and the touch of her hands (*S.R.*, pp. 27–28), the impression is conveyed that she is for Michael less an object deserving worship in and of herself than a sort of incitement to Platonic rapture.[9]

Like Stephen Wonham in *The Longest Journey* (1907), Michael Travis is addicted to sleeping outdoors.[10] As part 1 opens, Michael—whose given name sounds very much like "Macaulay"—is "awakening" under a "pink rose"[11] by a mystical river. The morning progresses, and all his exquisitely perceptive bodily senses—hearing, sight, smell, touch, and even taste— awaken in turn and synesthetize,[12] inspiring him to bodily and even to extra-bodily[13] ecstasies. Having become joyously aware of all the sights, sounds, and scents of a spring morning,

> Michael laughed and threw the blankets off him, and stood in a moment naked to the morning that flicked him through pointed leaves. Then he slipped down into the cool morning spaces [of the river], and they closed about his limbs and his warm body, and circled over his head. . . . [Michael] spread out his arms and let the slow stream take him and carry him, bearing him gently through shadow and light, between banks purely and mystically white with the may [*sic*]. . . . (*S.R.*, pp. 6–7)

In the course of a prolonged, onanistic nude swim during which his body caresses and is caressed by various phallic, vulvate, and other fertility symbols (*S.R.*, pp. 6–10), Michael

> paused to give good morning to the bobbing lily-balls, . . . slipping his fingers up juicy stalks and bending his face over the cups that were brimmed with delight and laughter and water and the sun. (*S.R.*, p. 9)

Subsequently, in a passage heavy with homosexual suggestion, thoughts of "the delight of the morning," and "the touch of slippery stalks ad wet gold cups against his body," give way in Michael's mind to thoughts of Jim, "the friend he loved" (*S.R.*, p. 11). Michael's sun-browned friend

> was tall and supple, and walked with a lounging gentleness that veiled strength. To the frail-bodied Michael this strength was as the beauty of his face, a thing to smile at for sheer pleasure. (*S.R.*, pp. 13–14)

Michael's thoughts of Jim give way to a suggestive meeting with Jim himself, and some suggestive[14] talk between them (*S.R.*, pp. 14–16). Among a plethora of oral and phallic images comes the expressed intention of Michael to purchase a mattress as a gift for Jim, but to sleep on it himself (*S.R.*, p. 16). In the course of the story, such a "sharing" will indeed occur. First, amidst a quantity of philosophical speculation, mystical vision, and rather limp heterosexual foreplay, Michael experiences a sexual "climax" with his fiancée Cecilia in a canoe on the river:[15]

> Then the rose filled the earth and sky . . . and the slumberous afternoon was on the slow, green river like the burden of a dream, and the weeds swayed to a mysterious rhythm, and presently a canoe slid gently down between sedgy banks, drifting from light to green shadow with a faint gurgling sound of water eddying.(*S.R.*, p. 29)

Next, Jim elopes with Cecilia on the day before she is to be married to Michael, and she spends a number of years living luxuriously on the Continent as Jim's mistress. Finally, when Jim casts Cecilia off, she returns to England where Michael marries her. On their low-budget honeymoon they go to Europe. There they see the same sights and socialize with the same people Cecilia and Jim had encountered previously (part 9).

Michael ascribes his quick and quiet acquiescence in a loveless and stifling marriage with Cecilia to "pity" and "weakness" on his part (*S.R.*, pp. 107–10). However, in view of his previously strong love for her former lover, there are strong homoerotic implications in this sexual "sharing" of the same woman by two erstwhile mutually affectionate men: one frail, fair-complected, and effeminate; the other strong, sunburnt, and virile.

Two Macaulay novels in which the author's own sexual rage and frustration are sublimated into print at the expense of the vital energies of male characters are *Non-Combatants and Others* (1916) and *What Not* (published 1919).[16] *Non-Combatants* depicts the agonies of the First World War from the perspective of the Home Front. The principal focus of the story is on "Alix Sandomir"; her many painful and ambivalent responses to the war, in which, as a woman, she can take no meaningful part; and her failed relationship with the soldier, "Basil Doye" (Rupert Brooke). In happier times, Basil and Alix, both artists, had enjoyed an intellectual camaraderie and a personal "intimacy" that may have been "very deep indeed."[17] But now the uncivilizing effects of global conflict have diminished their receptiveness to each other.[18] Wounded in the field, Doye has been shipped to a hospital in

London. There he has been threatened with the amputation of his fingers, and does, in fact, have "the middle finger of his right hand cut off." This mutilation is disastrous since he, like Alix, is an artist. Obviously the amputated finger is an emblem, both of his phallus and of his artistic power.[19] With equal symbolism Basil later breaks a pipestem in front of a fireplace while verbalizing a rejection of Alix that has long since taken place in his mind (N.-C., pp. 115–16, 214). As the novel concludes, Basil is back at war in a desolate and storm wracked spot when his "tent" collapses while he is tormented with longing for Evie, Alix's brainless, beautiful, voluptuous rival (N.-C., p. 301).[20]

Similar castration imagery occurs in *What Not* (1918), a post–World War I satire on the foibles of paternalistic government. Intermingled with the satire is a love story in which Macaulay's real-life married lover, Gerald O'Donovan, is represented as government minister "Nicholas Chester," while Macaulay herself appears as a ministry underling, "Kitty Grammont." Macaulay had strongly ambivalent feelings about her relationship with Gerald[21] which explain the continuing series of mutilations and other torments to which the hapless "Nicky Chester"[22] is subjected. These sadistic episodes do little or nothing to enhance the content or advance the true action of the story. For these reasons we must see as wholly cathartic[23] the scenes in which "Nicky" is observed:

1. pricking his finger with a poison thorn sent to him by a would-be assassin (*W.N.*, p. 80).
2. slicing out a section of that same finger with his own pen knife and going about his duties with his left hand in a sling (*W.N.*, pp. 80–81).
3. biting his own tongue in an aeroplane accident so severely that his handkerchief is "scarlet-stained," and his speech is impaired while he is attempting to declare his love to Kitty (*W.N.*, pp. 126–27).
4. dangling over a balcony while members of a mob are accusing him of being married and are swinging him "to and fro" by a leg and an arm (*W.N.*, pp. 220–23).
5. stumbling down steps in the grasp of an assailant who calls him a "bloody married imbecile," and falling headlong into a melee from which he will emerge—but just barely!—with "a broken head and three smashed ribs" to lie "inert through quiet snow-bound days and nights, and no one knew whether or not he was going to recover" (*W.N.*, pp. 223–27).

Exploring a similarly "cathartic" tendency in the murder mysteries of Rose Macaulay's contemporary, Dorothy L. Sayers,[24] Janet Hitchman observes:

V. S. Naipaul has said, "An autobiography can distort; facts can be realigned. But fiction never lies: it reveals the writer totally." The only way Dorothy could get herself through a crisis was to write it out as fiction, to see it laid down as though it had happened to someone else. It was as if the typewriter were her psychoanalyst or father confessor. Then, when it was all written out, why waste it? Why not publish it? Murder in print the person who had deceived or hurt you. It assuaged the bitterness of her soul and enabled her to forgive and carry on. But she was wrong if she thought it did not show.[25]

Constance Babington Smith confirms that Rose Macaulay had a similar propensity for revealing herself "obliquely" in her novels."[26] In *Non-Combatants and Others* and *What Not* Macaulay does not "murder" Rupert Brooke and Gerald O'Donovan, but she most certainly debilitates them obliquely and with a vengeance. As is obvious from their imperiled fingers and other bodily and mental afflictions, the fictional surrogates for each of these men are confronted with the symbolic *threat* of castration. In yet another novel, *The Valley Captives* (1911),[27] having been angered beyond endurance by her father, Rose Macaulay actually carries out that threat.

The Valley Captives was dedicated by Rose Macaulay "to MY FATHER." To subject it to analysis is to understand Rose Macaulay's anguish at the time it was written. Its male co-protagonist[28] and his father are both cripples: physically, emotionally, and professionally. In the course of the action this co-protagonist's best friend—also a failure in his life and in his work—is horribly tortured and castrated by religious fanatics.

Emilie Rose Macaulay was a college professor's daughter with a sound religious upbringing. What incited her to perpetrate such horrors in print? A probable answer emerges from data provided by her biographer. Constance Smith records Rose Macaulay's longtime friendship with the poet Rupert Brooke, with whom "she was, for a time a little in love." Smith also discusses Brooke's possible influence on *The Secret River*, and his very definite influence on *Views and Vagabonds* (1912) and *Non-Combatants and Others*. In addition, Smith records that "somewhere about" the time of "the summer of 1910," Brooke

> invited Rose to accompany him on a caravan expedition, 'a sort of camping holiday'.[sic] But the invitation had to be declined, to Rose's intense disappointment. Her father frowned sternly on the idea of a caravan holiday à deux, and although by now she was nearly thirty she accepted the paternal veto. In *Views and Vagabonds*, however, there is a [remark in a] chapter entitled 'The Conscientious Bohemian' . . . [which] suggests that her father's ban continued to rankle for some time.[29]

Smith indicates that, because of this incident, Macaulay was "quietly de-fiant"[30] towards her father in certain passages of *Views and Vagabonds*. However, Smith makes no mention of the way in which Macaulay takes a far less "quiet" revenge in *The Valley Captives*. In this very somber novel she unmans the author of "the paternal veto" by means of three surrogates named "Oliver Vallon," "Tudor Vallon," and "Laurie Rennel."

Most of the action of *The Valley Captives* takes place in a rural setting on the western edge of Wales. Macaulay describes this locale as

> a secluded, remote, and extraordinarily lovely country between the hills and the sea [which perhaps] . . . had a paralysing effect on the energies of those who lived there.[31]

It was in such a locale that Macaulay herself was obliged to spend a most stultifying and unhappy period of time as one of three grown daughters living at home with her parents.[32] Perhaps this explains why her characters are, indeed, "captives"—each in her or his own way—and why there is in the novel the repeated imagery of entrapment—of "nets" and "walls"; "cellars" and "pits"; "prisons" and "chains"—to characterize their various situations. Moreover, in Tudor Vallon's desperate and continually thwarted desire to go to London and learn painting there is certainly a depiction of Rose Macaulay's own early artistic dilemma:

> . . . Tudor was trying at this time, hopelessly, despairingly, savagely, to teach himself to paint. Somehow he had to learn; if not from others, then by himself. So in his secret hours he laboured vainly. But it was absurd. Tudor was artist enough to know that he knew nothing. What he did he hated. And—this was a strange thing—it was not merely that he had not learnt to draw or paint; there seemed to be in his attempts an oddly repulsive element. . . . If the technique had been good instead of bad, this evil note would still, where it appeared, have made ugly and repulsive pictures. . . . Why he, who hated ugliness, should produce it despite himself, was a problem. (*V.C.*, pp. 40–41)

The narrator goes on to imply that it is the "hate" and "ugliness" in Tudor's home life that have poisoned his perceptions and tainted his art.[33]

The Valley Captives appears similarly tainted. For instance, there seems to be a certain autobiographical poignancy in the "young Vallons'" recollection of spoiled opportunities for enjoyment, of bygone holidays when "the elders of the household took their amusement [on the croquet lawn], inaccessibly near" (*V.C.*, p. 9).[34] It is likely that this sort of failure of communication between Macaulay and other members of her family may have helped to engender the reclusive, impotent, failed men and pushy, shrill, somewhat successful women who populate many of *The Valley Captives'* pages.

The father of the family with which the story is primarily concerned is "pale, tired-faced," physically handicapped Oliver Vallon. He is described in the first sentence of the first chapter as "the ineffectual, cynical cripple" (*V.C.,* p. 1).

> It was difficult to forget when one talked to Oliver Vallon that one talked to a failure. The creed of inert scepticism that he applied to the world in general sprang straight out of his own experience of life as it was lived. What *was* the use of fighting when one never won? (*V.C.,* pp. 3–4)

Having limited finances and scant ability to augment them, Vallon, a widower, has been pressured into a loveless and mercenary second marriage by the widow Bodger. It is she who holds the purse strings, and she dominates him in other ways as well. The widow Bodger has a viciously sardonic daughter and a coarse and brutal son by her first marriage. This sadistic pair, Cecily and Phil Bodger, anticipate by seventeen years Virginia Woolf's observation in *A Room of One's Own* concerning the deficiencies of minds "purely feminine" and "purely masculine."[35] Cecily's caustic tongue and Phil's beefy fists are an unending source of torment to Oliver Vallon's virile daughter and effete son, the offspring of his first marriage. Vallon is unwilling and unable to prevent familial strife. He has no meaningful interaction with his own children; he is incapable of feeling anything other than "repulsion" for the stepchildren with whom his own are interminably in conflict. Vallon defends himself against "the discordant clash of actualities that made life in the house on the hill" by mocking the family members involved, or by escaping from them into his library. There in fiction, like Rose Macaulay's own father in fact, he writes books that bring him neither reputation nor remuneration (*V.C.,* p. 8).[36]

The reader's awareness of Oliver Vallon's weakness and impotence is heightened by the contrast of his ineffectual personality with the strong personalities of his sister and his wife. An effective contrast to the limp passivity of Oliver is the energy and decisiveness of his "clever cosmopolitan" sister, "Miss Kate Vallon," who is characterized as

> a fine-lipped, keen-eyed lady of erectly-carried head and alert brows, grafting on to her brother's fineness and ironic discernment a militant vigor not his. . . . (*V.C.,* p. 111)[37]

In keeping with Miss Kate's "militant vigor," she is invested with a masculine emblem of power—a sword:

Oliver Vallon looked at his sister rather nervously. She always came upon him with something . . . of the suggestion of an impatient knight-errant, sword in hand, eager to cleave prison bars. He shrank from such eagerness; cleaving swords do not bring peace, and his peace, hardly won, was the thing he most prized. . . . To go out into the arena . . . and fight for victory was a very bitterness of imagination to the defeated man. . . . Yet his militant sister goaded him continually to the field. (*V.C.*, pp. 117–18)

The "arena" in question is a marital one, not a martial one, although it is described in martial terms. In the ensuing "combat"—an argument over whether or not to send Oliver's unhappy children on a much needed Italian holiday with Aunt Kate—Vallon is symbolically castrated by his second wife:

There is no need to describe in words the hurling of a feather-bed against a very brittle lance; it suffices that it was hurled, gathered together, and hurled again, and finally became moist with [Mrs. Vallon's] salt water [tears], and the extra weight it gained thus did the business. The fragile lance shivered; the haft dropped weakly from a nerveless hand. "I've no doubt, my dear, that you are entirely in the right," the defeated combatant hastened to admit. . . . (*V.C.*, p. 120)[38]

Vallon's unmanning is foreshadowed earlier in a scene with his daughter, "John." Deaf to her pleas that he act towards her brother with compassion and understanding, "Oliver Vallon played with an ivory paperknife, balancing it on long, delicate fingers" (*V.C.*, p. 92).[39]

Oliver Vallon's fragile, timid son Tudor ("Teddy") resembles him greatly. During one dramatic encounter between them a lamp illumines "the delicate, similar features of both" (*V.C.*, p. 80). Also like his father, Tudor is a cripple. The cause of the elder Vallon's disability is never mentioned, but it is stated that Tudor was disabled when, as a child, he was locked in the cellar by his stepsister and stepbrother. In the course of his futile attempt at escape, he had a bad fall. Consequently,

His spine was hurt, and his right arm broken, and he never completely mended of either. To the end of his life he was left-handed and walked with a slight limp. . . . (*V.C.*, p. 19)

Like Michael Travis in *The Secret River*, Tudor Vallon writes poetry. He also draws (*V.C.*, p. 20) and desperately yearns to study painting in London. Also, like Michael, Tudor has a finely honed aesthetic sensitivity; his delicate, frail body has the responsiveness of an aeolian harp:

The luminous eyes were of no color; their essence was merely light, whose hue followed the changing colors of its environment, reflecting and absorbing all tints in turn. . . . They lit a face delicately mobile, a boyish face, refined rather than strong, with a broad, clever forehead and a fine and nervous mouth. . . . The boy was of a light and nervous build, he might be swept by quick laughter and sudden angers, as finely stretched strings by wind; he seemed to have an excess of nervous sensibility that might have made for vital vigour and force of living, but that seemed in him to make rather for weakness. (V.C., pp. 67–68)

Tudor's "excess of nervous sensibility" causes him to start at sudden noises and to flee in terror from dangers real or imagined, as when he knocks his maiden aunt off a bridge in his terrified haste to escape from a friendly cow (V.C., pp. 110–11). Another manifestation of his nervous disorder is his exaggerated abhorrence of conventionally acknowledged heterosexual interchanges. For example, merely having been introduced to a young woman classmate of his during the day causes him to experience a nightmare from which he wakes "in a cold sweat" (V.C., p. 39). Similarly, observing his stepbrother flirting with a young woman causes him to "shudder . . . for both of them" (V.C., p. 47). The actual sight of an embrace between his stepbrother and another young woman affects him with assorted negative feelings, most notably "an almost physical nausea" (V.C., pp. 132–34).[40]

"Tudor did not personally like any girls much" (V.C., p. 133), but the reader is not told why. Two explanations suggest themselves, and they are not mutually exclusive. One is that he suffers from extreme castration anxiety, mingled with, or perhaps provoked by, religious terror. This first hypothesis is substantiated by specific passages in the text.[41] The second explanation is that Tudor is a latent homosexual. With his effeminate appearance and preferences, his fear and hatred of most young women, his appreciation of a few young women only insofar as they are objects he would like to paint, or mannequins for whom he yearns to design "very queer" clothes (V.C., p. 134), he strongly suggests this possibility.

But whatever his sexual orientation, when Laurie Rennel is castrated, Tudor Vallon is identified with him in several ways. For example, Tudor and Laurie lie down together near the place where Laurie's mutilation will occur a few weeks later (V.C., pp. 68ff., 130). On the night of Laurie's ordeal the foppishly clad Tudor is said to be wearing a "sword" as part of his costume for a New Year's Eve ball. In some unknown fashion the sword disappears after Tudor flees "shaking like a girl"[42] from the scene of Laurie's distress. Tudor is then compared to "an unarmed man" whose cowardice will cause him to be tortured by opprobrium "like Laurie Rennel in the hands of the Hughes brothers" (V.C., p. 203). Further on there is also the realization that "so they divided it, he and Laurie: to Laurie the horrid fate, to him the indelible shame" (V.C., p. 205).

The setting in which Laurie meets his "horrid fate" is a very Gothic one. It is after midnight, in a raging storm, on a desolate bog, in a "dreadful upstairs room" (*V.C.*, p. 187) equipped long since with dreadful implements of torture. A helpless young woman screams in terror as an accompaniment to the action (*V.C.*, p. 170), which is carried out by two madmen in the grips of a religious frenzy. But, although the machinery is part of the Gothic novelist's stock in trade and cannot be considered original, the emotions that compelled Rose Macaulay to utilize that machinery were intensely personal.

Phillip Rizzo comments:

> The incident of Rennel's castration has elements of the sensational, elements perhaps too far out of what she [Macaulay] was to indicate as her range.[43]

The peculiar nature of Rennel's fate may seem excessively cruel; however, Rose Macaulay's tendency to sublimate her rages into print was certainly healthy. That Rennel's mutilation does indeed constitute a revenge fantasy appears almost certain. Her father had kept her immured at home, when she hungered to go to London and learn the art of writing. Her father had kept her—at age twenty-nine!—from the company—and possibly, as she may half have imagined, from the arms—of handsome, charismatic Rupert Brooke, with whom she had much in common, and with whom—Constance Smith's demi-disclaimers notwithstanding[44]—she was at the time very much in love. Rose Macaulay must have felt driven to sublimate in the novel dedicated "to MY FATHER" a very great deal of rage indeed.[45] For example, the discovery by Laurie Rennel's friends of his ordeal is brought about by a young woman whose first name, "Blodwen," is translated from Old English as "blood expectation,"[46] and whose surname, "Hughes," is a homonym for "hews."[47] Moreover, the pertinent pages are so unnecessarily overladen with phallic and castration symbols[48] as to suggest that the author was deriving some sort of release in depicting them. Perhaps the most startling of these symbols is the dressing gown in which Rose Macaulay three times laps her "languid" eunuch. The gown is "fat and soft, with pink rosebuds."[49] Having, in effect, thrice left her signature on the surrogate object of her revenge, Macaulay subjects him to a final, painful interview with Dorothy Wynne, the young woman he had been courting. Dorothy, who at one time had decided "to give to Laurie Rennel . . . all of herself that he cared to take" (*V.C.*, p. 172), has now decided instead to bestow herself on "her earnest young tramping lover," an itinerant preacher. With this preacher, Dorothy asserts to Laurie, she intends to "tramp the roads."[50]

A combination of wish-fulfillment and a revenge fantasy is strongly indicated by this final encounter between Laurie Rennel and Dorothy Wynne. At the time George Macaulay prevented his daughter Rose from joining

Rupert Brooke in his horse-drawn caravan, Brooke was himself an itinerant preacher in the cause of Socialism.[51] Significantly, in no fewer than four of the novels written after this, characters are borne away by vehicles resembling Brooke's.[52] Writing of her fictional character's escape "into the roads and fields" with her lover Rose Macaulay exults, "Through love at last she had found her way into life" (*V.C.*, pp. 316, 319–20). In Dorothy Wynne's "breaking free" (*V.C.*, p. 310), there was a vicarious escape for the author from the "FATHER" whom she could, if only in print, punish, and from whom she could flee with her lover in fantasy if not in fact.[53]

When Tudor Vallon and Laurie Rennel are lying down together in mutual commiseration and despair, the narrative voice of *The Valley Captives* interpolates:

> [Full] Realization [of what has happened and why] is difficult when one has wrecked one's ship and is flung by the storm on to a lee shore, broken and stranded. It takes a little time. (*V.C.*, p. 72)

One year later, this concept of a final haven for those who have experienced a "shipwreck" of their lives formed the theme of a beautifully written, prize-winning novel, *The Lee Shore* (1912).[54] Although the title was probably suggested by chapter 23 of Herman Melville's *Moby-Dick*,[55] this particular "lee shore" is on the coast of Italy, where George Macaulay made his home for a number of years when his children were small. That Peter and Thomas Margerison, father and child, are last seen perambulating happily along that coast in a donkey-drawn *cart* appears to be proof positive that this happy melding of symbols of an adored companion and a solicitous father represents Rose Macaulay's resolution of an emotional conflict that had been provoked by her interactions with both.

Certainly there is much to admire in Peter Margerison: his innate dedication to art for its own sake; his absolute integrity, goodness, and gentleness, and his life of renunciation and poverty make him an appealing figure. Constance Smith is convinced that, in creating this protagonist, "Rose was striving . . . to convince herself that her father's failure by worldly standards was of no importance. For there were other values . . . which counted for so much more."[56]

Whatever other emotional issues Macaulay may or may not have been attempting to resolve by means of her fictional hero, he is also a very obvious manifestation of her androgynous mind. Peter Margerison's very surname sounds feminine, as though he were "Margery's son." As a boy he is "delicate to frailness" (*L.S.*, p. 7). He has a whole-souled crush on an older boy, and there is more than a hint of the homoerotic in the imagery describing their encounters.[57] Peter is not a great success on the playing field, and his attempts to participate in sports cause him frequent injuries: "He was easy to break and hard to mend—made in Germany, as he was frequently told. So cheaply made was he that he could perform nothing" (*L.S.*, p. 11). In appearance and in manner Peter resembles his late mother— so much so that a former admirer of *hers* becomes smitten with *him*.[58] In temperament Peter is "gentle" (*L.S.*, p. 21) and non-aggressive. His approach to life manifests his "gentle philosophy of acquiescence" (*L.S.*, p. 35).[59] At least one woman perceives him in his early twenties as "so sympathetic, you might be a young lady" (*L.S.*, p. 114).

Like the gentle St. Francis, whom he professes to abhor, but ends by emulating, Peter Margerison is frequently associated with animals. He is consistently kind and gentle to even the most unattractive and troublesome small children; and, after the birth of his own baby, he bathes, feeds, dresses, reads aloud to and knits for the child with a maternal solicitude not evidenced by the child's biological mother (*L.S.*, pp. 204–5ff).

Another feminine attribute of Peter Margerison is his nickname: he is called "Margery" by his male associates throughout school, university, and into his adult working life. There is also his "immense love, innate rather than grafted, of the pleasures of the eye" (*L.S.*, p. 23).[60] In grammar school he enjoys looking at attractive males (*L.S.*, p. 13). At Cambridge he expresses his love of beautiful objects in the aesthetically pleasing way he furnishes his rooms (*L.S.*, p. 23). Peter delights in fine old china, in lovely antique tapestries, and in other art objects. His chosen profession is "art dealing" (*L.S.*, p. 32), and he has a passion for needlework:

> Peter was quite good at embroidery. He carried pieces of it (mostly elaborately designed book-covers) about in his pockets, and took them out at tea-parties and (surreptitiously) at lectures. . . . The embroidery stood for a symbol [*sic*], a type of the pleasures of the senses. . . . (*L.S.*, p. 23)

Peter's close personal relationships reflect his "feminine" nature. For example, he courts his cousin Lucy so passively that she never even notices (*L.S.*, p. 51) and marries a more aggressive man. Later, Peter is pushed into a relationship with Rhoda Johnson by Rhoda's mother. It is Rhoda who takes the initiative in suggesting marriage, although Peter pretends to have proposed (*L.S.*, p. 183). Similarly, it is Rhoda who suggests they leave their boarding house because she

> wanted a little place to themselves. Peter, who didn't really care, but who would have rather liked to stay and be with [his sister-in-law and brother] Peggy and Hilary, pretended that he too wanted a little place to themselves. (*L.S.*, p. 191)

This passage makes plain Peter's obvious unsuitability to enter into an exclusive heterosexual relationship. The verb "pretended" is crucial to an understanding of Peter's psychosexual make-up. Throughout the story he is attempting to live up to a standard of masculinity that in no way represents his real self. For example, as a youth he *pretends* to prefer the rigors of the cricket field to the contemplation of Bow china, in order to live up to his best friend Denis Urquhart's expectations of him (*L.S.*, p. 21). As a young man, he *pretends* to other young men that he vigorously defended Rhoda Johnson's honor when her would-be seducer spoke of her improperly, but in point of fact he simply fled from the man in embarrassment (*L.S.*, pp. 107, 109). Still later on, a widowed Peter *pretends* to himself that he is capable of stealing Denis Urquhart's wife. But, within hours of arranging an elopement Peter renounces the woman for love of the man. He is last seen vagabonding through Italy in the company of a sensuously handsome Italian youth.

The great passion of Peter's life—the "dominant motive" of his existence (*L.S.*, pp. 30–31)—is his whole-souled adoration of his friend Denis Urquhart. Peter is small, weak, and sickly; Denis is tall, strong, and handsome. Denis's sensual appeal for Peter is reminiscent of Jim's sensual appeal for Michael in *The Secret River:*

> On the shores of the Lido, . . . Peter laughed for the sheer pleasure of seeing Urquhart's lazy length stretched on the warm sand. (*L.S.*, p. 104)

Likewise, Urquhart's voice is special to Peter (*L.S.*, p. 296), and Urquhart's reactions to things are the ones that matter (*L.S.*, pp. 69, 126–29, 133). Since they first met at boarding school, Urquhart has been Peter's hero (*L.S.*, p. 11). In chapter 1 Peter's love for Denis and the adoring "deep blue eyes" with which he regards Denis are characterized as a "hereditary bequest" to him from his mother, who had loved and married Denis's father,[61] and had looked at the senior Urquhart "with just such eyes" (*L.S.*, pp. 9–10). At the age of fifteen, Peter is observed to pass from rapt contemplation of an exquisite eighteenth century bowl to mute adoration of Denis:

> "Keep that till you fall in love," [Denis's uncle Lord Evelyn] . . . had inwardly admonished Peter's back as the two [Peter and Denis] walked away together. "I daresay she won't deserve it any better—but that's a law of nature, and this is sheer squandering." (*L.S.*, p. 22)

Peter's "squandering" of his love on Denis is readily apparent to every other important character in *The Lee Shore*. Peter's employer Leslie resents it; Peter's cousin Felicity defends it (*L.S.*, p. 47). Peter's brother and sister-in-law, Hilary and Peggy, attempt to exploit it (*L.S.*, pp. 17, 166). Peter's wife Rhoda is jealous of it (*L.S.*, p. 197). Peter's cousin Lucy, who is unhappy in her marriage to Denis, cancels her planned elopement to Italy with Peter when she fully realizes the extent of it:

> "Peter we can't do it. . . . the reason is in you, not in me. It is that you love Denis too much. So you couldn't be happy."[62]

In his life style, Denis Urquhart, the object of Peter Margerison's obsessive admiration, seems a masculine enough man. For example, his personal "things were nice enough to look at without being particularly artistic" (*L.S.*, p. 156). He excels in sports (*L.S.*, pp. 1, 21), slays quantities of grouse during the hunt (*L.S.*, p. 209), courts a wife with vigor and decisiveness (*L.S.*, pp. 152–53, 155, 157), and includes among his college exploits a prank involving "actresses" (*L.S.*, p. 167). Denis is obviously gratified by Peter's hero worship (*L.S.*, p. 7), but he is not himself demonstrative, and there is no evidence that he reciprocates Peter's adulation with comparable sentiments. That Denis enjoys basking in Peter's open admiration (*L.S.*, p. 7), that Denis almost invariably acts towards Peter with courtesy, kindness, and interest, but that his friendship cools when Peter's fortunes wane, are the only facts that can be established.

Still, various of the images in *The Lee Shore* suggest powerful homoerotic feelings—if not experienced by Denis toward Peter, then certainly experienced by Peter toward Denis. One of the most striking instances occurs when Denis's scientist cousin Rodney explains Denis's appeal for Peter in socioeconomic terms, but then summarizes the situation with imagery more applicable to a relationship between a woman and a man than to a friendship between adult males.[63] Imagery suggesting a love triangle occurs when Peter and Denis "share" Peter's cousin Lucy Hope in a manner similar to the sharing of Cecilia by Michael and Jim in *The Secret River*.[64] However, it is not entirely clear just who—Lucy or Denis—is at the apex of the triangle, especially in view of the use made of phallic and other sexual symbols and suggestions in conjunction with meetings between the two males.[65]

A third category of feminine men in Rose Macaulay's writings were real individuals of whom she had read or with whom she came increasingly into contact as her literary career prospered. Sometimes such men were generalized beyond recognition, as in the case of Hindley Smith-Rimski of *Orphan Island* (1924).[66]

As this story opens, Victorian castaways—and their numerous progeny—have been stranded for sixty-eight years on a Polynesian Island. They constitute a society which, despite its uniqueness in certain particulars, functions "roughly, along the same lines as the societies of the larger world" from which it has been isolated for so long (*O.I.*, p. 190). Over the decades social changes in this fascinating South Seas community have paralleled "in microcosm" social changes elsewhere (*O.I.*, p. 190). For example, arriving in the 1920s and examining the journal of island happenings kept over the years by the Victoria-like matriarch, Miss Smith, Cambridge sociologist Mr. Thinkwell "detected parallels even to the European aesthetic movement" of the 1890s. The young men in this turn-of-the-century movement oiled their skins "all over," wore flowers behind their ears, drew pictures and wrote poetry. In her journal Miss Smith charged these "mincing" young men with "a loss of true Manliness" (*O.I.*, p. 186). Chief among these unmanly youths she named her own grandson, Hindley Smith-Rimski.

Subsequent to reading Miss Smith's chronicle of the island, Mr. Thinkwell encounters Hindley himself, now middle-aged:

> There appeared at the barber's entrance a very neat elegant, slim, young-old gentleman, who seemed in the earlier forties. There was something in his aspect, and in the air with which he wore his close-fitting costume of smooth gray bark fabric, and neat lizard-skin shoes, which indicated the dandy. Behind one ear he had stuck a small scarlet hibiscus bud, and he swung a light cane. He was exquisitely shaved and perfumed, and had a cared-for looking white skin. . . .
>
> He seemed an exquisite man, the flower of island civilization. One could imagine that he might hold the office of Arbiter Elegantiae among his peers. (*O.I.*, pp. 242–43)

In keeping with the "bland" and "well-bred" (*O.I.*, p. 253) Hindley's dandyish demeanor are his "languid voice" (*O.I.*, p. 281), his often flippant style of speech, and his elegant life style, made possible by inherited wealth and position. In his temperate, leisurely fashion he enjoys such amenities as the island affords him in the way of food, drink, drugs,[67] recreations, and discourse. His household servant is "beautifully trained" (*O.I.*, p. 254), and his tastefully appointed home reflects his personality:

> The house of Mr. Smith-Rimski was a small, elegant building, its wooden walls tastefully plastered with oyster shells. Inside it was carpeted with plaited palm, and on the walls hung paintings. A table stood at one side, holding bowls of brilliant flowers and a chess-board with roughly-cut wooden pieces.
>
> "I must," said Hindley, "have beauty about me." (*O.I.*, p. 252)

Hindley is the island's "librarian" to whom the writers of its "modern literature" entrust their productions. In his youth he generated a great deal of indifferent verse, but the prose of his more mature years shows to advantage his gay, amusing pen; his descriptions were entertaining and his comments apt. A tendency to a rather Petronian wit was held in check by a natural well-bred discretion. . . . Decidedly Hindley Smith-Rimski had talent, for all his foppish airs. (*O.I.*, p. 253)

As a sociologist, Mr. Thinkwell sees in the "suave, talkative" Hindley, "something rather tiresome . . . , in spite of his intelligence and his bland charm" (*O.I.*, p. 246).

He was an eternal type; one had met him in ancient Greece and Rome, and one met him in Cambridge, in Oxford, in London; even, it has been said, in Manchester, if not in Glasgow, and [likewise] on this island that they all persisted in calling Smith. (*O.I.*, p. 246)

Rose Macaulay presents this urbane "eternal type" as a sexless being. With a characteristically clever turn of phrase Hindley confides, "I have a passion for celibacy; it is more elegant—don't you agree . . . ?" (*O.I.*, p. 245). Hindley is equally susceptible to male and female beauty, admiring asexually and from afar. "I am half in love with him and half with his Flora," he remarks of one attractive young couple; "It would seem a pity if they should ever marry and become staid unromantic parents" (*O.I.*, p. 245). In every way, save in his sexual abstinence, Hindley is a precursor of the three aesthetes in *I Would Be Private* (1937). It is likely that he was suggested by a real person or persons in the London literary world in which Macaulay now circulated freely. The witty and sophisticated manner in which Macaulay portrays this simultaneously admirable and "tiresome" cosmopolite is an indication of the formidable expansion of her own personal and professional horizons. Hindley Smith-Rimski of *Orphan Island* (1924) is as far removed in space and time from Tudor Vallon of *The Valley Captives* (1911) as was Rose Macaulay's florescence in London, England, from her rustication in Aberystwyth, Wales.[68]

One very feminine man in a Rose Macaulay novel is an easily recognizable figure from the past. As already noted, Macaulay's nonfiction study of Milton's life and work conjures up the picture of a somewhat effeminate young gentleman:

Let us picture, then, the undergraduate of sixteen and a half, the pride and darling of his home, the prodigious pupil of his school, so delicately beautiful of face and form, so elegantly nice in demeanor and habit as to be nick-named in Cambridge, "the Lady," . . .[69]

Macaulay paraphrases Milton's own characteristically allusive retort to this nickname, which retort, she unsympathetically writes, was delivered "petulantly" (*M.*, p. 15).[70] But Macaulay was even less sympathetic to the poet three years earlier when she utilized "the lady" in a cameo role to lend verisimilitude to *The Shadow Flies* (1932),[71] a historical novel set in seventeenth century England on the eve of the Interregnum. Julian Conybeare, the story's fictive heroine, is overawed when, in the course of a visit to Cambridge she encounters her idol in person:

> As they left the White Horse Inn, they met a gentleman that entered it; a small slight man of somewhere round thirty years, fair-skinned, delicately and austerely featured, with long, smooth, chestnut hair on his shoulders. . . .
> Mr. Milton, a grave, distant and rather shy young man, bowed [in response to Robert Herrick's greeting] while Julian gazed at him. . . .
> So this beautiful, elegant, noble-faced gentleman, who seemed to be a little bored, a little in haste to be on his way, even a little impatient, was Mr. *John Milton, the one time lady of Christ's* [College] whom extraordinary fortune had brought to visit Cambridge at the very same time as themselves. . . . (*T.S.F.*, pp. 188–89; emphasis added)

A dedicated and gifted poet and scholar herself, and the prized pupil of Robert Herrick, Julian is at first ecstatic to be staying at the same inn as Mr. Milton. Back home in rural Devonshire she has studied his verse and has herself acted the part of the Lady in *Comus*, but in Cambridge she learns that the poet who so idealizes Woman in the abstract, will not even condescend to speak to a female who is staying under the same roof:

> He never will say a word to us. He don't hold with females. I don't want to speak with him neither; I should never dare, knowing how he scorns us. Why do men scorn women? 'Tis great pity. (*T.S.F.*, p. 258)

Not only doesn't Milton, as he is depicted in *The Shadow Flies*, see women as human beings; he doesn't even see them as sex objects. In fact, he fails to see them at all (*T.S.F.*, pp. 231, 233–34). In one scene the Pan-like[72] Robert Herrick commends "women, wine, and tobacco" to his pale, proud, and cold colleague in poetry. These enjoyments are, Herrick tells the too serious and too dainty young man, "good cordials to revive thin blood and drooping spirits" (*T.S.F.*, p. 234). After Milton's "rather aloof good-night," Herrick reflects:

> He's a very fine poet, John Milton, but his blood runs too thin i' his veins. *The lady of Christ's—aye, he colours up like a very lady at a coarse word. He could well play his own Lady in Comus.* He's something of a cold, distant, unfriendly man, with his mind all set fast on reforming education, and no time to stay and take's pleasure by the way. He was never one o' Ben's [Jonson's] merry circle, nor could'a been. *We never*

went to bed when we might'a stayed up to talk and to drink. . . . (*T.S.F.*, pp. 234–35; emphasis added)

In another scene, at a gathering of almost every poet in Cambridge except the unsociable Mr. Milton, John Cleveland tries and fails to put across a malicious story of his own invention concerning the absentee:

The tale of John Milton bore an unveracious air, and Mr. [Henry] More dismissed it with a smile.

"John Milton could invent likelier tales of thee than that, Jack Cleveland. And I dare say that he do, for he hath a very satirical malicious wit."

"I grant, I grant. Rat the fellow, he's all the gifts, set aside the right politics and a trifle of pleasant friendly levity." (*T.S.F.*, p. 279)

The mingled animosity, envy, and admiration of Cleveland's emotions here are perhaps the key to Rose Macaulay's own, and may explain why she "beladys" Milton perhaps to excess. She was herself a published—though indifferent—poet.[73] She was deeply read in and enamoured of the seventeenth century. Like Julian Conybeare, Robert Herrick, and John Cleveland in the fictional situations created by her, she could not fail to be impressed by Milton's genius—nor, like these same characters, to be offended by what she perceived to be his ostentatious virtue and egocentric aloofness.

There are at least five men in *I Would Be Private* (1937),[74] all of whom are feminine in a variety of ways. At least two of these men were real contemporaries of Rose Macaulay, who transplanted them to a West Indian Island and produced in the process a partial roman à clef: In 1930 the celebrated novelist Edward Morgan Forster met Robert Buckingham, who was to become the great love of his life for the next forty years.[75] In 1932 Buckingham married May Hockey, and she and Forster remained rivals for Buckingham's affections and attentions for the next several years. In 1933 May Buckingham gave birth to a son, Robert Morgan, who become Forster's godchild. And in 1937 Rose Macaulay became the first person to allude to these events in a published work with her (disguised) references to them in her novel, *I Would Be Private*.[76]

Forster's fiction had become a powerful influence on Rose Macaulay's novels at least as early as 1909.[77] During the 1920s, according to Constance Smith, Macaulay and Forster met personally, and Macaulay's biographer characterizes her as being at that time "Forster's ardent disciple."[78] This adulation found expression in a volume of literary criticism, *The Writings of E. M. Forster* (1938), while Macaulay's personal knowledge of Forster and sympathy for his plight as the homosexual admirer of a heterosexual man had been attested to the year before with *I Would Be Private*.

In this most curious work of fiction, Ronald McBrown, a tall, handsome London policeman, becomes simultaneously disillusioned, by witnessing a miscarriage of British justice, and dismayed, at the invasion of his privacy after his wife has given birth to quintuplets. He resigns from the police force and flees with his wife and family to the Virgin Islands. There he hopes to find some peace and privacy. On the island of Papagayo[79] the McBrown party encounters various other people who have taken refuge there with a similar ideal.

Among these are three homosexuals—John Stowe, Francis Axe, and Charles Mendle, whom McBrown had protected from rowdies on one occasion back in London. It is in the love of Charles Mendle for Ronald McBrown that Rose Macaulay pays homage to E. M. Forster's enduring love for Robert Buckingham.

The homosexuality of Stowe, Axe, and Mendle is established: all three are "arty" young Cambridge men—John is a surrealist painter; Francis and Charles are writers—who prefer aesthetics to athletics. The young men make their first appearance in the novel "sitting indoors . . . and talking about books" (*W.B.P.*, p. 57), while outside "the Oxford hearties" are on a drunken spree on Oxford vs. Cambridge boat-race night. When these "lusty . . . Oxonians" attempt to intrude on them uninvited, the arty young men prefer summoning a nearby policeman to defending themselves (*W.B.P.*, pp. 52–54). The young men are described as behaving with "pride and affectation" (*W.B.P.*, pp. 54–55), and the voices of John and Francis when first heard are "languid" (*W.B.P.*, p. 52); while the voice of Charles is "high" (*W.B.P.*, p. 51).

These close-knit young men prefer the company of one another to the company of anyone else:

> [having] been at Cambridge together, [they] liked at intervals to find some sequestered and exotic part of the earth where they could stay for some months and work. Sometimes it would be Spain or Africa, some-times New Mexico, or Central or South America, once it had been Tristan da Cunha. (*W.B.P.*, p. 157)

While they reside on Papagayo the kindly black matron who delivers food to them is aware of their sexual orientation, although most of the islanders are not (*W.B.P.*, p. 200). The young men are compulsively misogynist (*W.B.P.*, pp. 160–61, 217). They are ignorant of women (*W.B.P.*, pp. 183–84), are bored by them (*W.B.P.*, pp. 185–86), are entirely heedless of the nature and permanence of the marital bond (*W.B.P.*, pp. 301–2). This is quite obvious when gentle and sympathetic Francis Axe expresses his admiration for those who—like his own parents—endure the rigors of begetting and raising children. Francis has, however, no desire to do any begetting of his own (*W.B.P.*, p. 213). In a similar—but far more waspish—vein temperamental John Stowe fulminates at "Family life! No good ever came of it!" (*W.B.P.*, p. 306). With like—but silent—disfavor, moody and speculative Charles Mendle concurs with Francis and John that Ronald McBrown's wife and children are "of course, a pity" (*W.B.P.*, pp. 181, 185). To the three arty young men, marriage and children are incomprehensible abstractions, and they are obliged to resort to literary allusions in an attempt to elucidate these abstractions to themselves (*W.B.P.*, pp. 214, 241, 301–3):

> "None such true friends, none so sweet life," Charles quoted, with skepticism, "As what between the man and wife. . . . But I can't really grasp that. Marriage is a mystery to me; I don't try to grasp it. I can't imagine myself marrying. . . . It must be an extraordinary queer tie to feel." (*W.B.P.*, p. 302)

Hostility towards and/or ignorance of women govern both the aesthetic perceptions and the artistic productions of Francis, John, and Charles. For example, when consuming art, "these young men. . . . on principle read only gentlemen writers" (*W.B.P.*, p. 168). And, in their innermost feelings, and hence in the creations inspired by those feelings, John and Charles perceive images of mutilated women coupled with images of "death," "putrefaction" (*W.B.P.*, part 2, chapter 1), and "abortion" (*W.B.P.*, pp. 192–94). Only the misogyny of Francis Axe is said to be "more theoretical than actual, owing to getting on with his sisters." He is capable of feeling a liking for women and takes "more interest in human beings" than his companions (*W.B.P.*, p. 217). But for John Stowe and Charles Mendle females are "idiotic" and "cow like" (*W.B.P.*, p. 163). They are *"stupid,"* "irrational," "mad" (*W.B.P.*, pp. 183–84). They bite like "sandflies," buzz like "mosquitoes," and twitter like "shrill . . . birds" (*W.B.P.*, pp. 161, 167). They play havoc with a man's creativity and destroy his peace (*W.B.P.*, p. 165).

By contrast—for all three of the arty young men—a physically attractive and "charming" young man like Ronald McBrown can be "adored" for the way he speaks (*W.B.P.*, p. 184), esteemed for his strength of character (*W.B.P.*, pp. 221–22), admired for his "strong, graceful back" (*W.B.P.*, p. 295); "loved" with a motherly solicitude (*W.B.P.*, p. 295), or with hope and happiness (*W.B.P.*, p. 181), or unrequitedly and with despair (*W.B.P.*, pp. 292–96), even across the miles (*W.B.P.*, p. 319).

The three arty and aloof young men might *seem* unsympathetic characters at first glance, but there are lengthy passages in the book which belie this.[80] As a homosexual, Rose Macaulay's friend E. M. Forster might well have taken pleasure in the portrayal of Charles Mendle and Ronald McBrown on walks together: "two tall and handsome young men, descending gracefully through the woods like gods" (*W.B.P.*, p. 178). But, even more, he must have taken pleasure in recognizing himself with three decades or so lopped off his age, as well as in the representation of his beloved Bob Buckingham. This friendship, in *I Would Be Private*, of the Cambridge intellectual and the street-wise London police constable, has marked similarities to the Forster/ Buckingham relationship. Like "Ronald McBrown," Robert Buckingham was a tall, handsome London policeman, knowledgeable about the life of the streets. The first meeting of "McBrown" and "Mendle" is occasioned by the annual Oxford vs. Cambridge boat race; the first meeting of Forster and Buckingham was occasioned by that race.[81] "McBrown" has a wife and children to whom he is devoted, and of whom "Mendle" is jealous; Buckingham was similarly devoted to his wife and child.[82] "McBrown" defends the police; "Mendle"—like Forster—assails them.[83] In "Charles Mendle's" temperament E. M. Forster might have recognized his own:

> Writing did not make Charles a happy man, for nothing did that, owing to his temperament, but it relieved often the tension of his mood. (*W.B.P.*, p. 157)[84]

In "Charles Mendle's" political tendencies E. M. Forster could have recognized his own:

> I should want to help the democratic side against Fascism, in any country, I think. . . . Well, anyhow, you see how hard I find it to write anything, with all this afoot in Europe. To write anything not connected with these vital things, with all these strugglings and clashes, I mean something that may be constructive, it seems not pulling one's weight like fiddling while Europe burns. (*W.B.P.*, pp. 297–98)

In "Charles Mendle's" aesthetic theory E. M. Forster *would* have recognized his own:

> If one could reach that fusion of art and life; the *right* fusion; art not *using* life, just as fuel for its flames, but letting life use art, and yet letting go nothing of craftsmanship . . . that would be to find one's place in the scheme; it would be what, I suppose, finding God is to the religious; or finding the ideal and lasting love is to the lover. (*W.B.P.*, p. 298)

"Charles Mendle's" "fusion" is simply a paraphrase of E. M. Forster's "Only connect."[85]

Several phallic and oral images are used when Ronald McBrown and Charles Mendle are alone. These suggest, if not the nature of McBrown's feelings for Mendle—since the former's mind is usually on his wife or children or some other domestic or practical matter—then surely the nature of Mendle's feelings for McBrown.[86]

With a fine feminist irony, Rose Macaulay has seen to it that the most virile man in *I Would Be Private* is also the most feminine. Ronald McBrown, a stalwart ex-policeman, a father of quintuplets, an expert horticulturalist, a manly carpenter, also cooks adeptly (*W.B.P.*, p. 4), washes dishes more adroitly than his wife (*W.B.P.*, p. 68), and shares fully in the duties of infant care.[87]

McBrown's tending of his own infants with "maternal" expertise is viewed with an equal lack of enthusiasm by men who are boastfully heterosexual, and by men who are unobtrusively homosexual (*W.B.P.*, pp. 195, 213). McBrown readily acknowledges to himself and to others the tedium involved in tending numerous infants. Yet he is equally aware that his willingness to endure this tedium makes it possible for his wife to experience life more fully: "My wife likes seeing things as well as I do. . . . It would not be fair did we not take turns" (*W.B.P.*, pp. 99–100). McBrown sees his wife as a human being of equal worth and sentience with himself. Thus, "justice" impels him to share a lifetime of arduous duties with her; love compels him to remain "attached" to her;[88] and both love and justice inspire him to feel the want of her presence when pleasure and adventure are at hand (*W.B.P.*, p. 193).

The living arrangement designed by Rose Macaulay for use by several of the sojourners on Papagayo Island provides a clue not only to the interaction of social and sexual values in *I Would Be Private*, but to the extent of Rose Macaulay's affection for and indebtedness to E. M. Forster.[89] A failed "loony asylum" has been converted into a prestigious lodging house. "The madhouse" is described as

> a long white building facing south, and partitioned into twelve numbered cabins, with a covered verandah running all along in front of it. (*W.B.P.*, p. 212)

Cabins one through three are occupied by the heterosexuals; cabins ten through twelve are occupied by the homosexuals; "the intervening cabins were empty" (*W.B.P.*, p. 212). There are, as has been indicated, differences among the various perspectives and personalities of the homosexuals. There are likewise differences among the various perspectives and personalities of the heterosexuals. For example, Gert Grig, in number one, is a happy-go-lucky, sexually liberated, self-centered hedonist. Her brother Leslie in number two is an underprivileged but aspiring and aggressive young man, a Leonard Bast figure,[90] but one obviously destined to make good. In the next cabin are their partly masculine sister, Win, and her partly feminine husband, Ron, who happily—albeit often wearily—obey the imperatives of domesticity. The intervening rooms may yet be filled with individuals of still other personalities and perspectives.

Each of the numbered cabins in this "madhouse" is linked by the same verandah. This, of course, is the common thread of humanity that joins the disparate characters, homosexual and heterosexual alike. For Rose Macaulay's "madhouse" is a microcosm of the world, each of whose sojourners has, like the characters in a well-known E. M. Forster novel, her or his own "room with a view."[91]

3

"Femme coupée en morceaux"

IN AGATHA CHRISTIE'S *Murder in Mesopotamia* (1935), arch-detective Hercule Poirot finds his chief clue to the murder of Mrs. Leidner in the personality of the victim herself. That personality is best revealed, asserts Poirot, by an analysis of the volumes on Mrs. Leidner's bedroom bookshelf. Among the readings found there, at the scene of the crime, is Rose Macaulay's

> *Crewe Train*, [which] seemed to show that Mrs. Leidner had a sympathy and an interest in the independent woman—unencumbered or entrapped by man. . . . *Crewe Train* is a study of a passionate individualist.[1]

The "passionate individualist" referred to is Denham Dobie, the motorcycle-riding, cave-exploring, penknife-wielding heroine of Macaulay's 1926 novel about a splendid love affair that becomes a squalid marriage.[2] Similar "passionate individualists" abound in several novels of Rose Macaulay. They are always female. They are often semi-autobiographical. They are usually young. They are true to themselves only when they dress, act, play, work, think, or dream in a way that others in their social milieu regard as more appropriate to males. They are invariably allied with, and/or in conflict with, a father, a brother, a lover, a husband—or some combination thereof. They make their debut with Joanna Vallon in *The Valley Captives* (1911), disappear for a time, return in the 1920s, and then persist as a type until *The Towers of Trebizond* (1956). Unlike their cognates, the feminine men discussed in chapter 2, these masculine women are the products not of particular circumstances in Rose Macaulay's life, but of a persistent state of Rose Macaulay's mind, epitomized by Imogen Carrington's passionate feminist declaration to her horrified mother in *Told by an Idiot* (1923)[3]:

> *Marry* the navy? Oh, no. I couldn't do that. I should be too jealous of him. You see, I want to be in the navy myself, and I know I should hate his being in it when I couldn't. It would only rub it in. I want to do nice

things myself, not to marry people who do them. . . . it's *my* life I want to enjoy, not anyone else's. (*T.b.I.*, p. 267)

The feminist scholar would argue that, although various of Rose Macaulay's "passionate individualists" are collected in this and in a subsequent chapter that also refers to them as "masculine" women, a great part of their "masculinity" consists in their author's wanting them, like Imogen, to enjoy "my life . . . not anyone else's."[4]

In a vignette from act 3 of Henrik Ibsen's *A Doll's House* (1879), Torvald Helmer advises the widow Mrs. Linde to abandon her knitting because "that can never be anything but ungraceful." Instead, Helmer asserts, Mrs. Linde should take up embroidery because "it's far more becoming."[5] The message is plain: a woman, even one who is no longer the property of a father, a brother, or a husband,[6] and even one who is usefully—if trivially—occupied, is "feminine" only insofar as she gratifies the sensibilities of a man, of *any* man who might walk into a room and catch her knitting when she would please his eye more by embroidering. It is therefore no accident that Stanley Croft, one of the masculine women in *Told by an Idiot*, is shown reading *A Doll's House* just prior to filing for divorce (*T.b.I*, p. 111). Although yet another in the lengthy series of her husband's indiscriminate amours precipitates her action, his "idiotic opinions about one half of the human race" are no less a factor in the disintegration of the marriage (*T.b.I.*, p. 142).

Imogen Carrington of *Told by an Idiot* is said to be congenitally opposed to the stereotyping of sex roles while she is but "an infant of one summer" (*T.b.I.*, pp. 74–75). While Rose Macaulay's views were just as ingrained as Imogen's, they were not effectively incorporated into her fiction until her fourth novel, *The Valley Captives* (1911).[7] No fewer than three young females in this novel—"Cissie" Bodger, "Dolly" Wynne, and "John" Vallon—are useful in elucidating the motivation for, and the nature of, Rose Macaulay's protest against the traditional roles of women. The first two young women are vehicles which explain the plight of the would-be "womanly" woman; the third provides an opportunity for exploring the struggle of an individualist who desires merely to be "herself" (*V.C.*, p. 331).

The femininity of Cecily—also called "Cis," "Cissie," or "Miss Bodger"—is unadulterated sham: she *plays* at being a woman, and she and her family suffer greatly as a consequence. As Cissie passes from girlhood to young womanhood, she submits to the ever-increasing restrictions which are placed on her capacity for action. These restrictions are attributable not to bodily infirmity, but to the conventions regulating the behavior of the sexes. Insofar as she is beginning to subscribe to these conventions, she is in the process of developing into a "womanly" woman. Thus, for instance, Cissie becomes so concerned with the need to keep her clothes in order that she is virtually stymied in the physical expression of anger (*V.C.*, p. 23). As a consequence she becomes skillful at using her tongue to gossip maliciously and to instigate others, especially her brothers, to physical combat (*V.C.*, pp. 83–84). Afterwards, she affects to be horrified at the outcome (*V.C.*, p. 85).

Cissie's choice of costume for the New Year's Eve Ball is as significantly symbolic as the choices of her stepsiblings, Tudor and John. At the dance she is clad in imitation of "a snowdrop" (*V.C.*, p. 171),[8] a long, white, and particularly limp kind of flower. In keeping with this metaphor, Cissie's dress trails on the floor to such an extent that it is repeatedly stamped upon and torn under the feet of her partner, a "manly" man she will later marry (*V.C.*, pp. 179, 334).

As a "womanly" woman, Cissie is never observed in transit or in action without a companion or an escort. She has learned to fear driving the family pony and carriage because driving makes her "nervous" (*V.C.*, p. 303). When there is danger to others, she is useless. When there is danger to herself, she is resourceless. Whenever peril is imminent, she can only shriek or sob or laugh hysterically.[9] Although she is brutish by nature, as the story's narrator cynically observes, Cissie is a hypocrite "certain always to act and speak in [what she deems to be a ladylike] character." This is a result not of her true nature, but of her perpetual worry "lest the men should hear" (*V.C.*, p. 141). For this feminine but far from admirable woman, matrimony is the only possible career and life imposes only one overwhelming criterion: "What will a *man* think?" (*V.C.*, p. 210).

Also needing a man for a "prop" (*V.C.*, p. 220)[10] is Joanna Vallon's friend, Dorothy Wynne, a far more appealingly "womanly" woman than Cissie Bodger. Dorothy is beautiful in face and form; she is graceful in motion. From her "Botticelli lips" (*V.C.*, pp. 58–59) proceed the trite phrases and parochial prejudices of her upbringing among the country gentry. She is repeatedly referred to by her friends as "Dolly." Certainly, this nickname stems from Rose Macaulay's desire to place Dorothy in a class with Nora Helmer of *A Doll's House*. Like Ibsen's Nora, Macaulay's "Dolly" is destined to experience a moral and spiritual awakening, and to renounce some of what her society regards as her femininity in the process. Also like Ibsen's protagonist, Rose Macaulay's "Dolly" has been "smothered and stunted" in her moral growth by the comfortable "atmosphere" of her surroundings (*V.C.*, p. 57). Her conceptions of right and wrong stem from received opinion rather than from moral insight or personal preference and feeling. The opinions she is accustomed to receiving are snobbishly squirearchical.

Like the "snowdrop" Cissie Bodger, Dorothy Wynne is associated with flowers. We are told that her hapless suitor, Laurie Rennel, had long admired her "flower-like charm" (*V.C.*, p. 311); that she participated in the hunt "with her small head set flower-like on a slim white-stocked neck" (V.C., p. 141); that "her dark, flower-wreathed hair tossed about her shoulders" at the New Year's Eve Ball (V.C., p. 172).

Dorothy's costume, like those of the other characters who attend the Ball, effectively expresses her personality. She is dressed "as a wood-nymph" (V.C., p. 171). In a previous scene depicting the hunt, she is said to resemble "some dryad of the woods" (V.C., p. 142). But she is a "dryad" who is not quite comfortable in her role: her hunting costume "drags a little bit at the arms" (V.C., p. 141). Graceful though she looks, she is not quite at ease in her wealthy, well-clad, bland complacency. Ultimately, her moral sense is stirred by the "religious revival" that comes "raging" through the valley "like a fire before wind." She begins to question "her lifelong habit of conformity" (V.C., pp. 152, 157). Very prominent in the religious revival is Lloyd Evans, an idealistic young Church of England minister of humble origins who renounces his living to "tramp the roads"[11] preaching the Gospel. Dorothy's decision to join him as his wife enables her to abjure her worldly goods and her fashionable ways and to "depart . . . with him into the roads and fields" (V.C., p. 320).

Dorothy Wynne's resolve to give up "being worldly and comfortable" (V.C., p. 317) is only possible because she has found a man of great physical and moral strength who "had given her to herself" (V.C., p. 316). His "strong hands" lend both support and impetus to her moral regeneration:

> It was not for such as her to be caught and possessed by the greatness of an idea, like her earnest young tramping lover. For such as her personal love must be the revealer. . . . (V.C., p. 316)[12]

While she is still in a transition phase Dorothy is compared to "a lovely Undine with a newly found soul which she resents" (V.C., p. 225). Undine, a legendary Greek water spirit who could earn a soul by marrying a mortal and bearing his child, could be humanized only by commerce with a potent male. Similarly, when Dorothy acquires the crudely masculine Lloyd Evans for a "prop," she is humanized by possession of *his* phallus. Armed with his maleness, she can renounce several of her feminine activities for others which are more masculine. She can, for instance, exchange a homebound existence of meaningless frivolities—of "clothes, games, parties" (V.C., p. 316)—for a peripatetic life of purposeful endeavors. Under the protection of a husband she can abandon a life-style that is feminine and static for one that is masculine and kinetic.

Cissie Bodger's feminine suppression of herself leaves her immobile and vitriolic.[13] The trampling of her dress under the feet of her macho husband-to-be portends their future relations. By contrast, Dorothy Wynne is able to realize herself, but only as an adjunct to a powerful male. Of the three principal female characters in *The Valley Captives* only Joanna Vallon is not married by the story's end; but she, too, will become more fully "herself" only by totally annihilating a man she loves—her brother—and then incorporating his most salient characteristics into her own personality.

When Tudor and "John" (Joanna) Vallon[14] attend the New Year's Eve Ball, the costumes in which they appear provide an accurate indicator of the femininity of the brother and the masculinity of the sister. Tudor, the young man, is foppishly clad in pale blue silk, with a "black patch," a "tie-wig and ruffles" (*V.C.*, pp. 171, 178, 200). John, the sister, is costumed "as a silver-mailed Joan" of Arc (*V.C.*, p. 171). On the way home from the ball the pair are among a group called to the aid of Laurie Rennel. Concurrent with the New Year's Eve festivities Rennel has been kidnapped, tortured, and castrated by religious fanatics in "a dreadful upstairs room" (*V.C.*, p. 187). While the more feminine of the women in the party shrink in fear; while her frail and pale brother flees in abject terror, and her oafish drunken stepbrother "fumbled and stumbled below" (*V.C.*, p. 193), John is the first rescuer to burst in and confront the malefactors. For her bravery, she is later praised by her stepbrother as "a sportsman" (*V.C.*, p. 207).[15] In her emulation of "Joan of Arc" Joanna Vallon is the only true hero in the book.

As the actor of a heroic role, Joanna exhibits many masculine traits. For example, she is invariably called "John," not only by her family and friends, but also by the narrator. In childhood she speaks in "her deep little voice" (*V.C.*, p. 15). In young adulthood she is stolid, sturdy, square-jawed, laconic, calm, practical, unimaginative, aggressive, brave, and true. Eschewing feminine modesty, she looks directly at men with her "steady gray eyes" (*V.C.*, p. 13).[16] In fact, she bears a striking physical and temperamental resemblance to the romantic heroes of old.

Tudor Vallon recalls that, when he and his sister were children, he would invite her to act out with him the stories in adventure books. Often, for example, he would ask her to imagine herself as "Ralph," and to join him "on the Coral Island." But, invariably, she ridiculed the idea. Tudor attributes this to his sister's innate deficiency of imagination (*V.C.*, pp. 281–82). However, years later, as a young adult, she has no trouble dressing the part and emulating the exploits of St. Joan of Arc, a derring-doer with whom she could identify. Similarly, Rose Macaulay portrays in *The Valley Captives* a heroine with whom *she* can identify. Joanna Vallon transcends the sexual stereotypes of her author's day, performing well those tasks on the family farm requiring practical knowledge, manual dexterity, and vigorous bodily activity.[17]

> She loved the valley and the garden and all things out of doors, and
> when in doubt built a hen-house. She had also a knack of getting on
> with people; . . . her most intimate friends were the farmer people of
> the hills and valleys. Most of the girls she knew—and she was quite fond
> of some of them—talked about clothes, not occasionally, which is
> pleasant, but continually, which . . . is tedious. John preferred to talk
> [with her farmer friends] about incubators and vegetables, and . . . the
> deep mysteries of the fertile earth. . . . (V.C., pp. 49–50)

As a child, "John" prefers tools to dolls and dreams of becoming a carpenter.
Later on, as a young woman of marriageable age, she is heedless of any
impression she *should* be making on the young men she encounters. She
makes it abundantly clear to them that she prefers farming textbooks to
frothy romances. She pays little heed to her clothes. When she plays mixed
doubles tennis, she plays to win (V.C., p. 59). When she drives with others—
male or female—she is the first to reach for the reins (V.C., pp. 180, 303). She
anticipates a career not as a wife, as her father Oliver Vallon has insisted, but
as a farmer. She longs eagerly for the formal agricultural training that her
father denies her solely by accident of her sex. Simultaneously, he is attempting to force that identical training on her brother, who is totally unfitted for
it and disgusted by it.

Oliver Vallon's sister—John's Aunt Kate—vigorously opposes this stereotyping of sex roles. Kate insists that her nephew should be allowed to
study art as he desires, and that her niece should be allowed to study
agriculture. Forcing them to deny their true selves solely because of their
gender is, she insists, "immoral. All silliness is, of course, and that most—
not letting people live" (V.C., p. 119).[18]

In life, John and Tudor Vallon are a particularly close-knit sister-brother
pair. But, when Tudor dies saving John from a fatal carriage accident, some
curious imagery comes into play. First of all, Tudor's fatal injury occurs
when he is struck on the side of his head by "the point of the shaft" of his
sister's runaway cart. Elsewhere in the book the shaft of a cart is deliberately
used as a phallic symbol.[19] Second, John's cheek is described as having been
"cut open on a flint" (V.C., p. 307). Not only does the flint itself have sexual
significance in a poem earlier alluded to in the novel,[20] but the blood from
the sister's wounded cheek drips onto the dead brother's forehead. Thus, the
imagery surrounding Tudor's death suggests an incestuous—albeit mystical—union of the masculine sister and the feminine brother into one being,
partaking of the qualities of both and having "two lives to live at once."[21]
Sister and brother are merged into a single intensely aware and appreciative
self which regenerates "like a cramped growth restored to light and air"
(V.C., p. 331). The vegetable simile is an apt one: the interpenetration of sister
and brother suggests the fruitfulness—both physical and metaphysical—of
the union of Rhea and Saturn:[22]

[John] made friends with life, with people and animals and vegetables and herself, and dug in the garden. She realized and fulfilled her kinship with the earth; more and more its forces made, in her recognition of them, for beauty and good. . . . practical farming. . . . gave her its slow, progressive revelation of the liberty which . . . rises sublimely superior to law. . . . The walls of materialism had shattered. . . . (*V.C.*, p. 331)

If "Cissie" Bodger is a paradigm for the brutal subjugation of women, and "Dolly" Wynne is an archetype for the graceful submission of women, then "John" Vallon is the prototype for a new type of woman: one who is destined, in the process of self-realization, to make the heretofore exclusively masculine pursuits, prerogatives, and transcendent experiences of men her own.

Dangerous Ages (1921)[23] is a sensitive study of the predicament of being a female—of any age—in a society in which "Men must work and women must weep" (*D.A.*, p. 184). Of the seven women related by blood or by marriage who figure in the story, no less than four—Neville, Pamela, Nan, and Gerda—exhibit Macaulayesque masculine tendencies. Most prominent is Neville Bendish, the lovely, intellectually gifted wife of a British M.P., who has sacrificed her personal ambition to become a doctor for the sake of her children's well-being and her husband's career. Neville is fiercely competitive with other attractive women for her husband's attentions. For Rodney's sake she spends her winters in London drawing rooms and dining rooms "being the political wife" with well-bred ease (*D.A.*, pp. 19, 185).

But in the summer, in the privacy of the family estate, Neville—whose given name is masculine[24]—displays some behavior that is likewise remarkably masculine. This is particularly true of the first chapter in which androgynous Neville Bendish, like androgynous Michael Travis before her, celebrates a birthday with a nude swim at dawn (*D.A.*, pp. 11–14). If, in this opening passage of *Dangerous Ages*, masculine pronouns are substituted for feminine, Neville could very easily be mistaken for the boy-hero of an adventure tale: She rises at break of day, feels the morning chill on "her bare throat and chest," and departs for the woods in her pajamas, overcoat, and sand shoes. She is munching chunks of "bread and marmalade."[25] Momentarily, she hesitates under the window of the companion she habitually whistles awake for such expeditions—her daughter, Gerda. But she decides instead to go on with only her dog for company. Once in the woods, she strips off her clothes to reveal a forty-three-year-old female body that could just as easily be that of a young boy:

a slight and naked body, long in the leg, finely and supply knit, with light, flexible muscles—a body built for swiftness, grace and a certain wiry strength. (*D.A.*, p. 13)

After Neville's swim, she dries herself off on her coat, resumes her pajamas, finishes her bread and marmalade, and swarms[26] up a tree trunk to sit astride "a broad branch. . . . whistling shrilly," in imitation of various birds (*D.A.*, p. 13). Clearly, Neville's doings in the first few pages of the first chapter of *Dangerous Ages* read far more like those of an adolescent or pre-adolescent boy than of a middle-aged English society matron.

Neville's relationship to her spouse and offspring is a curious one: she loves them (*D.A.*, p. 15); she conscientiously and appropriately fulfills every wifely and maternal function; yet her family are also the playmates whom she excels at any sport: "she could beat any of the rest of them at swimming, walking, tennis or squash" (*D.A.*, p. 15). Just as her athletic prowess suggests a youth rather than a mature woman, so do the birthday presents her immediate family bestows on her. They include "a splendid great pocket knife" from her son, an "oak box" carved by her daughter, and "a new bicycle" from her husband (*D.A.*, p. 18).

If Neville's avocations are not traditionally feminine, neither is the vocation to which she has aspired for decades in spite of her own mother's vehement opposition:[27]

> I must be a doctor. . . . It's my job. The only one I could ever really have been much good at. The sight of human bones or a rabbit's brain thrills me, . . . (*D.A.*, p. 55)

Neville's innate interests and abilities have always been in the biological sciences; yet, ironically, it is her own sociobiological role that has hindered her:

> How to be useful though married: in [her husband] Rodney's case the problem was so simple, in hers so complicated. She had envied Rodney a little twenty years ago; then she had stopped, because the bringing up of Kay and Gerda had been a work in itself; now she had begun again. Rodney and she were more like each other than they were like their children; . . . Only Rodney's [temperament and outlook on life] had been solidified and developed by the contacts and exigencies of his career, and Neville's disembodied, devitalized and driven inwards by her more dilettante life. . . . (*D.A.*, p. 19)

The resumption of her pre-medical studies after a lapse of twenty-three years is an uphill struggle for Neville: her powers of concentration are dormant and diminished; her family actively opposes her; her daughter is smashed up in a bicycle accident and requires continuous nursing. With the cards thus stacked against her, she is predestined to failure even before she starts. In consequence, she suffers a physical and mental—a "nervous"—breakdown, and is ultimately reduced to sitting on charitable committees and trying to subdue the ego that had caused her to aspire to an ambition that was unattainable as a direct result of her marriage.[28]

By contrast, Neville's thirty-nine-year-old lesbian sister Pamela is happy and fulfilled in her career as a social worker. Her professional achievements have brought her, as Neville observes with admiration, "recognition, even fame, in the world you work in. You count for something" (*D.A.*, p. 190). And, while Pamela comforts Neville with the assurance that "Most people" would prefer Neville's situation to Pamela's, there is not the slightest indication Pamela herself feels this way (*D.A.*, p. 190).[29]

In many ways, Pamela Hilary conforms to the stereotype of a masculine woman. Her voice is "crisp, quick, and decided." Her body is "tall, and straight." Her "pince-nez" enhance her "distinguished-looking" appearance; while her pleasant and sometimes humorous manner, and her perpetual tact and good breeding, make her impervious to intimacy, save with her lover, Frances Carr. Pamela is very "capable" at her work, "the very type of the professional woman at her best," but her relatives are well aware that she is obsessed with Frances Carr, and the home that they have made with one another for eighteen years. It is this home that provides the very "roots" for Pamela's existence.[30]

Like Pamela, who calls her "Frank," Frances Carr is a dedicated social worker. Physically and temperamentally the pair complement each other: while Pamela is tall, fair and stately, Frances is small, brown, and merry. These women—both in their late thirties—are reciprocally nurturant: they fortify one another against illness and fatigue with bread and milk, with cushions and admonitions to rest. Pamela's sister Nan characterizes them as "Women . . . of the mothering type," who expend their maternal feelings on one another in lieu of children (*D.A.*, p. 77). But Nan, who is sexually sophisticated in her own right, is perfectly aware of the strong sexual component in their relationship. Chapter 4 of *Dangerous Ages* provides Nan—and the reader—an opportunity to see this lesbian household for what it is, to ponder it, and then to accept it. These devoted "friends and their friendship and their anchored peace" (*D.A.*, p. 80) are in a state preferable to that of the spinster, the widow, or the heterosexual woman who changes partners indiscriminately. Only a happily married state is preferable.

Symbolism and suggestion skillfully imply in chapter 4 what Rose Macaulay is too reticent to state plainly. The chapter opens as Pamela fits her "latch-key"[31] into the door of the lodgings she shares with Frances Carr. Pamela lets herself into "the hot dark passage hall" that leads her to her room where Frances awaits her with a "steaming bowl" of "pap,"[32] an invitation to "lie back" in a "deep chair" piled with cushions, and a pair of "moccasin slippers" which Frances slips onto Pamela's feet after removing her street shoes. All of these images indicate some sort of interpenetration by these women. Quite suggestively, the narrator interrupts a recital of these events in medias res with a double-entendre implying that, although there were those among Pamela Hilary's acquaintance who "complained that they couldn't get to know Pamela," yet "Frances Carr *knew* her."[33]

The relationship of Pamela and Frances is, in my opinion, based on the lifelong companionship of Rose Macaulay's sister Jean and her colleague in nursing, Annie—"Nancy"—Willetts.[34] Therefore, when she felt motivated to write about this sort of living arrangement, Rose Macaulay had ample reason to do so with discretion and kindness. Like their real-life counterparts, Pamela and Frances are "all right"; they are idealistic dispensers of charity and sympathy, a refuge for the troubled and a support to the needy. Their sexual orientation—a textbook case of arrested psychosexual development[35]—does not preclude their being "decent people," calmly and cheerfully "doing one's job" (*D.A.*, pp. 77, 79). They do not make a spectacle of themselves; are "not sloppy, not gushing." Macaulay presents them as not terribly extraordinary or shocking; as, in fact, "rather boring," since "Most sorts of love were rather dull, to the spectator" (*D.A.*, pp. 77).

The first chapter of *Dangerous Ages* begins with a reminder "that there are a million more women than men in this country" (*D.A.*, p. 21).[36] The institution of "some system of polygamy" is advocated by Pamela's twenty-year-old niece Gerda[37] as a way of dealing with this "surplus" (*D.A.*, pp. 20–21). Pamela and Frances have found their own alternative, their own "something solid," their own "anchor," their own "Roots" (*D.A.*, pp. 79, 81). Perceiving this, Nan Hilary yearns, for the first time in her frenetic and promiscuous life, to settle down. She decides to marry Barry Briscoe, a wealthy and attractive man of good character, who has been courting her unsuccessfully for months. Ironically, this good resolve comes too late: Barry has already fallen out of love with Nan and has begun to fall in love with her niece, Gerda. A duel, very nearly to the death, fought by these two women during a bicycling holiday on the Cornish coast settles the matter for good.

At the beginning of the holiday with her brother Kay, her aunt Nan, and her aunt's suitor, Barry, the normally dreamy and passive Gerda is playfully mocked by her brother as a "Coward" and tauntingly enjoined to "act like a man" (*D.A.*, p. 145). While Nan is swimming fearlessly through the high seas "with the arrowy straightness of a fish or a submarine," and while Barry and Kay are being "dashed about by the waves" in a futile attempt to keep up, the far more timid and far less agile Gerda is placidly rolling and paddling "in the surf by herself" (*D.A.*, p. 145). This placidity is expressive of her essential nature; but, before the conclusion of this episode she will "act like a man" indeed.

Nan is thirty-three years old. Her "supple body excellently trained"

(*D.A.*, p. 146) surpasses Gerda's childishly "flat body" and "thin white arms" (*D.A.*, p. 149). Likewise, Nan's superb intellect outshines Gerda's vague and dreamy consciousness, just as her brilliant novels and literary criticism excel Gerda's mediocre poetry. Yet Gerda wins Barry Briscoe away from her aunt and marries him.

The contest for Barry's heart and hand may be abstracted into a clash of Youth with Age, of Idealism with Cynicism, or even of Virtue with Sin; since Gerda, although advocating "Free Love" in principle, has been as pure as the driven snow in practice, while Nan has been a freewheeling "rake" (*D.A.*, p. 24) with a seeming preference for married men. In keeping with romantic convention, Gerda's childlike undeveloped body, her blond hair and fair complexion epitomize her moral purity, while Nan's "lissome" form, her darker hair and skin indicate the instincts of a "lower animal" (*D.A.*, pp. 23, 28). All this is strictly in keeping with the romance convention. However, in a startling variant from that convention, it is the two *women* who will ultimately engage in a duel of "honour" for the purpose of impressing the man:

> They would prove to one another which was the better woman, as knights in single combat of old proved it, or fighters in the ring to-day. As to Barry he should look on at it, whether he liked it or not. (*D.A.*, p. 151)[38]

Thus a *man* is cast into the passive role of a spectator and a prize; and at one point it is a *man* who faints[39] while two women engage in deeds of derring-do. Rose Macaulay's reversal of the customary sex roles in an otherwise archetypal situation is astonishing. Traditionally, two men loving the same woman would engage in physical combat, but one or both of two women loving the same man would resort to guile, rather than force.

In the most exciting action scenes she ever wrote,[40] Macaulay depicts two women diving from dangerous heights, swimming in treacherous seas, confronting ferocious bulls, and hurtling their bicycles down tortuous mountain paths until one of them—Gerda—goes off the side of a cliff "straight into space, like a young Phoebus riding a horse of the morning through the blue air" (*D.A.*, p. 163).[41]

Gerda's injuries are serious, but not life-threatening. Her courage in enduring pain earns her the accolade of "sportsman," which had before belonged to Nan (*D.A.*, p. 159), and secures to her exclusively the affections of Barry, whom she had previously hoped to "share" with her aunt (*D.A.*, pp. 132–33, 167).

Probably the most masculine of Rose Macaulay's women characters is Miss Montana, known until the concluding pages of *Mystery at Geneva* (1923)[42] as "Henry Beechtree," and referred to until then with masculine pronouns. "Henry," the transvestite antihero of the story, is a shabby, impoverished, yet gentlemanly, young reporter for the not-too-influential *British Bolshevist*. He has been assigned to cover a session of the League of Nations at Geneva. When several of the most admired and influential delegates are spirited away in a sinister plot to discredit and destroy the League, Henry sets out to "expose" a British member of the Secretariat, Charles Wilbraham, as the mastermind of the plot. Instead, Henry succeeds only in exposing himself as Wilbraham's "former lady secretary . . . in the Ministry of Information. . . . Dismissed . . . for incompetence" (*M.G.*, p. 208).

Although *Mystery at Geneva* seems to have many of the elements of farce—Macaulay subtitles it "An Improbable Tale of Singular Happenings"[43]—it also constitutes a kind of half-serious, half-ironic catalog of the evils inflicted by nation on nation, by men on men, and, more especially, by men on women: white slavery, prostitution, pornography, involuntary servitude, battered women, job discrimination, the exploitation of women by the news media—all are at least touched on in the course of this "Improbable Tale."

Miss Montana's assumption of masculine dress is justified first as a "disguise" to prevent her former employer, Charles Wilbraham, from knowing her if they meet, and thereby to facilitate her desired revenge on him (*M.G.*, p. 243). Second, it is the means whereby she is able to replace her injured lover, Denis O'Neill, as a newspaper correspondent, and this gives her a mobility, an opportunity for experience and adventure, that was customarily denied to women at the time the novel was written. In "his" "coat" and "trousers," with "his" "monocle," "hat," and "cane," (*M.G.*, pp. 2, 54), "he" can roam freely alone about Geneva at all hours of the night, while the only other women who do so are prostitutes; even lady delegates to the League of Nations walking in pairs through the streets in the early evening may feel—and prove to be—more vulnerable because they are women (*M.G.*, pp. 147–49).

Professor Alice Bensen calls the disguise of Miss Montana "A game element."[44] If it is that, it is also considerably more than that. If a woman decries the abuse of women, as Mlle. Binesco, a minor character in *Mystery at Geneva*, does, she can be dismissed as hysterical. Mlle. Binesco, a "womanly woman" (*M.G.*, p. 144), does in fact become hysterical when she observes, for example, "the iniquities of the traffic in women and children all over the world" (*M.G.*, p. 110). But if a *man*—or someone believed to be a man—is critical of the exploitation of women, for instance, by pornographers, then *his* opinion will carry greater weight:

> [Henry sought to pass the time reading] *L'Humeur* which he found on the [café] table before him. But *L'Humeur* is not really very funny. It

has only one joke, only one type of comic picture: a woman in-
completely dressed. Was that, Henry speculated, really funny? It happens, after all, to nearly all women at least every morning and every
evening. Was it really funny even when to the lady thus unattired there
entered a gentleman, whether M. l'Amant or M. le Mari?

Was only one thing funny? . . . Henry, . . . tried hard to think so,
but failed. . . . He could not see that it was funnier that a female should
not yet have completed her toilet than that a male should not. Neither
was funny. (*M.G.*, p. 11)

Likewise, if a man, or someone believed to be a man, takes exception to
clerical excesses of prudery, his opinion seems more valid than that of a
member of the class towards which that prudery is directed:

"I see," said the clergyman, "that you have one of the French comic
papers with you. A pity their humour is so much spoilt by suggestiveness."

Suggestiveness. Henry could never understand that word as applied
in condemnation. Should not everything be suggestive? Or should all
literature, art, and humour be a cul-de-sac, suggesting no idea whatsoever? Henry did not want to be uncharitable, but he could not but
think that those who used this word in this sense laid themselves open
to the suspicion . . . that their minds were only receptive of one kind of
suggestion, and that a coarse one. (*M.G.*, pp. 39–40)

As a "man" and a journalist, Henry also gains a greater credibility in his
condemnation of the inherent sexism of the daily newspaper:[45]

*Women are, inherently and with no activities on their part, News, in a
way that men are not.* Henry had often thought this very singular. He
had read in accounts of public gatherings (such as criminal trials, tennis
tournaments, and boxing matches) such statements as "There were
many well-dressed women present." These women had done nothing to
deserve their fame; they were merely present, just as men were. . . . *A
. . . question arose: were women News to their own sex, or only to
men?* . . . All sorts of articles and letters appear in the papers about
women. Profound questions are raised concerning them. Should they
smoke? Should they work? Vote? Take orders? Marry? Exist? Are not
their skirts too short, or their sleeves? Have they a sense of humour, of
honour, of direction? Are spinsters superfluous? But how seldom similar inquiries are propounded about men. How few persons discuss
superfluous bachelors, or whether the male arm or leg is an immodest
sight, or whether men should vote. For men [since the press is controlled by and for men] are not news. (*M.G.*, pp. 160–61; emphasis
added)

Speaking with the authority of a "man," Henry can even object to the sexist attitudes bred into women:

> "Are you a Catholic, Miss Longfellow?" [Henry inquired].
> "I was brought up Catholic. Women believe what they are taught, as a rule, don't they?"
> "I hadn't observed it," Henry said, "particularly. Are women so unlike men then?"
> "That's quite a question, isn't it? What do you think?"
> "I can't think in large sections and masses of people," Henry replied. "Women are so different one from another. So are men. That's all I can see, when people talk of the sexes."
> (*M.G.*, p. 68)

As a woman, "Henry" had been Miss Montana, a secretary typist trapped in a low-status, low-paying, and monotonous job. She had been regarded—and treated—with contempt by her employer, Charles Wilbraham. For having, among other stenographic sins, "spelt Parliament with a small p," she had been dismissed by Wilbraham in favor of "some one . . . more thoroughly efficient." Since that time Wilbraham, "with first one bullied secretary, now another, had moved on his triumphant way" to hobnob with world leaders (*M.G.*, pp. 240–42). Rose Macaulay concludes with the assertion that Wilbraham is regarded by Miss Montana with "such rancour as Serb-Croat-Slovenes scarce feel against Albanians, or Bolsheviks against Bourgeoisie" (*M.G.*, p. 248). The political analogy is deliberate: the economic and social subjugation of women has always been a political issue.[46] In fact, when Miss Montana assumes male dress and becomes "Henry Beechtree," "he" cannot help, to a limited extent, also donning male politics and cruelty towards women. So, for example, although "Henry" empathizes with Wilbraham's current secretary, the pretty but witless Miss Doris Wembley, "he" plays on Miss Wembley's sexual attraction to "him" and exploits her, solely in order to obtain compromising information about her boss: "He did not think that Miss Wembley was going to be amusing, but still, he intended to cultivate her acquaintance" (*M.G.*, pp. 55–56).

Since "his" masculinity is purely an illusion of dress and of manner, Henry is severely limited in the ways in which he can manifest it. "He" can, for instance, arouse Miss Wembley emotionally, but "he" cannot consummate the relationship physically. Sexually, "Henry" is a "man" in appearance, but not in performance. As it is with sex, so it is with violence: as a pseudo-man, "Henry" can be involved in abstract cruelty, but not in actual cruelty. It is relevant to recall here that when Shakespeare's Lady Macbeth begins to instigate the murder of King Duncan, she first invokes

> . . . you spirits
> That tend on mortal thoughts, *unsex me here,*

And fill me from the crown to the toe top-full
Of direst cruelty!

>   (*Macbeth* 1.5.41–44; emphasis added)

"Direst cruelty" is see by so astute a student of human nature as Shakespeare as unnatural behavior for a woman. She must be "unsexed" *before* she can practice it. Similarly, the perpetration of deliberate physical violence generally is as impossible for the transvestites and tomboys in Rose Macaulay's fiction as it is for the more feminine of her women.[47] "Henry Beechtree" can enjoy violence in the abstract: headlines such as "Femme coupée en morceaux"—"Woman hacked to bits"—add zest to "his" morning coffee and rolls (*M.G.*, p. 101); but the actual sight of a goldfish being devoured by a cat makes "him" dizzy and nauseous (*M.G.*, pp. 92–94), and reveals "him" as a woman, despite "his" disguise (*M.G.*, p. 235). By contrast, a "manly man" like Charles Wilbraham is undisturbed by any amount of genuine violence and cruelty: he can not only shake hands with M. Kratzky, the bloodstained Russian "Butcher of Odessa," but he can calmly and without a qualm sit down to a substantial lunch with this torturer and murderer of young and old. The mere thought of such a meal turns "Henry" physically "sick" (*M.G.*, pp. 49–50).

Thus, although Henry warns Miss Longfellow against the practice of making sweeping generalizations about the sexes, paradoxically Henry becomes the subject of such a generalization in "his" own right. Even if a woman assumes a man's mannerisms, dons a man's clothes, and follows a man's occupation, the sight or thought or practice of physical cruelty will invariably arouse in her a negative visceral reaction. Rose Macaulay calls this at one point "womanly sympathy" (*M.G.*, p. 149), and at another "squeamishness" (*M.G.*, p. 50). This "squeamishness" is the touch-stone by means of which even the most "manly" of women will be revealed for what they are. For, as the plot's real villain, ex-Catholic Cardinal Silvio Franchi,[48] explains his early perception of Henry's true biological sex, "Masculine nerves are, as a rule, more robust" (*M.G.*, p. 235).

Whether Father Hamilton Johnson ever read *Mystery at Geneva* is perhaps an irresolvable mystery.[49] Still, curiously enough, its heroine, like Laurie in *Trebizond*, has an androgynous analogue in another of the Abbot Daniel stories he translated and sent to Rose Macaulay in 1951.[50] In this case the story, "De Eunucho,"—"Concerning a Eunuch,"[51] could not have influenced the contents of the novel. But the contents of the novel might very well have reflected Rose Macaulay's receptiveness to the story. "Concerning a Eunuch" tells of a venerable hermit who has dressed in rags and dwelt alone in a desert cave in humble circumstances. This monk, the "Abbot Anastasius," summons his old friend the Abbot Daniel to him, receives communion, and, with a radiant face, gives "his soul to the Lord" ("D.E.", p. 149). Only when preparing the body for burial does Abbot Daniel's disciple learn "he was a [Noble] woman. . . . really called Anastasia when she was in the world" ("D.E.", pp. 150–51). When the monastery she founded in Alexandria failed to offer her sufficient security from the importunities of the Emperor and the wrath of his wife, she sought refuge in Scithis with Abbot Daniel. It was he who "clothed her in mannish garb" ("D.E.", p. 151), concealed her in a cave far from the town, and kept her location a secret for twenty-eight years while the officers of the Emperor and the Pope sought her in vain. Anastasia's transvestism was, then, the means by which a virtuous and much persecuted woman renounced "an earthly and human kingdom" and "sought" instead "the Kingdom of Heaven" ("D.E.", pp. 147–48). Abbot Daniel concludes his revelation to the disciple that "Anastasius" was really "Anastasia" by voicing his prayer that the two of them might someday prove as "worthy" of salvation as she ("D.E.", p. 151).

"I must get hold of the *Liber de Miraculis*," wrote Rose Macaulay to Father Johnson after receiving his translation of this tale. She was capable of reading it in the Latin original, although it cannot be established that she did so.[52] She did, however, visit a Cypriot restaurant and inquire about the foods consumed in this and yet another of the Abbot Daniel stories.[53] Naturally, for, to the author of *Mystery at Geneva*, "De Eunucho" would have been "paximatia" (Easter bread)[54] indeed.

Two "masculine" women figure prominently in *Told by an Idiot* (1923),[55] the Rose Macaulay novel that appeared a year after *Mystery at Geneva*. These women are Stanley Croft (née Garden), who will be discussed in this chapter, and her niece, Imogen Carrington, who will be of major concern in chapter 4. Stanley, also called "Stan," is her father's spiritual heir: like him, she is "an ardent hunter of the idea" (*T.b.I.*, p. 16); but whereas he is a theologian and spends a lifetime in pursuit of the true faith, she is a social activist and devotes the greater part of her efforts to "something one ought to do, or join, or help, which might avert" the "shipwreck" of our so greatly troubled world (*T.b.I.*, pp. 20–21).

Like women in Rose Macaulay's other novels, Stanley makes generalizations about the differences in female and male "nerves." While women, she decides, behave like "nervous children," and go "frothing about with words and ideas," men go calmly and serenely after what Stanley recognizes as:

> The elemental, enduring things: sex, fatherhood, work. They knew what mattered; they went for the essentials. . . . Men were somehow admirable, in their strong stability. Their nervous systems were so magnificent. They could kill animals without feeling sick, break the necks of fishes, put worms on hooks, shoot rabbits and birds, jab bayonets into bodies. Women would never amount to much in this world because they nearly all have a nervous disease; they are strung on

wires. . . . It seems fundamental, this difference between the nerves of most women and most men. You see it among little girls and boys; most little boys, but how few little girls, can squash insects and kill rabbits without a qualm. It is this difference which gives even a stupid man often a greater mastery over life than a clever woman. He is not frightened by life. Women, for the most part, are. (*T.b.I.*, pp. 143–44)

Stanley does not wish to kill a rabbit or to jab a bayonet into a body, but she does work an entire lifetime to expand the parameters of behavior possible for females in England in order to give them, too, "a greater mastery over life." At eighteen Stanley Garden becomes one of the first twelve women to attend the newly established Somerville College, Oxford. Her first year there—1880—is a time of high hope for women:

> There was proceeding at this time a now long-forgotten campaign called the Women's Movement. . . . Women, long suppressed, were emerging; women were to be doctors, lawyers, human beings, every- thing; women were to have their share of the earth, their share of adventure. . . . (*T.b.I.*, p. 41)[56]

In praise of the young women of Stanley's generation, Rose Macaulay writing in the 1920s remembers for us:

> The [eighteen] eighties were . . . a great time for women. What was called *emancipation* then occurred to them. Young ladies were getting education and it went to their heads. No creature was ever more solemn, more eager, more full of good intentions for the world, than the university-educated young female of the eighties. We shall not look upon her like again; . . . (*T.b.I.*, pp. 55–56)[57]

The account of Stanley's life begins when she is a "sturdy," "sexless" Oxford undergraduate of eighteen, filled with idealism and enthusiasm; the account ends forty-four years later when Stanley, grown stout and matronly but still idealistic, still enthusiastic, is happily boarding a train to Geneva, where, as an employee of the League of Nations, she is confident she will help to "save the world yet" (*T.b.I.*, p. 336). Between the ages of eighteen and sixty-two Stanley has been, among other things, a settlement worker, a suffragist, an aesthete, a Christian, a Fabian Socialist, an adherent of Celtic mystical poetry, a jingoist, a pacifist, a propagandist for working women, a political candidate, and a feminist. Her varied and passionately felt experi- ences have included homosexual crushes, heterosexual love, marriage, moth- erhood, divorce, and single parenthood.

Three of Stanley's male relatives regard her as unwomanly in many of her actions and aspirations: her grandfather, a high-ranking clergyman; her younger brother, a "Philistine"; and her husband, a "reactionary." An older brother is sympathetic insofar as his congenital cynicism will allow. Stanley's masculinity can best be understood in the light of certain of the attitudes and reactions of these men.

In 1894 Stanley is a young wife with a key to her own front door. She is also a new mother who bicycles—"now her son has safely arrived" (*T.b.I.*, p. 108)—for pleasure and for the restoration and maintenance of muscle tone after childbirth. It is about women like her that a boldface headline in the *Sunday Observer* demands, "What is the modern girl coming to, for she opens her front door with a key?" (*T.b.I.*, p. 129). But Stanley's "grandpapa" has already asked the same question of the *Manchester Guardian*, and also of Stanley's husband, since Stanley has her own "latchkey" (*T.b.I.*, p. 112):

> "Poor grandpapa [said Stanley's sister Vicky]. He's writing to the *Guardian*, as usual, about the Modern Woman. She's dreadfully on his mind. Latchkeys. He doesn't think women ought to have them. Why not? He doesn't explain. Men may open their front doors with keys, but women must, he thinks, always ring up the unfortunate maids. He can think of no reasons why; he is past reasons, but not past convictions. . . . [And] he thinks women on bicycles really indecent, poor old dear." (*T.b.I.*, p. 108)

It is perfectly in keeping with grandpapa's militant anti-feminist character that he is brought to his death bed by influenza, but blames his imminent demise on a lady bicyclist, instead (*T.b.I.*, p. 127). He proves to be sincerely religious, undeniably courageous, and "dignified to the last" as he departs to meet his "Maker." But he is also an unreconstructed old reactionary who takes the entire Bible[58]—even the marginal annotations—literally (*T.b.I.*, p. 23); who cleaves to the Established Church, to the calculations of Bishop Ussher that the world "had been created in six days in the year 4004 B.C.," and to an arbitrary standard of "morality" for young females which—he has found it convenient to forget—was not in force when he himself was young:

> What were unmarried young women coming to? . . . The untrammelled . . . freedom of intercourse enjoyed by modern young men and women (especially young women) continually shocked him. Grandpapa had enjoyed much free and untrammelled intercourse in his own distant youth, during the Regency, but fifty years of Victorianism had since intervened, and he believed that intercourse should not now be free. (*T.b.I.*, pp. 88–89)

While his granddaughter Stanley is "continually" chafing at the unwarranted restrictions placed on women by "the conventional prudery of the age" (*T.b.I.*, p. 89), grandpapa is simultaneously attempting to shore up those same pruderies by an ongoing series of anti-feminist diatribes in speech and in print.

Stanley's grandpapa actively opposes "the New Woman" on principle, but Stanley's younger brother Irving merely disapproves of her out of inertia and selfishness. Irving is self-centered, self-seeking, and self-satisfied; invariably he enjoys the status quo and utilizes it to his own best advantage. Nevertheless, in 1880, when both he and Stanley are teenagers, although he "recked not of the Woman's Movement," he

> amiably held [their older brother] Maurice's high bicycle while Stanley, divested of her [absurd, caught-in-at-the-knees] tight skirt and clad in a pair of his knickerbockers, mounted it and pedalled round and round the quiet square. It was Irving who knew that a lower kind of bicycle was on its way. . . .
> "But girls'll never ride it," he opined. "That's jolly certain."
> "Girls will probably be wearing knickerbockers in a year or two," Stanley, always hopeful, asserted. "For exercise and games and things. Or else a new kind of skirt will come in, short and wide. Our clothes are absurd."
> "*Women's clothes always are,*" *said Irving, content that this should be so.* (*T.b.I.*, pp. 45–46; emphasis added)

In the 1890s Irving, now in his late twenties, enjoys life, ignores public controversies, and avoids extreme opinions and persons. He takes no interest in the Woman's Movement, which he considers "unattractive" (*T.b.I.*, p. 116). His attitudes towards his sisters' lives reflect his attitudes towards women in general: that their ultimate worth is a function of the social status and practices of the men they marry and of their own conformity to Irving's arbitrary standards concerning "what a woman should be." Because his sister Rome is over thirty and unmarried, he worries that people will soon begin to think of her as "an old maid": he uses the expression pejoratively. His beautiful sister Una is "all right," although she fell in love with a yeoman farmer and so "married down." He disparages his sister Stanley for her feminist friends, and Stanley's husband Denman for his aesthetic friends, "an affected and conceited crew, both the men and the women being unsexed, and for ever writing things one didn't want to read" (*T.b.I.*, p. 116). Of Irving's four sisters, only

> Vicky seemed to him what a woman should be. She looked pretty, dressed and danced well, was amusing, lived in the right part of London, and gave very decent, lively little dinners, at which people weren't always trying to be clever. (*T.b.I.*, p. 116)

Ironically, Vicky, too, has certain limited feminist aspirations, as she confides to Rome. She delights in her bicycle, despite male disapproval, and she enjoys the way cycling has transformed women's clothes so as to give them greater freedom of movement—"Short jackets and cloth caps are coming in. Bustles are no more" (*T.b.I.*, p. 108). She even aspires to cycle in bloomers and to smoke cigarettes, but is restrained by her husband's conception of bloomers and cigarettes as "unfeminine."

> "Charles doesn't approve. Conspicuous, he thinks. And, of course, so it is. Well, men will be men. They'll never be civilized where women are concerned, most of them." (*T.b.I.*, p. 108)

Among the "men who will be men" Vicky includes Stanley's "reactionary" husband. Stanley, "an individual, a human creature sensitively reacting to all the contacts of the engrossing world" (*T.b.I.*, p. 142), has had the grave misfortune to have been betrayed by sexual passion into marriage with a man whose very name—Denman Croft—epitomizes the decidedly recidivist nature of his Weltanschauung.[59] Denman and his set of "light-hearted and cynical aesthetes" influence Stanley against one of the more recent of Henrik Ibsen's "tracts" on the "emancipation" of women:

> What a play! What moralising! What purpose! What deplorable solemnity! There seemed . . . nothing to do about "A Doll's House" but to laugh at it. (*T.b.I.*, p. 111)

Denman Croft has good reason to trivialize Ibsen's play. In his "idiotic opinions about one half of the human race" (*T.b.I.*, p. 142), Denman resembles no one so much as Torvald Helmer. Rose Macaulay sets the scene for one effectively Ibsenesque episode by having Stanley read *A Doll's House* on the train as she returns from a day of bicycling in the countryside. Flushed with health and happiness, she meets Denman in the entrance hall to their home, and his criticisms reduce her from euphoria to temporary unease. Denman blames Stanley for being late, although he has only just returned home himself. He castigates her for her appearance: she is clad in knickerbockers and stout shoes; she is flushed and windblown and in need of a bath. Upstairs, while she looks in on their baby and prepares to bathe, he changes his clothes and continues his criticisms, sounding all the while like a hearty echo of Torvald Helmer:

> "Women ought to wear graceful, trailing things always [even if this imperils their cleanliness and safety]. . . .
> "It's better to be elegant, dirty and dangerous than frumpish, clean and safe. . . . The fact is, women ought never to indulge in activities, either of body or mind; it's not their role. They can't do it gracefully. . . .
> "An elegant inertia is what is required of women. . . . Any activity

necessary to the human race can be performed by . . . men. . . ."
(*T.b.I.*, pp. 113–14)

Ironically, Denman is prescribing "An elegant inertia" for women at the same time as he is dressing for dinner and demanding to know what his servant "girl" has done with his black socks. Even more ironically, while Stanley sings away her irritation at him in the tub, Denman, too, "would have liked a bath" (*T.b.I.*, p. 114), since he has just left the bed of his current mistress, an "exquisitely lovely" woman (*T.b.I.*, p. 135) of the inactive sort he likes. "Den-man," whom Stanley realizes she must divorce after two children and five years of marriage, is indeed a throwback to the time of the caveman. He believes that women exist for only three purposes: to wait on him hand and foot, to service him sexually, or to please his eye. Any other activities they might perform, any other aspirations they might have are "ungraceful," a pejorative which in his lexicon is the equivalent of grand-papa's condemnation of things "indecent" (*T.b.I.*, p. 108).

Rose Macaulay's sympathies during this scene are entirely with Stanley. The same cycling costume that Denman labels as "frumpish" is seen by the story's omniscient narrator as "that graceful and sensible fashion of our ancestresses" (*T.b.I.*, p. 110). And Vicky, the epitome of ladylike deportment and taste, tells Rome, "Stanley . . . looks delightful [cycling in bloomers], whatever Denman says" (*T.b.I.*, p. 108).

It is an article of faith with Stanley that

> "Things *need* doing. The world is so shocking....All this time women have been suppressed and kept under and not allowed to help in putting things rights, and now they're just getting free...." (*T.b.I.*, p. 50)

In the course of an altruistic and active lifetime, Stanley does much that is "useful" and a few things that are noteworthy. Her great and cheerful idealism survives the refusal of the younger generation—her daughter and son, her nieces and nephews—to carry on her work. Her great tragedy is in marrying—and in being obliged to divorce—a man who believes that others exist only to amuse him, that the children he begets are merely "amusing toys" (*T.b.I.*, p. 137), and that the burgeoning role of "one half the human race" in the cause of social reform can be trivialized to

> "All this feminine pedalling about and playing ridiculous games and speaking on platforms and writing books and serving on commit-tees. . . ." (*T.b.I.*, p. 114)

Stanley's relationship with her older brother Maurice is also significant, for it is with him that she conducts a lifelong debate about public affairs. Maurice, who shares many of Stanley's ideals, becomes a crusading journalist, but his mordant and contentious critical faculty generally make him seem far less sympathetic than he is. However, when he and his wife produce a son and a daughter, Maurice temporarily abandons his customary cynicism and sincerely expresses a desire to educate both his children equally. Unhappily, he hasn't reckoned on the "unjust" nature of his own wife, who

> was . . . the type of mother whose strong sex instinct leads her to prefer boys to girls, and she took no pains to hide this. Maurice said, "The girl shall have as good a chance as the boy, and as good an education. We'll make no difference," but Amy said, "Chance! Fiddlesticks! What chances does a girl want, except to marry well? What does a girl want with education? . . . Girls can't have real brains, anyhow. They can't *do* anything. . . ." (*T.b.I.*, pp. 61–62)

Years of personal and political disappointments exacerbate Maurice's congenital skepticism; when the Liberals finally sweep the Tories out of office in 1905 and Stanley is jubilant at the prospects for women's suffrage,

> Maurice grinned cynically at her.
> "If you . . . think you're going to get a vote, my dear, you're off it. . . . You may send all the deputations you like, but you won't move them. Women's suffrage is merely the House joke." (*T.b.I.*, p. 243)[60]

While Maurice spends his life bitterly commenting upon the wrongs he sees, Stanley spends hers actively striving to change them.

The writings of the Scottish mystic poetess Fiona Macleod are a source of solace for Stanley during her protracted and painful divorce (*T.b.I.*, p. 150). This is entirely appropriate to the conception of a masculine woman; for, by the time Rose Macaulay wrote *Told by an Idiot*, the true identity of the reclusive "Miss Macleod" had been known for several years. "She" was really William Sharp, a happily married, conventionally heterosexual man whose "transvestism not of the flesh but of the imagination"[61] enabled him to write about, and for, afflicted women with a truly womanly compassion. While William Sharp's "Fiona Macleod" reminds us of a man's "feminine" capacity for feeling, Rose Macaulay's "Stanley Croft" serves to proclaim a woman's "masculine" desire for active involvement in the world. Both of these efforts to promote androgyny help to expand the possibilities for human beings.

4

"That Outrageous Power of Inflaming"

UNFEMININE AND UNATTRACTIVE, but intelligent and sincere, Ann Dorland is cleared of suspicion of murder and supplied with a fortune and a future husband in Dorothy L. Sayers's *The Unpleasantness at the Bellona Club* (1928). While probing the secrets of Ann Dorland's love life, Sayers's ace detective, Lord Peter Wimsey, makes a fleeting but significant reference to "what Rose Macaulay referred to as 'nameless orgies.'"[1] His allusion is to the passage in *Dangerous Ages* in which Neville, indignant at the news that a friend of her daughter has just borne a child to the man she lives with without benefit of clergy, argues the matter, and then falls into a reverie:

> Neville, led by Free Love to a private vision, brooded cynically over savages dancing round a wood-pile in primeval forests, engaged in what missionaries, journalists and writers of fiction about our coloured brothers call "nameless orgies" . . . and she saw the steep roads of the round world running back and back and back—on or back, it made no difference, since the world was round—to this. Saw, too, a thousand stuffy homes wherein sat couples linked by a legal formula so rigid, so lasting, so indelible, that not all their tears could wash out a word of it, unless they took to themselves other mates, in which case their second state might be worse than their first. Free love—love in chains. How absurd it all was, and how tragic too. One might react back to the remaining choice—no love at all—and that was absurder and more tragic still, since man was made . . . to love. (*D.A.,* p. 22)[2]

"Free love—love in chains. . . . no love at all." Rose Macaulay's formulation of this age-old predicament was an intriguing one for Dorothy Sayers,[3] whose detective in *The Bellona Club* investigates not only a murder, but the interactions of women and men.[4]

Relations between the sexes also form the basis for the syllogism which Rome Garden of *Told by an Idiot* propounds to her shocked Victorian mama:

> Novels have always been about sex, or rather sexes. . . . People must
> have a sex in this life; it's inevitable. Novels must be about people; that's
> inevitable too. So novels must be partly about sex, and they're nearly
> always about two sexes, and usually largely about the relations of the
> two sexes to one another. They always have been. . . . (*T.b.I.*, p. 81)[5]

Instances of sexual experience or abstinence abound in *Told by an Idiot*. The
life stories of its numerous characters provide explorations into human
sexuality—whether inside or outside of marriage. Also explored is the
question of celibacy, as imposed by custom, divorce, death, or the death of
love. Perhaps a subsequent study will deal with these issues as they affect all
the personae of the novel—indeed, of the *novels*—in addition to the masculine women who fall within the parameters of this study. For now, the
complexities involved can only be hinted at by taking as exemplars Rome
Garden and her sister, Stanley Croft, and their niece, Imogen Carrington.
Rome is an "urbane," do-nothing, "blue-stocking" who frightens off most
men: her conduct is as "cool" as her utterances are unrestrained. Only after
the murder of the one man she is destined to love[6] does she freely acknowledge her sexual feelings for him (*T.b.I.*, p. 124). Conversely, Rome's sister
Stanley, having with "ecstasy" acknowledged her own sexuality "body and
soul" in her marriage with Denman Croft, compels herself "to shut off that
side of life" during and after her divorce (*T.b.I.*, pp. 72, 142). Thus, one of
these women recognizes her libido too late; the other suppresses hers too
soon.

   Neither Rome nor Stanley is regarded by her contemporaries as conventionally "feminine," although both are unquestionably heterosexual.
Rome is portrayed as

> a woman of the world, a known diner-out, a good talker, something of
> a wit, so that *her presence was sought by hostesses as that of an amusing
> bachelor is sought.* . . . *She knew her way about.* . . . (*T.b.I.*, p. 78;
> emphasis added)

Rome Garden possesses the wit, intellect, and learning more commonly
found in the men of her time. Wealth inherited from her grandfather has
made her financially independent. She enjoys her single existence with a self-
indulgent masculine freedom: dressing well, traveling frequently and un-
chaperoned—sometimes with her lawyer friend, Guy Donkin—and gambling astutely at "Bridge, whist, baccarat, poker, roulette" (*T.b.I.*, p. 178).
However, in Rome's case, propinquity does not promote prurience. The
hapless Francis Jayne was the one passion of her life, and one can probably
believe her when she asserts, "Guy and I do nothing not *comme-il-faut*"
(*T.b.I.*, p. 178).

   As selfless as her sister Rome is self-indulgent, Stanley is obsessed with social reform. This obsession has been a source of worry to their sister Vicky, who rejoices when marriage brings a temporary halt to Stanley's career:

> "I'm glad she's off that stupid trade union and sweated labor fuss. . . . I was afraid Stan was going to turn into a female fanatic, like some of those short-haired friends of hers. That's not what we women ought to be, is it, my Imogen?" (*T.b.I.*, p. 73)

But "Imogen, an infant of one summer," whom Vicky catches up in her arms and kisses while she speaks to her thus, is as masculine a woman as her Aunt Stanley. Because Imogen is the most autobiographical of all Rose Macaulay's characters,[7] her innate reaction to Vicky's words is Rose Macaulay's own:

> But Imogen, neither then nor at any later time, had any clear idea about what women ought or ought not to be. Anything they liked, she probably thought. If, indeed, there were, specifically, any such creatures as women....For Imogen was born to have a doubting mind on this as on other subjects. (*T.b.I.*, p.74)

The young Imogen who outperforms her male playmates "in climbing, running, gymnastics, and all active games," who gets dirty damming brooks and wading in them, who wants to capture bear cubs at the North Pole, who glides through the forest shooting real arrows at imaginary Indians, who slinks through the streets of London with a toy pistol in her pocket, who pretends that she is Sherlock Holmes, who is suspected of being mentally ill by an uncle who sees her playing at knights in armor in the woods, who knows by heart "the displacement and horse-power and knots of all the battleships and first-class cruisers" in the British navy, who daydreams that she is lieutenant-commander Denis Carton, sailor and popular metaphysical poet—this Imogen is autobiographical.[8]

When Imogen's uncle Ted says of these activities that "no sensible young fellow would like it," (*T.b.I.*, p. 252)—that Imogen's marriageability would be compromised by these pastimes—he restates Henrik Ibsen's protest in *A Doll's House:* that men may lead their lives to please themselves, but that women must lead their lives with reference to men.[9] Being forced to put aside her favorite occupations as fantasies when she "grows up," while the males she knows grow up to join the armed forces, travel, fight in wars, and otherwise experience the activities about which Imogen can only daydream, she has every reason to be resentful:

> Rotten it was, being grown up. Simply rotten. Because. . . . when you put your hair up, you had to hide all sorts of things away, like a guilty secret. . . . Your mother told people you were a tomboy. A tomboy. Imbecile word. As if girls didn't like doing nice things as much as boys.

Who started the idea they didn't, or shouldn't? Oh, it was rotten being grown up. (*T.b.I.*, p. 253)

When Rose Macaulay addressed the Oxford University Literary Society "on the creation of men by women, women by men, in fiction, drama and poetry," she proffered the suggestion that an author's portrayals of the opposite sex tend to be idealized, "whereas their own sex they often draw more from within, and achieve more realism."[10] If one applies this axiom to Imogen Carrington and her aunts Rome Garden and Stanley Croft, one can draw some useful conclusions about the kind of masculine woman Rose Macaulay was and about the kind of masculine women characters Rose Macaulay's works customarily portray. First, no matter which traditionally male-dominated activities they engage in, they are heterosexual as adults, even if they manifest homosexual tendencies in their youth. In girlhood, Imogen adores a succession of female teachers (*T.b.I.*, pp. 175–76),[11] just as, years before, her Aunt Stanley had been "in love" with a succession of female schoolmates (*T.b.I.*, pp. 42–43). But Stanley's first physical relationship is with her husband, and Imogen's first caresses come from a fiancé in the navy (*T.b.I.*, pp. 317–18).[12] Another characteristic of Macaulay's masculine women is their inborn emotionality. Rome is tortured by powerful emotions despite the "bland, cool, and composed" facade she presents to the world.[13] Far less "self-contained" than Rome is Stanley, who openly experiences life's pleasures and pains with great emotional intensity.[14] And very like Stanley is her niece Imogen who, at the age of eight, earns the opprobrium of her older brother Hugh because she is moved to tears by the sights and sounds accompanying the appearance of Dr. Nansen at Albert Hall:

> Boys did not understand the female weakness which wept at fire engines, poetry and clapping, and was sick at squashed insects. Imogen wanted (even still half hoped) to be a boy, so she tried to hide her weaknesses. (*T.b.I.*, p. 162)

The tearful habit is something Imogen does not outgrow. When, at age thirty-four, she leaves her married lover behind for a year to voyage to the Pacific Islands in fulfillment of a lifelong dream, characteristically she "wept" (*T.b.I.*, p. 336).

Finally, Rome, Stanley, and Imogen cannot commit any act of physical violence. Rome witnesses her lover being brutally stabbed to death and withdraws quietly to the country without so much as a *fantasy* of personally punishing his assailant. Stanley is callously wronged by the husband who pressured her into marriage, yet it is *she* who apologizes to him, blaming herself for the failure of their marriage (*T.b.I.*, pp. 139, 143–44). More liberated in her fantasies is Imogen, who slays wild beasts and ferocious warriors without number in her daydreams. She imagines that someday the trophies on her walls will include:

reindeer, sand-bok, polar bear, grizzly, lion, tiger, cheetah, wombat and wolf. [But] no birds. Shooting birds was no fun. Imogen knew, for she had shot her first and only sparrow last week, with her new catapult. The boys had been delighted, but she had nearly cried. It had been beastly. (*T.b.I.*, p. 192)[15]

In all her youthful fantasies, Imogen glorifies war. But in the concluding portion of *Told by an Idiot,* Imogen and all her friends and relations experience the horrors of the First World War. Imogen is very angry at being excluded from combat owing to "a mere fluke of sex." She "had never before so completely realized that she was not, in point of fact, a young man" (*T.b.I.*, p. 316). Yet the sights and sounds and smells of hospitalized soldiers make her—as they made Rose Macaulay—nauseous and faint (*T.b.I.*, p. 317).[16]

In only one of Rose Macaulay's twenty-three novels does a woman lay hands on another human being and murder him, but there is considerable ambiguity even about that one instance.[17] Likewise, in only one of the novels does a woman—Flora Smith of *Orphan Island*—willfully and wantonly injure an animal—and that woman is consistently portrayed as "cruel."[18] Imogen Carrington's masculine imaginings seem largely the product of the same powerful hunger for experience and the same intensely active imagination that caused her—and Rose Macaulay—to become a writer. Like her Aunt Stanley, Imogen chafes at the irrational restrictions that have been arbitrarily imposed on her sex. Since she cannot change that sex—in a world that values men more than women and allows them a considerably wider range of experiences—she imagines it as having been changed, just as she imagines other adventures for herself:

> She wanted to go to the Pacific Islands and bathe from coral reefs; wanted money and fame; . . . wanted to save a life, watched by cheering crowds; wanted a motor bicycle; . . . wanted to be a young man. But not now a naval man; she had seen through the monotony and routine of that life. She wanted in these days to be a journalist, a newspaper correspondent, sent abroad on exciting jobs, to report wars, and eruptions of Vesuvius, and earthquakes, and Cretan excavations, and revolutions in South America, and international conferences. (*T.b.I.*, p. 298)

The first of these fantasies provides the setting for Rose Macaulay's next novel, *Orphan Island.*

Nineteen-year-old Rosamond Thinkwell is a dreamy ingenue, a stockier version of Gerda Bendish in *Dangerous Ages*. Ninety-eight-year-old Miss Charlotte Smith is the autocratic, alcoholic matriarch of a small Pacific island who has succumbed to the delusion that she is Queen Victoria. Although both these women should be categorized as masculine, the mores by which each lives are brought into sharp contrast in *Orphan Island* (1924).

Rosamond is the daughter of a learned and industrious Cambridge sociologist. One of her older brothers is a promising young scientist; the other is a published—and attractive—author. But Rosamond herself displays gifts neither of mind nor of body, nor does she possess any special skills or knowledge, save an ability to read maps and a thorough knowledge of the lore of tropical islands.[19] She is a simple, happy, inarticulate person with bobbed blond hair, a sturdy boyish body, and a credulous nature. Her belief in God is "deep, childish, and romantic" (*O.I.*, pp.108–9). She has an instinctive and heartfelt aversion to the torture, entrapment, or killing of living creatures, whether they are worms on hooks, or men on chain gangs. At the sight of the latter she "blinked away tears" (*O.I.*, p. 196).[20] Primitive pleasures—eating, swimming, climbing trees, experiencing tropical flora and fauna—pervade her daydreams. On any subject other than food and Pacific islands she has "a vague and wandering mind" (*O.I.*, p. 33).[21]

Rosamond's brother Charles says of her, "She doesn't know the difference between any two things, unless they're to eat. She can't distinguish between men and women" (*O.I.*, p. 34). Most certainly this is true of the numerous times Rosamond has been "in love." Her passions have been bisexual, intense, and platonic.[22] With "pleasure" Rosamond had worshipped from afar heroines and heroes—ancient and modern, on stage or in books—as well as assorted sailors and athletes, classmates and teachers (*O.I.*, p. 156).[23] Initially she is "pleased and stirred" by Captain Paul, commander of the schooner that carries her and her family to Orphan Island (*O.I.*, p. 133),[24] but he falls considerably in her estimation after he kisses her:

> It was a step down on his part, unworthy, as it were, of a man of action and travel, whose heart should be all set on adventure. She preferred him to tell her stories of the sea. (*O.I.*, p. 51)

Later, Captain Paul is superseded in Rosamond's affections by Flora Smith, the sensuously beautiful daughter of the Island's Prime Minister and his Spanish wife:

> Was it . . . that, once you had seen Flora Smith, no one else counted very much? Such grace was hers, such mocking beauty and such pride...a mountain panther could not touch her for the kind of wild, disdainful elegance she had. (*O.I.*, p. 85)

At a glance and a smile from the exquisite Flora Rosamond is "as wax in . . . flame" (*O.I.*, p. 229). In the grips of a passion that lasts almost the length of the novel, Rosamond blushes at the mention of Flora's good looks (*O.I.*, p. 107), yearns for Flora's friendship and regard (*O.I.*, p. 79), is pained whenever she incurs Flora's displeasure (*O.I.*, pp. 130, 148), mentions Flora in her prayers (*O.I.*, p. 150), cheers herself with thoughts of Flora (*O.I.*,

p. 208), feels love for Flora "hurt and tear" her (*O.I.*, p. 157). By contrast, when Flora's handsome brother Heathcliff indicates some interest in Rosamond, she rebuffs him (*O.I.*, pp. 127, 131).

Rosamond's brother Charles is also susceptible to Flora's charms, and Rosamond begins "breathlessly" to hope that Flora will "one day love and marry" her brother. "To have Flora for sister . . . what felicity!" is Rosamond's conscious thought, but that she is in this manner sublimating her own sexual feelings for "her dear Flora" (*O.I.*, p. 288) is obvious. Flora's cheeks, throat, eyes, hair, skin, and limbs figure constantly in Rosamond's thoughts.

An episode that anticipates E. J. Scovell's lesbian poem, "After the Party," by eight years[25] depicts Rosamond and Flora climbing "a winding path up a thicketed slope" through the "green gloom" of a tropical forest (*O.I.*, p. 154) to a secluded place where Flora speaks of her desire to marry her boyfriend Peter, and Rosamond gazes rapturously at Flora in the painful ecstasy of unrequited love. Various sexual symbols are in evidence during this scene as the two young women talk about love, marriage, and children. Finally the two hide behind a mangrove clump and "swop" their dresses:

> Each took off her frock. Flora looked with interest at Rosamond's cami-knickers, Rosamond at Flora's under-petticoat of scarlet-dyed, cocoa-nut cloth. Flora slipped into the short-sleeved, low-necked white cotton frock, Rosamond into the tunic made of the scarlet feathers of many birds. Neither altogether fitted, for the wearers were of different builds; Rosamond was small, firmly built, stocky, like a sturdy little boy, without feminine elegances, or any of Flora's wild animal sinuousness. (*O.I.*, p. 160)

As in "After the Party," the lesbian implications of this encounter are latent but obvious.

When Rose Macaulay wishes to discredit a given viewpoint, a favorite device of hers is to have that viewpoint voiced by a character that is herself or himself somewhat less than reputable. Thus, as we have seen in *Told by an Idiot*, views critical of women's involvement in sports or politics or social reform are put into the mouth of the waster, Denman Croft. Likewise, in *Orphan Island*, a lapsed Anglican Missionary, Mr. Merton, whose soiled white trousers and alcoholic breath indicate his lack of credibility (*O.I.*, p. 44), distinguishes between "female virtue" and "male virtue" when whites and "niggers"—his word for Polynesians—intermingle in the Islands:

> "You'd find the women would sink, in one generation, to nigger notions of morality" [said Mr. Merton.]
> "The women, you think, more rapidly than the men?" [inquired Mr. Thinkwell.]

"Oh, the men....I was speaking of morality—female virtue."

"And what about male virtue?"

"Honesty, you mean, and industry, and so forth....Well, those qualities aren't so quickly affected."

"I perceive," said Mr. Thinkwell, "that you are one of those who think of virtue in the two sexes in different terms. An interesting state of mind, and one often to be met with, especially among persons rather of action than of thought. You can trace it back many thousands of years...." (*O.I.*, p. 47)

Tracing the evolution of the concepts of "female virtue" and "male virtue" so crudely voiced by Rose Macaulay's Mr. Merton, feminist scholar Jane Flanders draws on the findings of L. C. Knights and R. H. Tawney:

> By the seventeenth and eighteenth centuries, controls on female sexuality, which originated in misogyny, paradoxically led to an opposite concept: that women, armed by their greater purity, were obliged to uphold a standard of morality, spirituality and sanctity for society as a whole. This belief had an implicit economic rationale; clearly, the man in the marketplace or at the exchange could not be hampered by moral scruples.[26] The doctrine of economic individualism precluded the recognition of communal obligations and moral imperatives binding all members of society. It became the woman's duty to maintain moral order through her devotion to chastity, home and family. "Morality" and "honor" could be removed from the male economic sphere and instead identified with woman's sexual restraint and conformity to conjugal and maternal roles. When she "fell" from this obligation, she assumed the guilt for the community as a whole.
>
> . . . While the usual pattern for males was to leave home and to establish themselves in the public arena, females were being all the more closely confined and assigned the task of supporting affective relations within the family. Men were forced into aggressive competition within a context of pragmatic moral choice, while women were asked to be loving, nurturing, yielding, devoted to children (whose innocence required the protection of equally inviolate beings), while also making a display of liberal expenditure and conspicuous leisure.[27]

It is in just such a society that the Thinkwell family and their companions find themselves when they arrive on Orphan Island. It is a society in which the Victorian world view[28] and Victorian proprieties of language and behavior still prevail; in which boys are trained to play aggressive team games while girls are left to amuse themselves in a more "ladylike" fashion;[29] and in which young women have "no business to *know*" about topics relating to sexuality and must be sheltered from such "undesirable characters" as illegitimate children, lest they contract some sort of moral taint and become "er—undesirably entangled" (*O.I.*, pp. 89–90). In this society women of the upper—or "Smith"—class give dances and dinner parties, but as for any share in the government, "Fortunately *they* don't count. Or where *should* we be?" (*O.I.*, pp. 58, 225). And thus it is that, on the Island, Rosamond encounters the Misses Macbean, who know that they are illegitimate and hence "we aren't accepted in good society," but who also know that young ladies have "no business to *know* about things of that kind." Between the Misses Macbean and Rosamond, who played organized games like cricket at school, who leads a troop of Girl Guides back in Cambridge, who chooses her own friends and "speak[s] of anything we like...anything we do," and whose homeland has recently extended the suffrage to women,[30] there is a gap of some "seventy years" (*O.I.*, p. 89).

Orphan Island's concept of the "womanly woman" is exemplified by fat and placid Mrs. Albert Edward Smith, the "amiable" wife of its Prime Minister, who needs "protection" from overexertion, who supervises her servants conscientiously, who selects foods for her family's table personally, whose mind is almost invariably on her sewing—even when she is confronted with the first English visitors to her island in seventy years—and whose favorite remark is "Very pleased, I'm sure."[31] When her husband holds out to her the possibility of travel away from her desert island home, Mrs. Smith's reply is characteristic:

> "What say you, my love?" he inquired of his lady.
> "Oh, I," she said placidly. "I am a home-lover, you know, my dear. Travel is all very well for gentlemen; makes a nice change, don't it; but what do we women want with it? That's what your mamma has always said, Bertie. Women's business is in the home."
> Mr. Smith indulgently displayed his wife's womanly reply to the audience. (*O.I.*, p. 65)

Mr. Thinkwell reminds that same audience that Bertie's mama herself "travelled rather far afield"—was shipwrecked on a Polynesian Island in transit from England to California—but then

> Miss Smith's son's indulgent smile changed to a more reverent expression. "My mother, Mr. Thinkwell, is no ordinary woman. Almost a man's grasp, a man's intelligence and knowledge of affairs. And yet, sir, a womanly woman if ever there was one."
> [Mr. Thinkwell's son] Charles reflected that Miss Smith sounded much like the late Queen Victoria as viewed by herself and her subjects about the time of the Diamond Jubilee. (*O.I.*, pp. 65–66)

The Miss Smith who has "Almost a man's grasp" is a clergyman's daughter who was shipwrecked on the Island almost seventy years before with a Scottish nurse, an alcoholic Irish doctor, and forty-three orphans.

Not only did Miss Smith "marry" the doctor[32] and produce ten children with him before he was eaten by a shark; she also became the founder of "Quite a little nation. Houses, roads, and all that sort of thing" (*O.I.*, p. 58), with its own currency, social structure, Church, Parliament, laws, professions, trades, and prison system modelled after those of Victorian England. Like Queen Victoria, with whom she identifies herself increasingly as the years pass,[33] Miss Smith is the titular head of both church and state. But, in fact, the power and influence of "Miss Smith of Smith Island"[34] over her one thousand twenty-four subjects (*O.I.*, p. 76) far exceeds that of the English Queen.[35] For example, not only has Miss Smith ordained every successive "Anglican" clergyman on the Island, but what she remembers—or finds it expedient to remember—of the Bible and the Anglican Prayer Service constitutes almost all that the islanders know of religion.[36] Miss Smith's memory provides the text for the clergyman's Sunday sermon (*O.I.*, pp. 68, 163). Likewise, the very little Miss Smith has retained of English letters has become the basis for the Island's literature. Her influence over the Islanders' every conception of the world extends not only to institutions, but to factual knowledge as well. She has been their lexicon, and words she has not taught them do not exist (*O.I.*, pp. 57, 69, 125). She has been their encyclopedia and has imparted to them her scanty knowledge of natural history; however, because she cannot draw, animals like the "cow," "sheep," "dog," and "horse" are merely words to them (*O.I.*, pp. 200–1).

Miss Charlotte Smith is a masculine woman with certain affinities to Aunt Kate Vallon of *The Valley Captives*. Both women are practical, decisive, dogmatic, and energetic. The masculine nature of each is represented by a figurative "sword"[37]—which, in the case of Miss Smith, is said to have "snapped short abruptly at the hilt" after she has been deposed from power (*O.I.*, p. 312). Another male emblem of power and authority—a stick—is tellingly employed, first as a symbol of Miss Smith's puissance (*O.I.*, pp. 93, 95, 103), and then as a sign of her downfall and destruction. The climactic duel to the death between the island's two matriarchs recalls the classic confrontation, not of witches with their cauldrons, but of Biblical prophets, or of wizards with their staffs.[38] In this scene, Miss Smith denies the Scottish nurse, Jean—who has kept to "her duty and her place" (*O.I.*, p. 154) beside Miss Smith for sixty-eight years—the opportunity to return home to Aberdeen to die. Jean then "stepped forward, leaning on her stick, lifting one arm prophetically above her head for silence" (*O.I.*, p. 275). She pronounces doom upon Miss Smith by revealing that all of her children are bastards, since their father was already married when he contracted his alliance with Miss Smith. Miss Smith immediately suffers a stroke that proves fatal; the "stick" falls from her hand, and with it departs also her power to speak, to move, and even to live (*O.I.*, pp. 311–12):

Her lips worked, but no sound emerged; she grasped and shook her stick at Jean, at her people, at heaven, till it fell suddenly from her hand, and she seemed to collapse, with a loud and stertorous groan. (*O.I.*, p. 276)

Other masculine traits of Miss Smith include the fact that, "naturally, *her* name goes down" to her descendants rather than that of her deceased consort. However, the thought of any other name descending in the female line strikes her son, Albert Edward, as "an odd notion indeed" (*O.I.*, p. 60). Property and status also belong by right of birth to members of the "Smith Caste"—Miss Smith's ten children and their "legitimate issue";[39] however, political power is reserved solely for the males. Four of Miss Smith's children are sons, and these are trained in the arts of government in order to assume their hereditary role as leaders of the Island's people and Parliament.

As a sociologist, Mr. Thinkwell perceives Miss Smith's island as "The world in Microcosm" (*O.I.*, p. 190). It is a world in which—Godlike—Miss Smith creates the law and the Scriptures (*O.I.*, p. 312); but—Godlike also—she is above the law. Thus, although she inveighs against drunkenness (*O.I.*, p. 96), she is an alcoholic. Although she rails against sexual transgressions (*O.I.*, p. 188), she has been—albeit inadvertently—"a wanton" (*O.I.*, p. 28). Although she makes laws against bastardy, her ten children—as she has found it convenient to forget—are "bastards all" (*O.I.*, p. 275). Finally, although she imposes Victorian standards of masculinity and femininity on her subjects—gentlemen smoke and ladies don't (*O.I.*, p. 122); gentlemen govern and ladies don't—her own career has been a masculine one. "I have created a House of Parliament," Miss Smith noted in her journal of life on the Island,

> which shall consist of twenty-one of the most steady and virtuous Orphans, as well, of course, as my own four Sons, who will be their natural Leaders. Caroline says, why should not *she*, the eldest of the Family, be there, and I had to discourse to her at some length on the different functions of *Man* and *Woman* in the scheme of Creation, and how it would not be fitting that the gentler and frailer Sex should take an active part in the male arts of Government. She replied, 'But *you* do, Mamma!' and I had to explain to her the peculiar Position to which God had called me. I fear she gets no more docile as time goes by, . . . (*O.I.*, pp. 183–84)[40]

A month later the spirited Caroline is neutralized as a threat to Miss Smith's hegemony by the provision to her of "a Consort," in the person of a young man she has been pining to marry. Nothing else is heard thereafter of this rebellious daughter, save that the "eldest boy" of her union with Conrad

Rimski was the "far from manly" Hindley Smith-Rimski,[41] and that Caroline herself died twenty years before the arrival of the Thinkwell party on Orphan Island (O.I., p. 99).

All four of the principal female characters in Rose Macaulay's *Crewe Train* (1926) embody certain masculine traits. Thus, the treacly and gossipy novelist, Evelyn Gresham, has "closely cut" hair and a "boyish" body, despite her role as "the middle-aged mother of four adults" (C.T., p. 286). Evelyn's catty, "clever," and attractive daughter Audrey is an editor and author who sometimes resents being a woman (C.T., p. 211). Admired by her friend Arnold Chapel because she is "like an intelligent youth, with a girl's grace added,"[42] Audrey is bisexual in her own "admirations" (C.T., p. 84). Audrey's younger sister, Noel, an Oxford undergraduate and a feminist (C.T., p. 211), honorably avoids loose talk about the affairs of others; and, in the last chapter in which she appears, goes off alone by train from London to Cornwall with a rucksack on her back in search of her cousin Denham, for the expressed purpose of restoring Denham to her estranged husband. Noel finds Denham in a cottage on a cliff overlooking the ocean and joins her in consuming bread, jam, and tea. Their "virginal" communion over this sisterly meal gives way to the exploration of secret caves, steps and passageways—one a "slimy tunnel"—that lead from the cottage to the sea (C.T., pp. 296–98).

No overtly erotic activity is portrayed, or even intended, by Macaulay in the commingling of Noel, "the product of a fastidious civilization," and Denham, "the young barbarian" (C.T., p. 297). But it is an interesting sidelight on the novel that this and other of Denham's Cornish escapades, both real and rumored, seem highly reminiscent of Vita Sackville-West's visits to Cornwall with Violet Trefusis.[43]

Reviewing *Crewe Train* at the time of its appearance, critic Robert Morss Lovett observed that Denham

> plays the part allotted in eighteenth century novels, such as *Nature and Art* or *The Fool of Quality*, to a boy, . . . who illustrates the education of nature as opposed to that of artificial society.[44]

The clergyman father of Denham Dobie was a misanthrope and a recluse, who, after the death of Denham's mother, resigned his living and fled with his small daughter first to Mallorca, and then, when that island became overpopulated, to Andorra, in the vain hope of avoiding social contact and of evading responsibility. Unhappily betrayed by "life" into a second marriage with a handsome young Andorran woman,[45] Mr. Dobie soon found himself the father of four additional children, and the head of a household that was continually filled with his wife's very sociable friends and relations. Like other of the masculine heroines of Rose Macaulay, Denham has marked affinities with her male parent.[46] Likewise, Mr. Dobie's unhappy fate—he died as a direct result of the stress of having to deal with too many English visitors at one time (C.T., p. 23)—foreshadows Denham's unhappy future.

At the commencement of Crewe Train, Denham, its female protagonist, is a "grave, square-faced, brown-legged little girl," who is by nature "a very self-sufficing and independent child" (C.T., pp. 13, 11). She grows into an unkempt and silent young woman who finds housework and child care distasteful and unnecessary (C.T., pp. 15–16).[47] In accordance with her heredity, she lets others alone and wishes to be left alone herself. A description of Denham at age twenty-one "strolling up the rocky path behind Andorra town, full of bread and cheese and . . . animal content" conveys not even the slightest suggestion of the feminine:

> She was a long-legged, lounging, loosely-built young woman, brown-skinned, blunt-featured, with small dark eyes sunk deep under silky black brows and a big mouth screwed up into a whistle. She looked and was a loafer. . . . She was untidy; she was probably stupid. . . . She was obviously no lover of her kind; when she saw anyone whom she knew approaching, she . . . lurked hidden until they were passed by. If you had asked her why, she would have replied, "Dunno. It's a bother speaking to people when you're out." . . . Denham Dobie had no intention of giving herself unnecessary trouble. (C.T., p. 18)

The sudden death of Denham's father puts her in the hands of her maternal relatives, the Greshams, an urbane Chelsea family who hale her off to London and set about exposing her "animal" nature to "the higher life." They groom her, dress her, and subject her to books, parties, and people of culture. Exposed to civilization by the Greshams as a savage is exposed to religion by missionaries, Denham is compared to "a savage captured by life" who continually and ineffectually asks "Why?" in an earnest attempt "to grasp its principles," but who gets no satisfactory answers (C.T., p. 139).

> In all . . . things people had set up a standard, and if you did not conform to it you were not right, you were left. You wore thick stockings and high-heeled shoes in the town. You wore a hat if you gave a lunch party, a sleeveless dress in the evening. You had, somehow or other, to conform to a ritual, to be like the people you knew. You had to have, when you ate, one food brought in after another, each with fresh plates and different kinds of instruments to eat them with, as if on purpose to take time and trouble the servants. . . .
> Denham sometimes dreamed of a life in which one took practically no trouble at all. One would be alone; one would have no standards; there would be a warm climate and few clothes, and all food off the same plate, if a plate at all. And no conversation....(C.T., p. 58)

Denham, a truthful, literal-minded person, wants adventures instead of parties. She prefers maps to novels, radio weather reports to classical music or talk shows, and puttering around in the gardener's shed alone to joining her family and their friends in the parlor for word games or charades. Thus, her aunt perceives her as "a case of arrested development," and makes plans to "have her seen to" (C.T., p. 115). Arnold Chapel, a friend and business associate of the Gresham family, accuses her of being like a child of thirteen (C.T., pp. 96–97); but he succumbs to a sexual attraction for "her strong firm body" (C.T., p. 88), and to a fascination for her exotic background, appearance, and behavior, and insists they marry.

The physical and behavioral attributes of Arnold and Denham express his feminine and her masculine qualities. Arnold is slim, fair-complected, and refined, as befits a representative of "grace," "culture," and "civilization" (C.T., p. 88). Preoccupied with physical passion, he can still discourse learnedly—if distractedly—at dinner on the Russian ballet (C.T., p. 114). By contrast, his inamorata is large and muscular, brown-complected, a rude savage in behavior. She—not he—is "Physically . . . magnificent" (C.T., p. 115), a "primitive" (C.T., p. 215). Strong and silent, she strides through the forest in love with her beau but thinking much of the time instead about "wasps' nests, moles, squirrels, ants, or how many miles one walked an hour" (C.T., p. 112). Arnold's parents, who are anthropologists, classify her "as Cro-Magnon, . . . or Neanderthal" (C.T., p. 117).

Other traditional female and male qualities are reversed in the personalities of this wife and husband: her health is robust; his is frail. She is laconic, stoic, and practical; he is verbose, emotional, and imaginative. She accepts religion pragmatically; he embraces it devoutly (C.T., pp. 134–35). She is slovenly; he is tidy. She prefers solitude; he requires society. Her appetite exceeds his. Her athletic abilities and energies surpass his. Her practical and mechanical skills are far more in evidence than his. She is active and perambulatory; he is passive and stationary. She observes and describes real events or natural phenomena accurately and dispassionately; he romanticizes. When he writes a novel, Arnold positions "the literary moon" haphazardly and inaccurately, but Denham is quick to remind him of the astronomical verities (C.T., p. 154). While Denham, clad in "khaki breeches" in the manner of Vita Sackville-West,[48] is in a rowboat on the Cornish coast making maps, scaling cliffs, and exploring caves, Arnold is wading along the shore and gathering prawns (C.T., pp. 174–83). While Denham, dressed in "grimy overalls" (C.T., p. 228), is overhauling her motorbike at her seacoast cottage and planning a solitary trek through Cornwall with her dog, Arnold is entertaining and being entertained at parties, plays, and dinners in London.

Filled with a desire to please her during their courtship—and perhaps also with a wish to taste once again the delights of his own childhood—Arnold eagerly joins Denham in the pursuits she enjoys, although he regards them as better suited to a child of "thirteen" (*C.T.*, p. 96). During one weekend spent at her uncle's country house, he finds her alone in the gardener's shed and joins her in carving and sailing toy boats down a woodland stream. Here, as on subsequent occasions, behavior which Arnold perceives as enjoyable but regressive serves as a prelude to their serious heterosexual love-making. And, just as the toy boats launched by Denham and Arnold may have been suggested by the wad of flaming paper sailed by Rickie and Stephen in E. M. Forster's *The Longest Journey*,[49] the revelation to an inflamed Orlando of the boy-like Sasha's femininity as she skates along a frozen river may well owe something to Rose Macaulay's own streamside revelation, which preceded it by two years:

> He came up to her, his retrieved boat in his hand. He felt pleased, as if he had satisfied a small boy.
> The rain stopped, and the west was suddenly a sheet of yellow. The young man saw the young woman standing against it, the short ends of her damp black hair caught with light, her bare wet arms golden-brown. His heart turned in him, for she was no small boy, but a woman. Their eyes met, and the look in his filled hers . . . with consciousness of him.
> "I want to kiss you," he said. . . . (*C.T.*, p. 99)[50]

Their love affair leads to marriage, their marriage leads to Denham's first pregnancy, and that pregnancy causes her to be violently sick for the first time in her life.[51] While Denham loathes the pregnancy as an unwanted, unwarranted affront to her body and an intolerable encumbrance upon her freedom of action, Arnold has "a whim for a child or children" (*C.T.*, p. 172), and moreover sees in it an opportunity for his wife to become "feminised"[52]:

> Mammas do not go on being like small boys [of twelve]. That quality in Denham which he loved would make place for a new quality, of the kind commonly called deeper, which he would love even more. She would become feminised. Arnold regretted this in a way, for, in proportion as their child should gain a mother, he must lose a playmate; but still, life is like that, it marches on, and what you lose on the swings you gain (let us hope) on the roundabouts. (*C.T.*, p. 168).

When Denham disobeys her doctor and continues her normal round of strenuous activities, she has a miscarriage. This helps to create an ever-widening "rift" between herself and her husband. Later Denham is indeed "feminised" by the onset of a second pregnancy; she resolves to sacrifice her own essential nature out of regard for her unborn child and out of a genuine but inarticulate and undemonstrative love for Arnold. Ironically, when she makes this resolve, she is unaware that Arnold is no longer in love with her:

> Because she loved Arnold, she would go and live again as he lived,
> surrounded by people, civilization, and fuss, she would bear his child,
> tend it and rear it, become a wife and a mother instead of a free person,
> be tangled in a thousand industries and cares. . . . (*C.T.*, p. 312)

Early in their acquaintanceship Arnold had observed of Denham that her
nature was that of "an individualist" (*C.T.*, p. 96). A metaphor for the essence
of that individuality is a seaside cottage with a passage in its basement leading
to a cave with an outlet to the sea. This cave she discovers with "A deep,
heady satisfaction," such as that experienced by "a person in love, or a
religious who has found his vocation" (*C.T.*, p. 182). The cottage and the
cave are, in Robert Kuehn's interpretation of this episode, symbolic of
Denham's innermost "self, her soul."[53] From the moment she is seized upon
by "life," as her father was before her, she strives ineffectually to defend that
self from encroachment by others. In seeking to ward off intruders from her
cottage and her cave, "She is really," observes Kuehn, "fighting for her right
to freedom and privacy in the face of the world's compulsions and intru-
sions."[54]

That "freedom" and that "privacy" are best enjoyed by Denham in pur-
suance of a life style that her acquaintances regard as irresponsible, immature, and masculine. Had she been born a biological male, following her
innate inclinations and abilities might have made her a cartographer, a wood
carver or carpenter or shipwright, a meteorologist, a mechanic, a fisherman,
a sailor, a soldier of fortune, an athlete, an explorer, or a vagabond. But she
has been born, instead, a biological female, and—like all but one of such
masculine Macaulay heroines—a heterosexual as well.[55] And thus, tempted
into "life" by "love," as a mouse is tempted into "the trap" by "the piece of
toasted cheese that baited it" (*C.T.*, p. 313), Denham is perverted into a
passive, "stupid" creature, lying pregnant and helpless on a sofa, smothered
in a blanket, and listening to a disquisition on how to manage a household
by a woman who commends "The Cambridge and Oxford colleges" as
"excellent training schools for housewives" (*C.T.*, p. 318).

Young Cary Folyot of *Daisy and Daphne* (1928)[56] has a "secret life": She
alternates reading the works of Freud—which frighten and disgust her—with
making clandestine visits to an Anglican church. There she makes her
confession, receives absolution, and attempts without much success to argue
her religious doubts with the priest. Daisy Simpson, fiancée of Cary's older
brother, accidentally discovers the private dilemma of this precocious pre-
teenager and is moved by it to speculate:

> Is . . . [sex], then, really so disgusting, or is it we who are too readily
> disgusted? . . . *How fortunate are the animals, arriving into this world*

without the sense of fastidiousness that so deranges and dualises the mind of man. (D. & D., p. 198; emphasis added)

Caught, like her creator, amidst a complex of conflicting feelings concerning the dichotomies of flesh and spirit, Cary yearns alternately for matrimony or for celibacy; for thirteen children who would emerge from her body[57] or for a life spent writing books as a solitary nun in a convent and denying that same body.

The moral dilemma exemplified by Cary's internal conflict is one that was central to Rose Macaulay's own life: For decades Macaulay was involved with a married lover whom she could neither marry nor bring herself to relinquish.[58] Oscillating, like Cary, between sexual desires, sexual disgusts, spiritual longings, and spiritual doubts, Macaulay wrote in novel after novel of heroines who were themselves writers and who were invariably involved in adultery, actual or potential.

But Cary Folyot is of interest, too, because, being some twelve or thirteen years of age, she is among the youngest of Rose Macaulay's masculine women. Cary's "spindle" legs and coltish appearance, her nautical predilection,[59] her adventure fantasies set in exotic and far-off places, her yearning to be an explorer, her compulsive "literary efforts" (D. & D., p. 175), and her preoccupation with religious faith and doubt—especially vis-à-vis the Anglican Church—all of these make her, like her predecessor Imogen Carrington, a recasting of Rose Macaulay's youth into fiction.

Climbing trees and waging imaginary battles between settlers and Indians while in a forest with her younger brother Charles, Cary suddenly finds herself battling in earnest to save Charles from a wild boar. For this purpose she takes up a male symbol of power, a "stick" (D. & D., p. 54). With it she fends off the boar until she, her brother, and their governess are rescued by the timely arrival of her older brother Raymond who, of course, wields a more substantial "stick" (D. & D., p. 54).[60] When, some months later, Raymond is assaulted by burglars in the middle of the night at their London home, it is Cary who, unable to rouse Charles, "entered on her dark and frightful adventure alone" in an attempt to rescue him. To this end she is armed with a "cricket bat" belonging to the temporarily impotent Charles.[61] Along with her female readers, Rose Macaulay must have thrilled vicariously to Raymond's commendation of Cary—"You deserve a medal" (D. & D., p. 252)—and to Cary's own retrospective enjoyment of the adventure, which was, the youthful heroine exults, "Just like a night in a book" (D. & D., p. 253).

Cary's art is the mirror of her life; for, in her own "literary efforts," it is young women who have all the "adventures" (D. & D., p. 132). If a male character is permitted to appear in a novel, he occupies a subordinate position as a husband and father, and can be quickly and easily eliminated when the heroine wants to go exploring for treasure in Patagonia with her children and her faithful Indian guide (*D. & D.*, pp. 175–76). In her survey of the seven novels written by Rose Macaulay from 1918 to 1926, Margarete Kluge remarks:

> One could call R. Macaulay the English woman's writer par excellence. The chief and subordinate characters of her numerous novels are almost exclusively women. The man plays an entirely insignificant role in them, being mostly only mentioned because certain of her heroines are married and must therefore converse with the husbands in question.[62]

"When men come in [to a novel] there's love," observes Cary. And love between the sexes is something that causes Cary considerable distress as she oscillates between her Church's injunction "to think nicely" (*D. & D.*, p. 195) and Dr. Freud's observation

> that no other group of instincts has been submitted to such far-reaching suppression by the demands of cultural education, while at the same time the sexual instincts are the ones which, in most people, find it easiest to escape from the control of the highest mental agencies.[63]

Claudia Cradock of *Staying with Relations* (1930)[64] sheds additional light on the nature of Cary Folyot, and thence on the nature of Rose Macaulay herself. Claudia is deliberately misrepresented to the reader as "A spinster," "a virgin," "the celibate type" (*S. Rel.*, pp. 14, 158). Only midway through the plot is it revealed that Claudia has been involved intermittently for years in a love affair with a married man, Adrian Rickaby. Ultimately Claudia puts several thousand miles between herself and Rickaby and becomes engaged to a wealthy widower with five children on whom she plans "to gratify her maternal instincts" (*S. Rel.*, p. 314).[65] "And so much for your mother types," her now bereft lover bitterly complains to a novelist of his acquaintance.

> "You didn't guess Claudia was one, did you?"
> "No," said Catherine. . . .
> "Well," he said, sombrely and with spite, "she is. She wants to vent her instincts on a widower's five children, and doubtless five more of her own as soon as she can come by them." (*S. Rel.*, p. 314)

The "Claudia" who so wants to exercise "her maternal instincts" and the "Catherine" who witnesses the discomfiture of Claudia's cast-off lover both bear a noticeable resemblance to Rose Macaulay. As Cary Folyot was able, with a few strokes of her pen, to leave her heroine in possession of six or seven children who would serve as companions, and divest her of a troublesome mate, so Rose Macaulay was able to provide a ready-made family for Claudia and release her from a relationship which caused her a great deal of grief, guilt, and pain. It is no accident that the names "Adrian Rickaby" and "Gerald O'Donovan" are identical in their rhythm and number of syllables.

Rose Macaulay's propensity for generating fantasy children for herself is also quite evident in *I Would Be Private* (1937),[66] an escapist novel which begins with the birth of quintuplets to one of its heroines. There are three masculine women in this novel. First mentioned is twenty-two-year-old Winifred McBrown, the "sturdy, plump-faced, brown-eyed girl" (*W.B.P.*, p. 139) whose "unwomanly feat in technogenesis" (*W.B.P.*, p. 15)—the production of five live young at one birth[67]—begins the story. "Win" McBrown is the daughter of a sailor and "would have been very well pleased," as her husband appreciates, "if she could have been a sailor, too. . . . She likes to see strange countries" (*W.B.P.*, pp. 47, 185). Thus, lying wearily convalescent after the birth of her quints, Win fantasizes at length about "Mountains and jungles, deserts and islands," and paddles her solitary canoe about the "lagoons" of her imagination (*W.B.P.*, pp. 45–47). Win has read the narratives of the perils endured by women explorers and romanticized their sufferings, concluding "They have a grand time, women that can travel have."[68] She dreams that her daughters will grow up to be aviators and explorers and that she might someday accompany them on their explorations (*W.B.P.*, pp. 284–85). Using money earned by the quints for commercial endorsements and movie contracts, she is able to travel with her family to the Caribbean. But, so long as her children are young and her husband has needs, any prolonged and solitary rambles of her own become "selfish" (*W.B.P.*, p. 109). "To be a lover, a wife and mother, an explorer, all four; here was a job" (*W.B.P.*, p. 111).

Like Win, her sister Gert is an "adventuress at heart" by virtue of their father's influence (*W.B.P.*, p. 47). Although attractively feminine in appearance, Gert speaks of "street tarts" without a trace of "feminine" embarrassment. When her sister mentions "dancing girls" as one of the attractions of Japan, Gert counters:

> As to dancing girls, I never struck any shortage of *them*, that I remember. Now, if you know of a country that features dancing *men*, I'd always be glad to consider it. (*W.B.P.*, pp. 43–44)

In Gert's fantasies about travel to exotic places, traditional sex roles are reversed: men are slavish and ornamental; *she* is regal and sybaritic. Likewise, in Gert's fantasies, she is splendidly clad in a costume that could almost have belonged to Haroun al-Rashid: "white silk trousers and a scarlet blouse."[69] She reclines on the deck of a luxury cruiser and takes her refreshment like the master of a harem with "a young fellow each side of me" (*W.B.P.*, p. 43). Arriving at some exciting foreign port, she goes "swanking ashore among the blackamoors, me palm parasol held over me head by the [ship's] second officer, while I buy pearls the size of peas" (*W.B.P.*, p. 43). Her unsuccessful attempt to find and to purchase a small black slave when she actually does arrive in the Caribbean (*W.B.P.*, p. 108) demonstrates that she would indeed convert her fantasies into fact if circumstances permitted.

Sexually liberated—although, in her own sense of the word, "discriminating" (*W.B.P.*, p. 269)[70]—Gert takes for a husband Señor Tomas Monte, a brown-skinned Venezuelan of dubious antecedents, questionable character, charming manner, and virtually non-existent vocation. A "kind of gipsy fellow," his principal appeal for her is that "he embodied . . . some of the gay, titillating mystery and romance of abroad" (*W.B.P.*, p. 308). Although she goes through the form of marriage with him, just as she plans to go through the form of divorce with him if they should go their separate ways (*W.B.P.*, p. 270), Gert is well aware that "Monty" has left behind a wife—or wives—and that he is "father many times" in many places (*W.B.P.*, p. 102). Amoral, high-spirited, sufficient unto herself (*W.B.P.*, pp. 278, 302–03), Gert Grig loves for the moment and marries for the moment. She departs from the scene of her wedding on Papagayo Island with her new husband headed for Cuba and Florida amidst the following authorial meditations:

> Eternal adventuress, she would take Love in her stride, take lovers as they came and went; she would see them, yes, for a space, and, without heaviness, see them go, and go herself. It was Life she would grasp at and hold. (*W.B.P.*, p. 307)

Gert Grig's marriage to Señor Monte is one of three bigamous alliances in *I Would Be Private*. Perhaps fantasies centering around her own married lover influenced Rose Macaulay to bless these irregular unions with the Anglican marriage ceremony and to have each of these "marriages" promise well for the happiness of the individuals concerned.[71] Gert's disavowal of "silly police ideas" regarding arrangements entered into by partners who wish to be together, however permanently or impermanently (*W.B.P.*, p. 270), accords with her sailor father's pragmatic approach to marriage: "Bigamy has its bright side, as I always say" (*W.B.P.*, p. 279).

In one of the scenes of *I Would Be Private*, Dorothea Dunster, the third of the story's masculine women, rubs down "her hard, sturdy, naked body" with a rough towel, gets into her pajamas and ties the cord.[72] The costume in which Dorothea sleeps is masculine. The clothing in which she works— "khaki dungarees," "sea-going overalls," "shorts" (*W.B.P.*, pp. 127, 257, 166)—is masculine. The handkerchief she carries is "grimy" (*W.B.P.*, p. 179), most probably with the grease from the engine of her motor-boat, or from her solitary digging for treasure on the various cays of Papagayo Island.

The "stalwart tomboy" daughter of the island's Anglican priest (*W.B.P.*, p. 166), Dorothea recapitulates several of the salient characteristics of her masculine predecessors. She is sturdily-built and practical minded like "John" Vallon; she has well-developed musculature, seeks privacy, and has a secret refuge like Denham Dobie. She has the simple and unquestioning religious faith of Rosamond Thinkwell, and like Rosamond, loves to eat tropical fruit, loves animals, is compassionate concerning the trials of others, and is readily moved to sympathetic tears. Like Cary Folyot, Dorothea provides herself with imaginary babies (*W.B.P.*, pp. 239–40); but, unlike Cary, Dorothea seems curiously asexual. Calm and laconic like many of her predecessors, Dorothea is also the realization of every nautical fantasy of every heroine who has preceded her, for she is the captain of her own boat—although it is only a small dinghy—and the master of her own soul.

The quiet, ascetic Vicar of Papagayo Island perceives her as "the only sane one among his children" (*W.B.P.*, p. 313), for she is quiet, contented, and useful, and remains untroubled by the carnal passions that make her sister a laughingstock and her brother a wastrel. There is about Dorothea none of the feeling of being afraid, incompetent, and "lost" which assails even the sturdiest of her predecessors simply by reason of their femaleness. In *Staying with Relations*, for example, Isie Rickaby can ride a surfboard like a demigod and seek her prey in the jungles of Guatemala like Diana the Huntress (*S. Rel.*, pp. 17, 312), but she is revealed to be hopelessly dependent and neurotic. Likewise, Isie's young stepsister Meg Cradock, despite her sturdy body, her archery, fishing, swimming, and other down-to-earth boyish preoccupations, is shown to have the physical and mental weakness appertaining to a previous bout with "Meningitis" (*S. Rel.*, p. 93). These and other stalwart women in *Staying with Relations* are weighed in a balance with their male relatives and found wanting:

> Benet, so like . . . [his sister Claudia], had, among other differences, the differences of sex. . . . he, being masculine, could assert himself more firmly on the world, approaching it with more of familiarity and of confidence, seating himself in its saddle and seizing its reins with the triumphant control of the male rider whose steed it has always (if one comes to think of it) been. Feminine creatures too often appear and feel unseated, alien, and a little lost, as if they knew no way of coming to terms with a world too strong, swift, and overpowering for them. *Catherine had seen that lost look in the eyes of many little girls, while their brothers seemed to be immediately at home in the odd world into which they had strayed, recognizing it as something which their papas and grandpapas had bequeathed to them. . . . Baffled and afraid; that, thought Catherine, was what women were when they stopped to think. Men, on the other hand, seemed competent, assured, at home, full of energy and physical and mental robustness.* (*S. Rel.*, pp. 38–39; emphasis added)[73]

Catherine, as has been noted, is a novelist with a marked resemblance to Rose Macaulay. Catherine's explorations of "woman's incompetence and bewilderment in the face of the world's strangeness" (*S. Rel.*, p. 39) can be subsumed into those of Macaulay herself as she portrays the vast majority of her masculine women. Thus, for example, John Vallon is frequently "sick" with anger or worry. Stanley Croft, Rome Garden, and Catherine Grey lie sleepless and tormented at night; Imogen Carrington is suspected by her uncle of being mentally ill;[74] Denham Dobie becomes pregnant, passive, and hopelessly "lost"; Cary Folyot is a prey to nightmares and overwhelming bedtime fears; Isie and Meg are confined to their beds by stress and exhaustion; Alix Sandomir and Barbary Deniston are "nervy" from earliest childhood.[75]

Dorothea Dunster is distinguished from these and other of her masculine sisters by four qualities. One is, as has already been established, her absolute emotional stability and equanimity. Even the jolliest and most equable of Rose Macaulay's other outdoorswomen[76]—"sunny," "tomboyish" Molly Bellairs in *The Making of a Bigot* (1914),[77] "timeless" Una Garden in *Told by an Idiot*,[78] happy-go-lucky Rosamond Thinkwell in *Orphan Island*, "Amazonian" Pamela Deniston in *The World My Wilderness* (1950)—must pass through a Sturm und Drang period resulting from frustrated love before they can attain the possibility of the sort of contentment to which their essential natures seem best suited. Perhaps Dorothea's utter asexuality is the most influential component of her tranquil and untroubled nature. The only two men of importance to her are her father, a gentle, kindly, and genuinely spiritual cleric; and her friend Mr. Huggins, a cheerful retired sailor who serves as a second father to her. Dorothea is, moreover, as insusceptible to the homoerotic as she is to the heteroerotic. Unlike many of her predecessors, she finds no women who "excite" her, even from afar.

A second characteristic of Dorothea Dunster that makes her unusual is the high regard in which she is held by all the men who meet her. She is esteemed by her father, is highly praised by Mr. Huggins, and earns the accolades even of the island's most misogynist residents.[79] The only dispraise she receives results from certain of her masculine attributes. Gert Grig resents her for being "more of a boy. No sex, if you get me," because, unlike the other women of Papagayo island, Dorothea is impervious to the charms of Señor Monte and perceives him for the "lazy louse" he is (*W.B.P.*, p. 268).[80] And Dorothea's "nymphomaniac" sister Linda hates Dorothea for habitually exercising towards her the kind of "protection" commonly provided in the novels of an earlier era by a brother or other male relative.

A third of Dorothea's attributes—her "unfailing competence and calm" (*W.B.P.*, p. 273)—explains her popularity with men. With her "strong . . . hands" and skilled fingers, she can skillfully mend a fishing line, clean, oil, and otherwise care for her boat and its engine, navigate adroitly whether by day or by night even through waters avoided by others because they are difficult and/or because they are feared to be haunted.[81] On all occasions she lands her boat "neatly" (*W.B.P.*, p. 232).

A fourth quality, upward mobility, makes Dorothea Dunster unique among all of Rose Macaulay's heroines. Denied the educational advantages accorded to her lazy older brother solely by reason of his sex, she is practical, enterprising, and "not unintelligent" (*W.B.P.*, pp. 171, 237). She is the only masculine heroine in all of Rose Macaulay's novels to practice a trade rather than a profession[82] and to rise like the heroes of Horatio Alger— by dint of her own industry, ability, and enterprise, with, of course, the help of "fortune"—to a position of economic prosperity (*W.B.P.*, p. 315).

No character created by Sir Arthur Conan Doyle is more feminine than his most masculine woman: Irene Adler, the lovely actress and transvestite "adventuress" who beats Sherlock Holmes at his own game in "A Scandal in Bohemia."[83] Similarly, no character created by Rose Macaulay is more voluptuously feminine than her most masculine creation: Helen Michel of *The World My Wilderness* (1950).[84] Irene Adler's principal appeal for the king who has jilted her to make a marriage of state is her "soul of steel. She has the face of the most beautiful of women, and the mind of the most resolute of men."[85] Likewise Macaulay's Helen Michel combines "a woman's beauty and the mind, grasp and wit of a man" (*W.W.*, p. 33).[86]

Helen Michel's androgynous name reflects the equally powerful female and male qualities she possesses. As Helen of Troy is reputed to have kindled both Greeks and Trojans to a state of war, so this modern-day Helen is said to possess "that outrageous power of inflaming" (*W.W.*, p. 233). With the dark hair and "classical" facial features of a Greco-Iberian deity, the full-breasted statuesque body "of the Milo Venus," she compels the adoration of both men and women. Her "siren"-like charm inspires in her ex-husband, Sir Gulliver Deniston, a kind of "madness that has captured about all of me" (*W.W.*, pp. 226, 235). She has the power to dominate people merely "by her presence" (*W.W.*, p. 233). Lucien, married cousin of her late second husband Maurice, finds her irresistible. Barbary, her adolescent daughter, is held enspelled and suffering in the "net" of her "charm" (*W.W.*, p. 146).[87] Meeting Helen for the first time, an Irish nurse finds herself "trapped. . . . a slave to sudden passion" (*W.W.*, p. 203). Even Sir Gulliver's appropriately jealous and hostile second wife, Lady Pamela, allows Helen to "seduce" her into a temporary friendliness (*W.W.*, p. 211).

Helen's surname, "Michel," translates as "Michael," a name favored by Macaulay[88] and appropriate to the masculine qualities Helen displays. In *Going Abroad* (1934),[89] beauty expert Jeanne Josef deplores "that masculine absorption in study, . . . that made some English women so very strange" and so neglectful of clothes and cosmetics (*G.A.*, p. 295).[90] But Helen is "an intellectual courtesan" (*W.W.*, p. 225). She not only recapitulates classical antiquity in her heroically feminine person; she also ranges freely and familiarly over it with her gifted scholar's mind. In years gone by, Helen soothed her daughter to sleep with the Greek myths or with Herodotus (*W.W.*, p. 38). She was her son's first instructor in Greek and Latin (*W.W.*, p. 20). Thoroughly at home in "twelfth-century Provençal poetry," she invents fifty poems in the troubadour style. Some of these are printed in the *Nouvelle Revue,* and they completely deceive Provençal scholars (*W.W.*, pp. 84–85).[91] With an ease that would have done credit to an Elizabethan courtier, Helen maintains that perpetrating this sort of sophisticated literary fraud is merely a recreation for her "like embroidery, or patience" (*W.W.*, p. 86). Lounging in her garden in the south of France, she delivers to her eldest son a seemingly casual commentary on scholars who have committed "Fraud, forgery, plagiarism, falsification, theft, concealment and even destruction of documents, to win glory or to prove a theory" (*W.W.*, p. 86). Her lecture is in itself a masterpiece of erudition.

Helen admits to her son that, in matters of scholarship, as in other matters, "I've no conscience of any kind. . . . It seems to have been left out of me" (*W.W.*, p. 86). Baptized into the Anglican Church "too young to say no" (*W.W.*, p. 26), she wonders

> if people want gods, why not the Greek ones; they were so useful in emergencies, and such enterprising and entertaining companions. Capricious, of course, but helpful, unless one offended them. I don't know why paganism has so quite gone out in England; I suppose we're not naturally a god-fearing people. (*W.W.*, pp. 26–27)

Helen uses "god-fearing" in the sense of "god-propitiating." Half ironically, half in earnest she proposes a reversion to deities of the sort that can be pleased by an offering of fish on a stone altar, a practice which her friend, the Catholic Abbé Dinant, calls "apostasy" (*W.W.*, p. 27).[92] Unencumbered and unintimidated by the Judeo-Christian ethic, Helen speaks and lives in conscious defiance of commonly accepted but sexually repressive religious and cultural myths, particularly as they apply to women. Outspoken, freethinking, Helen derides the basic concepts that underpin the patriarchy: that "female virtue" is any more "frail" than "male virtue" (*W.W..*, p. 241); that women *need* to be "stupid," uninteresting, and lacking in initiative (*W.W.*, pp. 189–90); that work is desirable, that patriotism is laudable, that the family is a religious ideal:

> "And as to the family, [said Helen,] I have never understood . . . why it should be an ideal at all. A group of closely related persons living under one roof; it is a convenience, often a necessity, sometimes a pleasure,

sometimes the reverse; but who first exalted it as admirable, an almost religious ideal?"

"My dear Madame, not *almost*. It *is* a religious ideal." The abbé spoke drily, and did not add anything about the Holy Family at Nazareth, for he never talked in such a manner to his worldly, unbelieving friends. (*W.W.*, pp. 134–35)

It is this sort of iconoclasm that motivates Helen to paint a portrait of her late father-in-law, a prominent French mayor, in the nude.[93]

Equally iconoclastic is Helen's refusal to perform the traditionally feminine role of "supporting affective relations within the family,"[94] or anywhere else. That one can feel liking and affection for people within and without one's household, but that they should never be trusted, is the advice Helen gives to her daughter (*W.W.*, pp. 223–24), and it illustrates her masculine predisposition toward subordinating her emotions to her reason or her pleasure:

> She was one of the rare women who are almost as highly sexed as a man; yet she took sex casually in her stride; it was not an aim of existence, but a pleasure by the way, to be taken simply, directly, frankly, then laid aside for some other pleasure. . . . [Her lover] Lucien admired her enormously, finding in her a woman's beauty and the mind, grasp and wit of a man. He guessed in her, too, a masculine freedom and sensuousness; most women, he held, loved not with their senses but with their sentiments. (*W.W.*, p. 33)

Sometimes as casual in her maternity as many men are in their paternity, only when it suits her convenience does Helen reveal to her ex-husband that she has let him think for some seventeen or eighteen years that *her* daughter Barbary was really *their* daughter. She offhandedly describes the affair with the Spanish painter Vicente Rodriguez that produced the child by quoting Byron's comment concerning Don Juan's liaison with Donna Julia:

> What men call gallantry, and the gods adultery,
> Is much more common where the climate's sultry.[95]

In certain of her attributes Helen Michel resembles her Irish father,[96] a gambling, disreputable, still virile "dispossessed peer in Galway" (*W.W.*, p. 226). However, Rose Macaulay's conception of Helen owes far more to the life of Lord Byron's contemporary, Charles James Fox (1749–1806). Helen, like Fox, was brought up by her father "without the least regard for morality."[97] University educated like Fox (*W.W.*, p. 21), as thoroughly conversant with the classics as he, in her student days she—like he—succumbed to "extravagant and dissolute habits,"[98] which mark, and mar, their respective careers. Helen's son Richie remembers

> . . . the long nights of cards, when his mother had sat playing on and on, with a party of friends, mostly men, enveloped in cigar smoke, knocking back whiskey, brandy, vodka, with enviable . . . expertise. . . , acquiring and parting with piles of chips that stood for incalculable wealth. . . . Helen had always played to the end; she might be finished financially, but never in spirit; *she was like Charles Fox, her ancestor, who having played and lost a fortune, would stake his gold watch, his horses, his houses, perhaps his mistresses.* (W.W., pp. 41–42; emphasis added)[99]

As sincerely as her putative ancestor, albeit on a far smaller scale, Helen Michel is a "champion of liberty."[100] Of her politics she says, "I am an old-fashioned Whig. Like my volatile ancestor, Charles James Fox" (W.W., p. 148). Other parallels between the two are striking: Arthur Aspinall writes of Fox, "His charm could overcome the hostility of even the most inveterate of his foes."[101] The same has already been established regarding Helen Michel.[102] As Fox, in his later years, entered into an irregular and enduring union with Mrs. Elizabeth Armistead, whom he ultimately married, so Helen Michel, married to Gulliver Deniston when she first began to live with Maurice Michel, became successively Maurice's mistress, wife, and widow (W.W., p. 19). After his death, despite her peccadilloes, she remains devoted to his memory (W.W., pp. 32, 89, 223). In the home Fox made with Mrs. Armistead at St. Anne's Hill, he is said to have "indulged his tastes for classical literature and a rural existence."[103] Their life at St. Anne's Hill became the prototype for Helen and Maurice Michel's secluded life at their "Villa Fraises."

Thus, as Helen Deniston Michel lounges comfortably and colorfully clad in a hammock in her garden "idly translating Greek comedies into French," it is not merely the "*Michel* male tradition . . . of libertinage" that she is recapitulating,[104] but that of her "volatile" Whig "ancestor," Charles James Fox, as well.[105] In no other masculine woman character of Rose Macaulay is so much beauty combined with so much intellect. Next to Cleopatra-like Helen (W.W., p. 107), Sir Gulliver's attractive second wife, Pamela, an athlete and a huntress who "looked at once Amazonian and full of good sense," knows herself to be "crude," "uninformed," and "dull" (W.W., pp. 36, 225). Likewise, Helen's own daughter Barbary—depicted with all the customary boyish paraphernalia: the pocketknife, the wooden boats and whistles, the male garb, the fishermen friends, the solitary travelling and exploring, the adventures as a fringe "maquisarde"—seems merely callow by comparison.

5

"To Flirt with the Waiters in Restaurants"

A GREAT MANY OF Rose Macaulay's novels contain a young woman and a young man—frequently sister and brother; sometimes cousins—who often appear to be the feminine and masculine halves of one personality. Sometimes such characters are merely the expression of Macaulay's own innate "spirit of asexual independence."[1] On other, more notable, occasions, they serve as an oblique but strongly feminist assertion of "Rose Macaulay's increasing concern" over the years "with woman and her particular social role."[2]

The earliest occurrence of androgynous siblings is in Macaulay's first novel, *Abbots Verney* (1906). Here, a youthful sister and brother, Maggie and Johnny Denham, two would-be English artists in Rome, share not only "their workshop" and their "artistic leanings," but their rather immature physical appearance, as well. Both these minor characters "suggested a couple of bright-eyed and intelligent puppies" (*A.V.*, p. 79).[3]

But it is in the succeeding novel, *The Furnace* (1907), that such a sister-brother pair assumes the status of heroine and hero. In appearance, Betty and Tommy Crevequer, Italian-English "street-children of gregarious habits and wide tastes" (*T.F.*, p. 216) seem to be indistinguishable: "There did not seem to be any particular difference between them, externally" (*T.F.*, pp. 3–4).[4] Both are in their early twenties. Both are untidy in dress. Both stammer. Both—like their predecessors the Denhams—pursue pseudo-artistic careers: Betty as a part-time performer on the music hall stage; Tommy as a reporter-illustrator for a low-class illustrated newspaper. Repeatedly Rose Macaulay portrays this pair in such a way as to heighten the reader's sense of their physical and temperamental similarities. They are "as two twin babes"; they are "Tweedledum and Tweedledee" (*T.F.*, pp. 20, 100, 105–6).

Still, such a physical "oneness" serves merely as an indicator of the spiritual "oneness" of this female/male pair. Far more indicative of the strength of the bond joining them is a silent, shared epiphany, an "illumi-

113

nated moment of insight" experienced by them as they walk together to church to worship (*T.F.*, p. 83). Since both are disappointed in love by members of the opposite sex, the novel's conclusion serves only to reaffirm "this companionship of two . . . stronger than death, surer than the thing called love" (*T.F.*, p. 167).

Five years after the publication of *The Furnace*, Betty and Tommy Crevequer reappear as minor characters in *Views and Vagabonds* (1912). Here, as before, these look-alike, act-alike bohemians are "two minds with but a single thought" (*V. & V.*, p. 257).[5]

The Valley Captives (1911)[6] features another sister/brother pair as co-protagonists. Shared persecutions at the hands of a boorish stepsister and stepbrother in childhood; shared provocations from the same stepsiblings when all are in their twenties; shared neglect from their lame, reclusive father—these factors help to forge a link from earliest childhood between the doughty, stolid Joanna Vallon, and her weak-kneed, frail-bodied brother, Tudor.

Physically and temperamentally the two are polar opposites. To "John," the sister, are allotted the traits customarily considered masculine; while "Teddy," her brother, is accorded those attributes usually regarded as feminine.[7] Nevertheless, this very masculine young woman and this very feminine young man are united spiritually by a shared consciousness.[8] Moreover, after Teddy dies in the act of saving his sister's life, this shared consciousness transcends even his mortality. In the early stages of mourning John

> had given the most vital part of herself to Teddy and he had taken it with him and kept it; but now, keeping it still, he seemed to give it back to her, a gift to be passed on, together with his own vividness of life. . . . To have two lives to live at once—that made of it an exciting business. (*V.C.*, pp. 331–32)

Joanna/John first causes the death of her male counterpart, whom she "had always loved . . . more than . . . herself" (*V.C.*, p. 322). He dies saving her,[9] and she then incorporates him into her own personality. This integration of two opposing but complementary principles, female and male, yin and yang, produces one internally harmonious, androgynous, individual.[10] Such an individual can partake of a reciprocally nurturant communion with the earth and with all animate creation:

> John became at last herself, alive and free. . . . She made friends with life, with people and animals and vegetables and herself, and dug in the garden. She realized and fulfilled her kinship with the earth. . . . (*V.C.*, pp. 330–31)

Interestingly, Rose Macaulay's melding of a masculine woman with a feminine man in *The Valley Captives* anticipates Virginia Woolf's published manifesto on the subject by some eighteen years.[11]

A year after the publication of *The Valley Captives,* Rose Macaulay produced her prize-winning *The Lee Shore* (1912).[12] First cousins Lucy Hope and Peter Margerison provide the central love interest of the novel, albeit each very unwisely marries someone else: Lucy, unaware that her strong feelings of affection for Peter are anything other than "sisterly," is dazzled into matrimony by the wealthy and handsome Denis Urquhart; Peter, distraught over losing Lucy, marries the sickly and penniless Rhoda Johnson in order to protect her from her would-be seducer, the contemptible Guy Vyvian. The shock at learning of Lucy's engagement causes Peter to become painfully aware of how much she is

> rooted in the very fiber of his being; it wasn't so much that he consciously loved her as that *she was his other self.* (*L.S.,* p. 154; emphasis added)

Indeed, the affinities, physical and spiritual, displayed by Lucy and Peter are as obvious to others as to themselves. Denis tells Lucy:

> "You [and Peter] *are* rather like, you know."
> "I know," said Lucy. "It's not only looking and laughing and words; we think alike too." (*L.S.,* p. 161)

Rhoda perceives the same uncanny external likeness, but then realizes that it is merely the reflection of an inner reality:

> [Lucy was] absurdly like Peter . . . to look at and to listen to. . . .
> Then Peter came in. . . . After all, Rhoda didn't see now that they were so like. . . . But . . . , there was something...something inner, essential, indefinable, of the spirit, that was not of like substance but the same. *So it is sometimes with twins.* (*L.S.,* pp. 198–99; emphasis added)

Peter has long been aware that he and Lucy "have always been different from most cousins . . . more like brother and sister" (*L.S.,* p. 197). From earliest childhood Lucy, too, has thought the relationship to be one of "brother and sister," but a prolonged separation from Peter brings her to an awareness that, "I was only half a person without you" (*L.S.,* p. 262).

Peter's wife has deserted him and died; Lucy's husband has disillusioned her. Meeting in a wood, the cousins now desire a physical union as total as the union of their minds and hearts:

Peter and Lucy had come to the place where they couldn't share and didn't want to, and no love but one matured. They had left civilization, left friendship, which is part of civilization, behind, and knew only the primitive, selfish, human love that demands all of body and soul. They needed no words to explain to one another their change of view. For always they had leaped to one another's thoughts and emotions and desires. (*L.S.*, p. 263)[13]

This promised union of the cousins seems to portend a more complete conjunction than the partners-through-life companionship attained by Betty and Tommy Crevequer at the conclusion of *The Furnace*, or by the partners-in-death fusion achieved by Joanna and Tudor Vallon. But Lucy and Peter's planned elopement is thwarted by Denis's cousin and uncle (*L.S.*, pp. 268–83, 300–1), and the lovers[14] remain permanently sundered.

Perhaps the most bizarre pairing of female/male counterparts occurs in Rose Macaulay's *What Not: A Prophetic Comedy* (1919). This novel satirizes governmental attempts to legislate improvements in the lives of citizens.[15] Extrapolating from what she learned at first hand during wartime work as a British civil servant, Macaulay hypothesizes a post-war "Ministry of Brains" which attempts to upgrade the collective British I.Q. through a combination of "Mind Training Courses" and stringent financial incentives to selective breeding.[16]

The originator of this scheme and the driving force behind it is Nicholas Chester, the intellectually gifted "Minister of Brains," whose hatred of stupidity is obsessive. In his public orations the Minister "made intelligence a flaming idea, like patriotism" (*W.N.*, p. 175).

The motivation for Chester's fanatical abhorrence of feeblemindedness stems from his own family circumstances. His Anglican clergyman father and his mother had married, as Chester recalls bitterly, although they

had no right, of course, to have had any children at all; they were first cousins, and deficiency was in the family....(*W.N.*, p. 186)

Four children resulted from this union: Maggie, seemingly of normal or above normal intelligence; Nicholas, of overwhelmingly superior intellect; and the imbecilic Joan[17] and Gerald.[18] Curiously, all that Joan and Gerald have in common is that they have been born into the same family and share the same affliction. Extraordinarily, Joan is *Nicholas* Chester's "twin sister" (*W.N.*, p.185).

Owing to this unfortunate situation, Nicholas Chester has for years scrupulously heeded the dictates of his reason: he has conscientiously avoided marriage because of the strong likelihood that children born to him will be mentally deficient. Finally, when he does yield to emotion and marry, the public disclosure of his marriage causes the fall of his ministry and the temporary ruin of his career.[19] Some time thereafter Chester takes his new wife Kitty on a first visit to the home of his parents. There,

> they saw Chester's twin sister. She was harmless; she was even doing crochet work; *and her face was the face of Chester uninformed by thought.* (*W.N.*, p. 234; emphasis added)

Obviously, like their fictional antecedents, this sister/brother pair exhibits a remarkable physical likeness. However, in contradistinction to their predecessors, this pair does not *seem* to share any mental or spiritual affinities. Needless to say, Joan Chester's opportunities for meaningful interaction and/or competition with her brilliant and successful male twin are nil. In keeping with this discrepancy, his role in the story is a major one; hers is the merest cameo. Still, in her capacity of "idiot drivelling on a green" (*W.N.*, p. 89), Joan serves a two-fold function. First, her very existence is a strong motivation for certain of her brother's otherwise inexplicably cruel actions, such as his attempt to regulate matrimony by statute.[20] Second, she serves as an extreme example of that rampant stupidity so soundly satirized by *What Not*. And, linking her brother to her in light of this second function is the fact that Nicholas Chester himself has fallen prey to the irrationality and stupidity in his own psyche.[21] This most supremely rational and intelligent of men has thereby brought to ruin everything he himself has so painstakingly built. Quite definitely he has far more in common with his imbecile sister than is at first apparent. Of this reality, the apparition that appears to his new wife as she and he journey home from their visit to his parents is blatantly symbolic. In the train compartment with her and her husband Kitty suddenly "sees":

> a Being with a vacant face. . . . And the Being's face was as the face of Chester's twin sister. (*W.N.*, p. 235)

Both Nicholas Chester and his unfortunate sister are middle-aged, and the disparity in their relative abilities is astronomical. A far different sister/brother pair makes its appearance in Rose Macaulay's next novel. *Potterism* (1920)[22] is a clever assault on the "cant" promulgated by the popular press, incorporating both a love story and a murder mystery.[23] Virginia Woolf castigated it as donnish and "masculine."[24] This was an error; the novel is really donnish and *feminist*. It makes use of ratiocination, a traditional tool of the patriarchy, to assail patriarchal institutions and assumptions: to argue both explicitly and implicitly that women, even those who have every material advantage, must strive also for mental acuity; to protest the incessant and illogical abuse of the slogan "innocent women and children" as a rallying cry by nations and factions on every side of every issue. "Why is it worse that women should suffer than men?" speculates scientist Katherine Varick,

> As to innocence, they have no more of that than men. I'm not innocent, particularly, nor are the other women I know. But they are always classed with children, a sort of helpless imbeciles who must be kept from danger and discomfort. I got sick of it during the war. . . .
> [And] . . . now the appeal to [railway] strikers published in the . . . papers . . . said, "Don't bring further hardship and suffering upon the innocent women and children....Save the women and children from the terror of the strike."[25]

Potterism is a medicine compounded to cure all those who distort reality for diseased and selfish ends. As such, it is filled with explicit and implicit protests against the unequal status of women.

The most sustained of these protests employs a hypothetical pair of siblings in the laboratory of the reader's mind. As the story begins, Jane and Johnny Potter, twin children of a hugely successful press lord and a highly sentimental lady novelist, are in their early twenties, fresh from Oxford, bursting with literary—and other—ambitions, and fiercely competitive, especially toward one another. The use of a pair of twins, alike in almost every way—except their sex—makes it possible for Rose Macaulay to simulate and then explore the disadvantages of a female who is trying to compete in a male-centered society. Similarly, a comparison of the twins' sex lives provides the opportunity for broader speculations on the differences—real or apparent—in female and male sexual behavior.

Jane Potter is the first-born of the twins. She is also slightly more intelligent than her brother, but as she leaves the university she is fully aware of the disadvantage of her gender:

> Jane knew that, though she might be one up on Johnny as regards Oxford, owing to slightly superior brain power, he was one up on her as regards Life, owing to that awful business sex. Women were handicapped; they had to fight much harder to achieve equal results. (*P.*, p. 13)

Angrily, Jane plans to "wrest" for herself those career opportunities that "People" will freely offer to her less able brother, solely by virtue of his maleness:

> Young men possessed the earth; young women had to wrest what they wanted out of it piecemeal. Johnny might end a cabinet minister, a notorious journalist, a Labour leader, anything....Women's jobs were, as a rule, so dowdy and unimportant. Jane was bored to death with this

sex business; it wasn't fair. . . . She wouldn't be dowdy and unimportant, like her mother and the other fools; she would have the best going. (*P.*, p. 13)

Although Jane is deeply bitter about the male-centeredness of the society in which she lives, her brother is totally oblivious to it:

Johnny said to Jane, "War is beastly, but one's got to be in it. . . . Every one ought to go."
"Every one can't," said Jane morosely.
But to Johnny every one meant all young men, and he took no heed. (*P.*, pp. 33–34)

The impetus that Johnny's maleness gives to his career in wartime translates into a significant advantage after the First World War, when, as an up-and-coming young writer, he is able to capitalize on his blood-and-guts experience in print (*P.*, p. 65). Meanwhile, Jane's far more limited opportunities as a wartime Civil Servant and a post-war shorthand typist cause her to plan "a novel about a girl at school and college and thereafter. Perhaps it would be the first of a trilogy" (*P.*, p. 214). In a relatively short time, Jane's lack of experiential opportunity has dulled her creativity. Just a very few years earlier Jane herself would have thought such subject matter dreadfully insipid (*P.*, pp. 40–41).[26]
Jane's sex interposes the first obstacle to her professional success. The second, as she learns after being left a young and pregnant widow, is a corollary of that sex—motherhood. Jane's ambitions for achievement and enjoyment are powerful, but her maternal instincts are powerful as well. After the birth of her son, her day-to-day life becomes a juggling act in which she attempts simultaneously to manage the baby, her professional life, her love life, and her social life.[27]
In fact, it is as a dropout from the literary field that Johnny, her twin brother and chief literary rival, now chooses to see her.[28] Jane's first baby and Johnny's first novel are "just out" at one and the same time, and each sibling feels enormously jealous of the other. When Jane speaks aggressively to Johnny of her "future masterpieces," he condescendingly assumes she means future *babies*, while she intends him to understand that she is referring to her future *books*. With like condescension, Jane taunts her brother with the fact that she has produced a child, while he has not (*P.*, pp. 222–23). Motherhood provides Jane with a profoundly "sensuous," intensely pleasurable emotional experience. At the same time, as she is resentfully aware, far more is exacted from her by the parenting process than would be exacted from Johnny should he father a child. It is very much to Jane's credit that, despite the difficulties involved, she is able to nurture both her baby and her book-in-progress at one and the same time (*P.*, pp. 225, 245, 252).

Potterism covers the twins' experiences from 1914 through 1920. Shortly before the novel's conclusion Johnny is said to have already established a reputation as "quite a competent journalist." In addition, still "swimming on the tide of his first novel," he has been given a job as assistant editor of an important weekly.[29] Meanwhile, some few weeks or months later, his "shade cleverer" sister (*P.*, p. 65) remains a freelance writer with "her novel coming out next week" (*P.*, p. 252).[30]

Setting aside the more obvious social advantages inherent in Johnny's gender, and the immediate biological disadvantages involved in Jane's reproductive function, Macaulay's story makes it obvious that other, more subtle factors have also retarded Jane's career. These can be most fully elucidated by employing the viewpoint and methodology of Katherine Varick, the ostensibly "sexless" chemist friend of the Potter twins whom Professor Alice Bensen regards as "the author's raisonneur."[31] Katherine— and thus her creator—would wish us to examine Jane as a complex personality, speaking and acting inconsistently, from motives of which she herself may be partially or even totally unaware. For example, at the commencement of her career Jane appears to be highly idealistic and very ambitious in her own right. Like her "anti-Potter" friends she professes to despise the "mediocrity, second-rateness, humbug, muddle, cant, cheap stunts" of the newspapers owned by her father (*P.*, p. 76).[32] Jane projects a career for herself as, for instance,

> a journalist; a reporter, perhaps: (only the stories women were sent out on were usually dull), a special correspondent, a free-lance contributor, a leader writer, eventually an editor....Then she could initiate a policy, say what she thought, stand up against the Potter press.
> Or one might be a public speaker, and get into Parliament later on, when women were admitted. One despised Parliament, but it might be fun. (*P.*, p. 42)

Initially, then, Jane's ambitions center around the actualization of her own potential for the greater good of the society in which she lives. Over a period of time, by means of her own painstaking industry, and in spite of the obstacles she knows she will encounter because of her sex, Jane intends to work her way up from fledgling "reporter" to seasoned "editor," or from hustling politician to respected Member of Parliament. She dreams she will be able to advance in the world by means of her own unaided efforts because she has the potential to speak and to act in significant ways on significant issues.[33]

But the lesson Jane learns in wartime is that, while men "make history" in exotic locales, women "stay . . . at home."[34] The war brings Johnny every opportunity for adventure and self-aggrandizement on the Continental battlefield; simultaneously it causes Jane to be deprived of sufficient time and energy to write and immures her behind a Civil Service desk.[35] Only because of the Armistice is she able to travel across the Channel; but then she is merely an appendage to her influential father, who employs her as a shorthand typist and file clerk in his Paris office.

Jane's brief and unsuccessful post-war marriage to a man with a beautiful face but a vapid mind is merely her way of compensating herself for the "glamour," excitement, and opportunity of which she feels she has been unjustly deprived. This involvement with Oliver Hobart, the editor of one of her father's own papers, represents a compromise of Jane's anti-Potterite ideals under the influence of what she momentarily causes herself to think of as "love." But, as the reader is made deliberately aware, Jane's first marriage is also—whether she is fully conscious of it or not—an astute attempt to advance an insufficiently successful career by linking it to that of a man who has far less ability but far greater influence than she. As her longtime friend, Arthur Gideon, cynically observes:

> I began to see . . . where Hobart came in. Jane wrote cleverly, clearly, and concisely—better than Johnny did. But, in these days of over-crowded competent journalism—*well it is not unwise to marry an editor of standing. It gives you a better place in the queue.*[36]

However, Gideon, too, succumbs to Jane's ambitions and affections. Six weeks after Hobart is accidentally killed falling down stairs, Gideon becomes engaged to Jane, even though she is expecting Hobart's child.

At the time of this second engagement Jane feels as competitive as she always has toward

> Johnny, with the rubbishy books he was writing and making his firm bring out for him and feeling so pleased with. Jane knew she could write better stuff than Johnny could, any day. And her books would be in addition to Gideon, and babies, and other amusing things. (*P.*, p. 211)

By contrast, a few months later, after the birth of her child, Jane has become far less competitive on her own behalf. Although still very much concerned with "writing" as a way of "making a kind of a name,"[37] she has transferred onto her fiancé several of her unfulfilled professional aspirations and personal jealousies. When, for instance, rather than compromise his anti-Potter principles, Arthur resigns his assistant editorship of the *Weekly Fact* and his job is offered to Johnny, Jane is

> sulky, jealous, and contemptuous.
> "Johnny. Why Johnny? He's not so good as lots of other people who would have liked the job. . . . Oh, Arthur, it is rot, your chucking it. I've a good mind not to marry you. I thought I was marrying the

assistant editor of an important paper, not just a lazy old Jew without a job." (*P.*, p. 235)

Although she does not say so to Arthur, beyond a doubt Jane is pre-eminent among the "lots of other people who would have liked the job."

In part because the demands of motherhood have drained her of self-assertiveness; in part because so many of her once-cherished personal ambitions have failed to materialize; Jane now attempts to fulfill these identical aspirations vicariously through her husband-to-be:

> Jane was not seriously alarmed. She believed that this [desire] of Arthur's [to withdraw into a studious "quest for truth"] was a short attack; when they were married she would see that he got cured of it. She wasn't going to let him drop out of things and disappear, her brilliant Arthur, who had his world in his hand to play with. Journalism, politics, public life of some sort—it was these that he was so eminently fitted for and must go in for.
> "You mustn't waste yourself, Arthur," she said. (*P.*, p. 244)

Almost certainly, as Rose Macaulay constructs the situation, Jane's failure to advance as rapidly as her twin brother, owing to the "handicap" of her sex, has convinced her that, if one can't be born with the privileges of a male, one should attempt to enhance one's own opportunities by marrying a male and manipulating him for one's own ends:

> He loved her, and she was persuaded that he would yield to her in the end, and not spoil her jolly, delightful life, which was to advance, hand in hand with his, to notoriety or glory or both. (*P.*, p. 245)

Jane's intention is thwarted a second time when Arthur Gideon—like Oliver Hobart before him—meets a premature death.[38] Still, Jane Potter-Hobart-(almost) Gideon is portrayed as preternaturally "greedy" for worldly success, and therefore destined to achieve it.[39] *Potterism* draws to a close with the cynical reassurance that,

> Jane would, no doubt, fulfill herself in the course of time, make an adequate figure in the world she loved, and suck therefrom no small advantage. (*P.*, p. 255)

Very auspiciously, her first novel finally does appear among the book publishers' spring offerings. But, along with the notice comes a parenthetical suggestion that Jane's brother will be perennially slightly more successful than she.[40] Nevertheless, *Potterism's* final paragraph is a strident reminder that Jane has produced a *son*. This male child, who is the image of her father both physically and temperamentally, is the heir presumptive to her father's publishing empire (*P.*, pp. 221, 256). Thus, albeit at one ironic remove, the ultimate triumph in this tale of the archetypal "Jane's" sibling rivalry with the archetypal "Johnny" is destined to be "Jane's." Having "failed" in that she was not born a male, she has "succeeded" in that she has given birth to one.[41]

Jane Potter becomes romantically involved only with men of her own class with whom she makes, or tries to make, advantageous alliances. Apparently no such motive enters into the indiscriminate amours of her promiscuous male twin. I have already observed that, in *Potterism*, Rose Macaulay's twins provide her with a kind of laboratory in which she can conduct for the observant reader a species of controlled experiments demonstrating the social and biological disadvantages acting upon "modern" English women of the second decade of the twentieth century. Similarly, in order to lead her reader to investigate, in the manner of her "raisonneur" Katherine Varick, the differences—real or apparent—in various manifestations of female and male sexuality, Macaulay is likewise able to utilize her twins in an analytic capacity.

The reader is first presented with the attitude towards "sexual relations" young Jane Potter *thinks* she holds shortly after graduation from Oxford. These views appear quite liberal:

> It was, surely, like eating and drinking, a natural element in life, which few avoid. . . . Jane was quite willing to accept with approval, as part of the game of living, such episodes in this field as came her way; but she could not regard them as important. As to marriage, it was merely dowdy. Domesticity; babies; servants; the companionship of one man. The sort of thing [her not very intelligent sister] Clare would go in for, no doubt. Not for Jane, before whom the world lay, an oyster asking to be opened. (*P.*, pp. 41–42)[42]

A sexually "liberated" life style is what Jane anticipates for herself while she is still at Oxford; however, later, her actual involvements with men always tend toward matrimony. Thus, whether her feelings for a man are transient, as they are for suave Oliver Hobart; or transcendent, as they appear for cerebral Arthur Gideon (*P.*, pp. 206, 219–20), Jane invariably feels a need to marry the object of her sexual desires and to bear his children. There is considerable evidence that Jane is incapable of a selfless, enduring passion. Yet, all her "liberated" theories notwithstanding, she always becomes engaged to the man who arouses her affections. Save for their common profession of journalism, Oliver Hobart and Arthur Gideon are polar opposites.[43] The incongruity of replacing the former with the latter heightens the reader's sense of the indiscriminate nature of Jane's marital urges.

By contrast, Jane's promiscuous brother exhibits no such matrimonial tendencies. Rose Macaulay euphemistically characterizes Johnny Potter as "polygamous" (*P.*, p. 215). His simultaneous involvements with a lady violinist and a "painted" music-hall girl of the "kind you don't meet" evoke speculations from his twin on possible differences between female and male sexuality:

> Men were perhaps less critical; or perhaps they wanted different qualities in those with whom they flirted; or perhaps it was that their amatory instinct, when pronounced at all, was much stronger than women's, and flowed out on to any object at hand when they were in the mood. (*P.*, p. 216)[44]

Jane's fiancé Gideon accounts for differences in women's and men's sexual behavior with a simplistic assumption:

> "Men usually have, as a rule, more sex feeling than women, that's all. Naturally. They need more, to carry them through all the business of making marriage proposals and keeping up homes, and so on. Women often have very little. That's why they're often better at friendship than most men are. . . . Most men . . . want sex in their lives at some time or other. Some women are quite happy without it. They can be nearly sexless. Very few men are that." (*P.*, p. 216)

However, *Potterism* is rife with women of varying importance to the plot who contradict this assumption. First and foremost, there is Jane herself, who becomes engaged to marry her second husband long before she has given birth to the child fathered by her first husband (*P.*, p. 210). There is Jane's older sister Clare, "whom one can't think of apart from sex. No friendship would ever satisfy her."[45] There is Peggy Potter, wife of Jane's elder brother, Frank. Marriage to an Anglican priest inhibits neither her roving eye nor the maliciousness of her tongue when she is frustrated in a flirtation (*P.*, pp. 47, 53–54). There is Johnny's sometime girlfriend, Nancy Sharpe, who studies the violin with unwavering devotion, but who can take a love affair "with nonchalance" (*P.*, pp. 215, 226–27). There is the lovely music hall girl, who can be intimate with a man "merely to pass the time" (*P.*, p. 215). There are the "fast" women of the "dissolute" Juke household and their "theatrical friends" (*P.*, pp. 171–76). There is the nameless prostitute who solicits Arthur Gideon on a rainy night (*P.*, p. 231). Finally, most sublimely ironic of all, there is the "frosty blue"-eyed chemist Katherine Varick, whom Arthur Gideon cites to Jane as the quintessential "sexless" woman.[46] Jane readily concurs with Gideon that the seemingly frigid Katherine "isn't typical. . . . isn't a channel for the life force, like most of us" (*P.*, p. 217).[47] Yet the reader has seen Katherine's reluctant confession in her "Journal":

For the last five years I have cared for Arthur Gideon more than for any one else in the world. I see no reason why I shouldn't, if I like. It has never damaged any one but myself. It has damaged me in two ways—it has made it sometimes difficult to give my mind to my work, and it has made me, often, rather degradingly jealous of Jane. However, you would hardly (I hope) notice it, and anyhow it can't be helped. (*P.*, p. 168)

Textual evidence demonstrates that both of the Potter twins are susceptible to intense erotic feelings. Johnny's powerful libido means that he "usually had more than one girl on hand" (*P.*, p. 215). Jane, married to Oliver Hobart and expecting his child, becomes progressively more enamoured of Arthur Gideon, even when she mistakenly believes him to be her husband's killer (*P.*, pp. 102, 185, 206). For Johnny, women are objects providing him with companionship, entertainment, and sexual gratification (*P.*, pp. 215–16). For Jane, men are likewise objects—to be exploited as she attempts to exploit everything else. She is "ignorant of love except in its crudest form of desire for the people and things which ministered to her personal happiness" (*P.*, p. 108). Even when her passion for Arthur is turning her "hot and cold," Jane is able to wonder "how long it would last at this pitch" (*P.*, pp. 219–20). What the idealistic Arthur views as a passionate union of two people who love each other, the calculating Jane perceives as the yoking together of two careers (*P.*, p. 246). Arthur's sudden death is a shock to Jane, but it does not leave her inconsolable:

She had loved Arthur Gideon; but what [her mother the sentimental authoress] Lady Pinkerton and [her equally sentimental sister] Clare would call her "heart" was not of the kind which would, as these two would doubtless put it in their strange phraseology, "break." Somehow, after all, Jane would have her good time; if not in one way, then in another. (*P.*, p. 255)

All this evidence suggests that, in writing about her archetypal "Jane" and "Johnny," Rose Macaulay postulates no major differences in the basic sexuality of males and females. However, strong social pressures exist for Jane which inhibit her expression of that essential sexuality. For instance, Johnny can enter omnivorously into flirtations and/or intimacies with women of all classes without fear of compromise to his social or professional status. By contrast, a woman of the same class, like his older sister Clare, has so repressed her sexual urges that she feels compelled to wait passively for a suitable man to initiate a courtship before she can even acknowledge *to herself* that she has any desire for him. "I'm not that sort of girl, I never was," she proclaims, decrying female assertiveness in affairs of the heart (*P.*,

p. 184). Since Clare Potter makes this "proud" proclamation while confessing to a clergyman that she has murdered the man who courted and then jilted her, the pathological consequences of such sexual repression are all too tragically obvious.

Moreover, this double standard of conduct for men and women may explain why Johnny Potter feels free to consort with dance hall girls of the "kind you don't meet," and waitresses and any other woman who appeals to his eye and his instincts, while Jane says she would consider the conversation of "the equivalent man" boring (P., pp. 215–16).[48] This statement is meretricious, for at least two reasons. For one thing, as Jane must be well aware, there *is no* "equivalent man" to a dance hall girl readily accessible to her. For another, *conversation* is not the issue here; *sex* is the issue. But it is an issue that Jane cannot afford to acknowledge even to herself. The sex urge in a woman of Jane's class is almost always inextricably bound up with societal pressure on her to marry.[49] Since a woman's matrimonial bonding to a man is usually the chief determinant of her position and income in the homocentric social order in which Jane finds herself, what rational woman could *allow* herself "to flirt with the waiters in restaurants" (P., p. 216)? Thus it is that Jane experiences a physical attraction for *Daily Haste* Editor Oliver Hobart—"*And* all that Hobart will let her in to" (P., p. 72). Later Jane "wrote in . . . [Arthur Gideon's] paper, *and* she was always seeing him."[50] After their engagement, an ambitious Jane suggests to a world-weary Arthur that he "must do something worthwhile" in "journalism, politics, public life of some sort" (P., p. 244). In other words, Jane is now determined that her husband-to-be "must go in for" (P., p. 244) success in those very same fields in which *she* has been denied sufficient scope for achievement, solely by accident of her sex.

Not at all coincidentally in years past, Jane's mother, for whose life and for whose writings Jane affects such blatant contempt, made an advantageous marriage to an up-and-coming journalist whose successful career provided an enormous stimulus to her own.[51] Mrs. Potter—now "Lady Pinkerton"—married a man who recognized her "flair" for popular fiction and published her stories in his papers. Subsequently, she became a successful novelist, while he acquired a publishing empire, a peerage, and "a lordly mansion" (P., pp. 13–15, 38, 110–11).

> Funny old pater had, every one knew, begun his career as a reporter on a provincial paper. If funny old pater had been just a shade less clever or enterprising, his family would have been educated at grammar schools and gone into business in their teens. Of course, Mrs. Potter had pulled the social level up a bit; but what, if you come to that, had Mrs. Potter been? Only the daughter of a country doctor; only the underpaid secretary of a lady novelist, for all she was so conceited now. (P., p. 18)

The archetypal Johnny's various spheres of activity need not be interlinked. For Johnny manhood is an advantage bestowed on him at birth; sex is a recreation; and, as it was for his father before him, his career is a function of his own enterprise and initiative. He can *afford* to indulge in a relatively unrestrained expression of his libido. However, for the archetypal Jane—his twin in all but gender—womanhood is the "handicap" with which she was born; "nice" girls don't get involved with men they don't intend to marry; marriage and status are indissolubly linked. It is small wonder that Jane Potter-Hobart-(almost) Gideon doesn't have even the slightest appetite "to flirt with the waiters in restaurants."

6

"The Pattern and the Hard Core"

IN POTTERISM and in other novels, Rose Macaulay's art holds a mirror to our lives: the vast majority of her major characters fall prey to the promptings that cause most human beings either to marry or to burn. In the process women—for need and/or love of men—surrender their birthright to define and fulfill who and what they are. This act of self-renunciation has been imposed by men on women and by women on themselves throughout all of recorded history. Henrik Ibsen[1] wrote of it before Rose Macaulay, and Euripides wrote of it before Henrik Ibsen. When her husband, Jason, puts her away to marry a younger, prettier, wealthier woman, Medea laments that a woman must be a "seer" in order to successfully adapt herself to the customs and preferences of "her body's master."[2] There is no question of him adapting to hers. Woman's subordination to man is all the more painful, Medea implies, because woman is aware of it. She has "life and wit"— intellect—sufficient to make her wretched in the consciousness of her helplessness and subservience.[3]

Rose Macaulay's writings repeatedly remind one that the men of her own and of previous eras were conditioned to center their lives around work, while the women with whom they were allied were socialized to center their lives around men and around children. "A tradition has now for long been established," writes Macaulay in her essay, "Problems of a Woman's Life," around 1926,

> that cooking and cleaning are woman's work. As these occupations are among the most tiresome which humanity has to endure, this tradition is very unfortunate for women. But there it is; and the problem is how to get what is needful done as rapidly as possible, so that one can go and do something else, more lucrative, interesting, or amusing. There must be something to eat at stated intervals, and the house or the flat must be clean. . . .
>
> It sounds simple, but actually to secure both these results will often be found to take the entire time. All the time there is. . . . [A]nd so the grave yawns, and at the end you will be able to say, not "I have warmed both hands before the fire of life," but "I have Kept House."[4]

Man's desire to dominate and stereotype woman into mindless domesticity is epitomized by Milton's *Paradise Lost* (IV, 296–99 and VIII, 46–57).[5] A natural countertendency, woman's desire to escape from the meaningless drudgery of such an existence, is the theme of Canadian writer Alice Munro's short story, "The Office" (1968). Munro's brief but disquieting tale is a deliberate variation on Virginia Woolf's *A Room of One's Own*.[6] Munro's protagonist, an author of scant reputation, married and with children, has all the tools of the craft at hand in a corner of her bedroom. Nevertheless, the pencil, the paper, the table and chair will not suffice to make her an autonomous individual, productive in her art. For that, she must have an office of her own, must be able to escape:

> A house is all right for a man to work in. He brings his work into the house, a place is cleared for it; the house rearranges itself as best it can around him. Everybody recognizes that his work exists. He is not expected to answer the telephone, to find things that are lost, to see why the children are crying, or feed the cat. He can shut his door.[7]

But a mother who shuts her door against her children, or who thinks not of them or of her husband but of ideas and issues having no relevance to them whatsoever, is "known to be an offense against nature."[8]

I have noted that young Jane Potter of *Potterism* is just beginning the struggle to sustain the pursuit of her chosen career in despite of the social conventions, the biological drives, and the subtle psychological imperatives that impel her to marry and procreate.[9] Middle-aged Neville Hilary Bendish of Rose Macaulay's next novel, *Dangerous Ages* (1921), is about to realize— alas, too late!—that for her the struggle is all but over. After twenty-two years of marriage to a successful—but egotistical and imperfect—man, Neville feels unfulfilled.

> How to be useful though married: in [her M. P. husband] Rodney's case the problem was so simple, in hers so complicated. She had envied Rodney a little twenty years ago; then she had stopped, because the bringing up of [her son] Kay and [her daughter] Gerda had been a work in itself; now she had begun again. (*D.A.*, p. 19)[10]

Like youthful, Jane, middle-aged Neville is compared and contrasted with a brother with whom she has much in common and whom she initially excelled in ability. Thus, in this novel, as in its immediate predecessor, a sister/brother pair becomes the vehicle for a strong, if oblique, feminist message. Like Jane and Johnny Potter before them, Neville and James Hilary share a special closeness in youth so that, several years afterward, their mother still experiences a little sharp pang [of jealousy at the memory of]. . . . those two dear ones talking together, studying together, going off together, bound by a hundred common interests, telling each other things they never told her. (*D.A.*, p. 109)

During their early medical studies

Jim and Neville had worked together. Jim had been proud of Neville's success; she had been quicker than he. (*D.A.*, p. 109)

Now, however, Jim is a highly successful Harley Street surgeon, happily married, and the father of a family (*D.A.*, p. 103). By contrast Neville has sacrificed medical school for marriage and children and now, "with the jagged ends of her long since broken career stabbing her" (*D.A.*, p. 15), is engaged in a frustrating and ultimately fruitless attempt to pick up her vocation again after a lapse of over two decades.[11]

Jim Hilary is quite emphatic in his opposition to Neville's attempt. In his opinion, intellection is a non-renewable resource and Neville's

brain has lost its grip. She's not kept it sharpened; she's spent her life on people. You can't have it both ways—a woman can't, I mean. Her work's been different. She doesn't seem to realise [*sic*] that what she's trying to learn up again now, in the spare moments of an already full life, demands a whole lifetime of hard work. She can't get back those twenty years; no one could. And she can't get back the clear, gripping brain she had before she had children. She's given some of it to them. That's nature's way, unfortunately. Hard luck, no doubt, but there it is; you can't get round it. (*D.A.*, pp. 109–10)[12]

In response to his mother's harsh criticism of women doctors as a class, Jim expresses the opinion that his female colleagues are fully competent (*D.A.*, pp. 113–14). At one time his sister Neville had the potential to be a physician, but her brain was "spoilt" by disuse. However, Jim perceives the vast majority of women as solely biological entities:[13]

"It's all right as far as most women are concerned," he said. "Most women have no brains to be spoilt. Neville had. Most women could do nothing at all with life if they didn't produce children; it's their only possible job. *They've* no call to feel ill-used." (*D.A.*, p. 110)

Neville's decision to resume the study of medicine stems, in part, from her desire to be genuinely active and useful now that her children have grown:

"Oh, Lord, it's a queer thing, being a woman. A well-off woman of forty-three with everything made comfortable for her and her brain gone to pot and her work in the world done. I want something to bite my teeth into—some solid, permanent job—and I get nothing but sweetmeats, and people point at Kay and Gerda and say 'That's your work, and it's over. Now you can rest, seeing that it's good, like God on the seventh day.' " (*D.A.*, p. 189)

Another force impelling Neville to resume her career is her very powerful ego. She hungers for public acclaim on her own behalf, not merely because she is the socialite wife of Rodney Bendish, a prominent Labour M. P. "I want to count, to make a name," she confides to her sister Pamela, "I'm damnably ambitious" (*D.A.*, p. 189).

Neville experiences an intense need to compete with her own husband, son, and brother, all of whom she envies passionately.[14] She *feels* superior to these men who are closest to her, and sometimes exhibits a tendency to minimize their achievements, even while these achievements excel or promise to excel her own.[15] But it is Neville's own natural talents and proclivities that are perhaps her strongest motivation to recommence the study of medicine:

> Rodney . . . wanted her constant companionship and interest in his own work.
> "You've had twenty-two years of it, darling," Neville said. "Now I must Live my own Life, as the Victorians used to put it. I must be a doctor; quite seriously I must. I want it. It's my job. The only one I could ever really have been much good at. The sight of human bones or a rabbit's brain thrills me, as the sight of a platform and a listening audience thrills you. . . ." (*D.A.*, p. 55)

Neville's chief motivation is, then, "that need for self-expression which marriage didn't satisfy" (*D.A.*, p. 234).

The effort to prepare for medical school "in the spare moments of an already full life" proves "difficult beyond her imaginings" (*D.A.*, pp. 54, 109). Ultimately, while nursing her ill daughter by day and studying by night, she suffers a "nervous breakdown" which puts a permanent end to her medical aspirations (*D.A.*, p. 184). Neville's private tragedy graphically illustrates Rose Macaulay's own direct and personal interest in the way the accident of one's biological sex functions as a prime determinant of one's available career options.[16] Like *Crewe Train*,[17] both *Potterism* and *Dangerous Ages* explore and explain the often inexorable process by which someone born into the female gender gradually yields up her individuality in the performance of a social and biological role. Ultimately, that individuality is irretrievable.

As Macaulay presents the situation in both novels, three forces operate in this process of gradual surrender. One is social. One is biological. One is psychological. The first of these involves the artificial encumbrances imposed upon women from their earliest years by the society into which they are born. For instance, social custom dictates that little girls must wear garments, such as dresses, that limit their opportunities for physical experience and development. In childhood Jane Potter had "gotten round" this social convention, which thwarted her innate athletic ability, by assuming masculine dress—"knickerbockers" (*P.*, p. 215).[18] However, in adulthood, despite her resolve never to "be put off with" the "second-rate jobs" customarily foisted upon women (*P.*, p. 13), she is, as we have previously seen, obliged to become first a wartime Civil Servant and then a secretary-typist. By contrast, the outbreak of World War I brings Johnny Potter a lieutenant's commission, and Johnny makes good use of the opportunities that thereby come his way to become a be-ribboned British Army major by the war's end. With the peace, both sister and brother are able to resume their literary careers, but Johnny can and does capitalize in his writings on a range of combat experiences which his twin was not permitted to share. Because, as Jane has long since discerned, "People" readily "give" responsible jobs to young men in a way they don't give them to young women, Johnny is quickly transmuted from hustling free-lance writer and literary sycophant to respected assistant editor. Jane cannot, like Johnny, be part of an editor's coterie of "writing young men," but she does find that she can get her articles published by marrying the editor of the *Daily Haste,* and by becoming romantically involved with the assistant editor of the *Weekly Fact.*[19] Her affairs with these men, although fraught with a variety of other factors, are primarily attempts to ally herself to positions of power. As a woman she is prevented by social custom from occupying those positions in her own right.

In analogous fashion, human reproductive biology—"the life force" (*P.*, p. 217)—handicaps a woman like Jane, but not a man like Johnny:

> If Johnny married and had a baby it wouldn't get in his way, only in its mamma's. It was a handicap, like your frock (however short it was) when you were climbing. You had got round that by taking it off and climbing in knickerbockers, but you couldn't get round a baby. (*P.*, p. 215)

Finally, there is the psychological factor of the effect on an individual's development of her or his "role model"—the feminine or masculine ideal represented for a child by the parent of the same sex. Jane has for her model her mother, "Leila Yorke," a treacly lady novelist of limited insights and questionable grammar whom she perceives as "dowdy and unimportant," a "fool" (*P.*, p. 13). Meanwhile, Johnny admires and emulates his father, "Lord Pinkerton," an enterprising and trendy Press Lord and Peer.[20]

Like Jane Potter, her "successor" Neville Bendish (née Hilary) resolves the problem of certain social customs restricting the physical activity of the female sex by simply ignoring them. For instance, Neville is a superbly conditioned athlete who has never let garments inhibit her in the development of her motor skills. She greets the dawn of her forty-third birthday by stripping naked and going for a solitary swim (D.A., p. 13). Afterwards, she dries herself, dons her pajamas, and shinnies up a tree. However, all this is done in private, on the family estate. In public, social pressures very much control the eminently proper behavior of "Mrs. Rodney Bendish," wife of the well-known British M. P. Because of the stigma attached by her class to women who "work," there is very little in the way of meaningful activity to which a woman of Mrs. Bendish's class can put her hand. Sometimes she helps her husband with his constituency; sometimes she emulates her social worker sister Pam by sitting on committees and otherwise aiding the unfortunate. However, in none of these pis-aller[21] pursuits does Neville Bendish find personal or professional fulfillment (D.A., p. 188).

Also like Jane Potter before her, Neville Bendish must deal with the consequences to a woman inherent in subordinating or abandoning other life goals to the biological function of childbearing and its corollary of childrearing. A twentyish Jane looks forward to a lifetime of having to demonstrate that she is not "the mere mother" (P., p. 222), but a fortyish Neville fears the time is fast approaching when

> I shall have done being a mother, in any sense that matters. Is being a wife enough to live for? . . . And Rodney will die some time—I know he'll die first—and then I shan't even be a wife. . . . What will be left? (D.A., p. 185)[22]

Finally, as with Jane and Johnny, the psychological effect of role models must be considered in analyzing Neville's failure to pursue her chosen profession vis-à-vis her slightly less able brother's success in that same field. The late Mr. Hilary, the father of Neville and Jim, was a highly proficient scholar; Mrs. Hilary, their mother, is a hysterical and fatuous woman who, with the demise of her husband and the maturation of her children, is acutely conscious of having outlived her usefulness.[23] Such parental influences on Jim to succeed and on Neville *not* to succeed are revealed in such passages as the one in which Mrs. Hilary reflects on

> sex, which set Jim on a platform to be worshipped, but kept Neville on a level to be loved. (D.A., p. 66)[24]

In earlier years Mrs. Hilary had feared and resented Neville's non-domestic aspirations and efforts and the bond Neville thereby had with Jim. Now Mrs. Hilary fears and resents the resumption of "this ridiculous work of hers. It's so absurd: a married woman of her age making her head ache working for examinations."

. . . Mrs. Hilary, who had welcomed Neville's marriage as ending all that, foresaw a renewal of the hurtful business.

But Jim looked grave and disapproving over it.

"It is absurd," he agreed, and her heart rose. (*D.A.*, p. 109)

Quite perversely, Mrs. Hilary admires in Jim the very thing she finds so threatening to her in Neville. She takes pride in the achievements of her son, even when they interfere with his attentions to her, as, for example, when he must be absent from her on her birthday to perform

"One of those tremendously difficult new operations, that hardly any-one can do. His work must come first, of course. He wouldn't be Jim if it didn't." (*D.A.*, p. 37)

Significantly, after Neville experiences her nervous breakdown, it is she who draws the analogy between herself and her role model—her mother—whose fatuousness and emotionalism have heretofore been a constant source of irritation to her:

"This must be what mother feels," she thought. "Poor mother....I'm like her; I've had my life, and I'm too stupid to work, and I can only cry....Men must work and women must weep....I never knew before that that was true....I mustn't see mother just now, it would be the last straw...like the skeletons people used to look at to warn themselves what they would come to....Poor mother...and poor me...." (*D.A.*, p. 184)

The natural gifts with which Neville Bendish was endowed at birth were initially greater than those of her brother; but, tragically, a great toll has been exacted on those gifts by the social, biological, and psychological factors which have "handicapped" her as a woman, but which have not in the slightest impinged upon Jim as a man. By the time both are middle-aged, Neville has been rendered impotent to perform any work that would be meaningful to her, while Jim is at the peak of the profession that had been the cherished goal of both. It is by means of Neville's rivalry with her male alter ego that Rose Macaulay is best able to demonstrate the disparity between female potential and aspiration and male prerogatives and domination of the professions.[25] In one of the most unforgettable scenes of the novel Jim deliberately makes his forty-three-year-old sister "come a mucker" in a "practice" exam with the premeditated object of showing the woman whose natural abilities had once conspicuously surpassed his own that medicine is "not your job any more. It's absurd to try. Really it is" (*D.A.*, pp. 111–13).

Like Jane Potter before her, Neville Bendish has fallen prey to "the life force."

Gender-related patterns for the failure of females and the success of males affect not only Neville and her brother, but her children. Doubtless adversely affected by Neville's example, her daughter Gerda—who excels "at economic and social subjects"—turns away from these towards more traditionally "feminine" pursuits: she writes uninspired poetry; she draws undistinguished pictures; she daydreams. In order to be near the man she loves, she volunteers to do clerical work for no pay at the philanthropic organization he heads. Briefly, she denounces marriage, and then speedily marries,[26] without even attempting college. Meanwhile Gerda's brother Kay, with the example of his successful father ever-present before him, is singlemindedly "reading economics for his Tripos" at Cambridge (D.A., pp. 56–57).

Bitterly assessing the negative influence of marriage and motherhood on her own productivity over the years, Rose Macaulay's contemporary Storm Jameson rages:

> I am deeply convinced—so deeply that it will be no use citing against me married women who are famous scientists or architects or financiers—that a woman who wishes to be a creator of anything except children should be content to be a nun or a wanderer on the face of the earth.[27]

In both *Potterism* and *Dangerous Ages*, "twins," sister/brother pairs very much alike in all but gender, are used by Rose Macaulay to graphically demonstrate the ways in which the disabilities of the mothers are visited on the daughters, while the prerogatives of the fathers become the prerogatives of the sons.

Tomboyish, dreamy Imogen Carrington in *Told by an Idiot* (1923) is "a recollection of the author's childhood."[28] She is also part of a grouping of fictional blood relations into "triplets," which constitutes a variant on Macaulay's twins device and likewise communicates an implicit feminist message. Imogen is joined with two brothers, as are Alix Sandomir before her in *Non-Combatants and Others* (1916), and Barbary Deniston after her in *The World My Wilderness* (1950). With the younger brother, Tony, Imogen shares inclinations and activities. In a scene labelled "Gamin"—which is set in England, but which is highly reminiscent of similar scenes depicting Tommy and Betty Crevequer in Italy in *The Furnace*—Imogen and Tony, "a happy and untidy pair" of children, "enjoyed the streets with the zest of street Arabs" (T.b.I., p. 216). In one of Imogen's childhood fantasies she rescues Tony from a ferocious polar bear (T.b.I., pp. 163–64).

Like her creator, Imogen in her girlhood possesses a martial frame of mind. The daydreams which she acts out and/or chronicles for herself center around her heroic exploits as a young man, "Usually he was in the navy" (*T.b.I.*, p. 194). Watching British troops depart to fight the Boer War, Imogen is consumed by envy and experiences a tremendous feeling of rivalry toward her brothers, Tony and Hugh:

> Thank heaven, it was rather age than sex that kept one from . . . [going and fighting the Boers]; the boys couldn't go any more than Imogen could. If the boys had been old enough and gone, Imogen would somehow, she felt sure, have gone too. To be left out was too awful. (*T.b.I.*, p. 184)

But, some years later, with the commencement of World War I, "the boys" do go while Imogen finds herself excluded from combat "owing to a mere fluke of sex" (*T.b.I.*, p. 316). Imogen's lament for the death of her younger brother Tony in the war recalls the prior and parallel bereavement of Alix Sandomir in *Non-Combatants*, and of Joanna Vallon in *The Valley Captives*. Similarly, as Betty Crevequer in *The Furnace* prefers the "substance" that is her injured brother to the "shadow" that is her remorseful lover,[29] so Imogen prefers her deceased younger brother to her deceased fiancé:

> Neville took his place in her memory not as a personal loss but as a gay, heartbreaking figure, a tragic symbol of murdered, outraged youth.
> But when Tony was killed, the world's foundations shook. He was her darling brother, her beloved companion in adventure, scrapes and enterprises from their childhood up. She could by no means recover from the cruel death of Tony. . . . (*T.b.I.*, p. 319)

Imogen is consoled for the unhappiness of a subsequent, more complicated love entanglement by the company of her older brother Hugh, with whom she is last seen departing from her lover and England for a year of beachcombing in the Pacific Islands (*T.b.I.*, pp. 333–36). Imogen's relationships with her two lovers, and her two brothers, are virtually identical to those of her predecessor Alix Sandomir. Like Imogen, Alix becomes involved with one man whose appeal for her is primarily physical, and also with one for whom her feelings are more complex.[30] Alix likewise has a younger brother, Paul, with whom she has marked physical and mental affinities and whom she both envies and pities because his sex makes him eligible for experiences from which she, as a woman, is forever excluded.[31] Paul Sandomir dies, like Tony Carrington, in the First World War. An older brother, Nicholas, provides consolation for Alix's disappointment in love, and she is last seen alone in his company on New Year's Eve.

In *Non-Combatants* and *Told by an Idiot*, these groupings into "triplets" are atypical, but not incomprehensible. One woman is joined to two complementary men, who are her brothers. One, the younger, is her psychic "twin," with whom she has strong emotional ties. The other, the older brother, takes over after the younger brother's death as a kind of father substitute. This latter is her protector and consoler in her misery over an unhappy love affair. In each case, both of the brothers together combine psychic and protective functions identical to those exercised toward Betty Crevequer by her brother Tommy. Also in each case, the shared characteristics of sisters with brothers enhances awareness of the sexism by which these siblings are impeded or empowered. Hence, the "triplets" in *Non-Combatants* and *Told by an Idiot* are merely a variant of the "twins" motif.[32]

A unique pairing of siblings occurs in Rose Macaulay's *Daisy and Daphne* (1928).[33] This novel's co-protagonists are different not in their sex, but in their breeding:

> Born of one father, but of two quite different mothers, Daphne and Daisy looked alike, though Daphne was the better looking, the more elegant, and five years the younger. But in disposition, outlook, manners, and ways of thought, they were very different, Daphne being the better equipped for facing the world, Daisy for reflecting on it, though even this she did not do well. (*D. & D.*, pp. 12–13)

Daphne, having been greatly influenced by the genteel aunt with whom she lived from the age of eleven, is well-educated, refined, attractive, and twenty-five, with all the virtues and graces appertaining to a member of the upper class. By contrast, her half-sister Daisy, the illegitimate daughter of an alcoholic lower-middle-class matron, is dishonest, snobbish, unattractive, and thirty. She writes potboiler novels and "lowbrow" articles on "Women" for trashy papers under the pseudonym, "Marjorie Wynne." In medias res— on page 143 of a 334-page novel—"Daisy and Daphne, these apparently two young women" are discovered to be

> actually one and the same young woman, Daphne being Daisy's presentment, or fantasy (as the psychologists call it) of herself as she hoped that she appeared to others. Daphne Daisy her mother had named her. . . . And Daisy she had always been called at home, but Daphne by her father's sister. . . . Daphne was the educated, intelligent young person of cultured antecedents, Daisy the daughter of Mrs. Arthur of East Sheen, about whom Daphne's friends knew nothing. (*D. & D.*, pp. 143–44)

The "catastrophic" revelation of this dual identity causes the break-up of Daisy/Daphne's engagement to a distinguished young scientist,[34] and her mutation to yet a third "self," "Marjorie Wynne," the best-selling novelist. Daisy/Daphne/Marjorie is last observed sailing away from England to commence a lecture tour in America. Meanwhile, her true self, "a frail little spirit, overshadowed by the three who formed its cage, fled shivering for cover" (*D. & C.*, p. 334).

In the story's "moral," the paragraph which concludes the novel, this particular dilemma of one human being who manifests a spurious and divided self in response to life's exigencies is generalized to include us "all" (*D. & D.*, p. 334).[35] But *Daisy and Daphne* should strike a particularly responsive chord in women. It will have meaning for any woman writer who, like Daisy, and like Rose Macaulay herself, has ever been compelled by an editor to misrepresent the nature, needs, and aspirations of her own sex in order to publish her work and to earn a living.[36] Especially meaningful in light of what Macaulay elsewhere satirizes as "the problems appertaining in particular to women"[37] are Daisy's efforts to appear younger, prettier, of better family and greater refinement than she really is in order to attract— and to keep—the man she loves and wishes to marry. That her love affair collapses along with the illusion she so earnestly tries but fails to sustain is less a comment on her than on our culture.

The Shadow Flies (1932) is a superbly wrought historical novel set in seventeenth-century England. Like *Trebizond*, it may well owe its inception to the influence of Father Hamilton Johnson.[38] The plot deals primarily with two youthful, adolescent sister/brother pairs of the sort Rose Macaulay customarily uses to point out culturally imposed limitations on women. These siblings are Julian ("July") and Christopher ("Kit") Conybeare; and their friends since childhood, Meg and Giles Yarde.

Meg and Giles play supporting roles. The former is a foil and companion to Julian; the latter becomes a foil and adversary to the poet John Cleveland. Like other, similar pairs in Rose Macaulay's fiction, Meg and Giles display a strong resemblance in their physical appearance (*T.S.F.*, p. 221), and their mutual tastes and temperaments. Both sister and brother are red-haired, freckled, long-limbed and robust. Both are anti-intellectuals, preferring boisterous outdoor sports and games to more "adult" pursuits. Back home in the small Devonshire village of Dean Prior, the "tomrigg" (*T.S.F.*, p. 180) Meg resists all efforts by her grandparents to teach her housewifery and "lady like" deportment. Simultaneously, at Cambridge, Giles excels in athletics, but has not the slightest aptitude for scholarship.

When Giles devotes himself too exclusively to Julian at a Cambridge festivity, Meg's jealousy seems less like a sister's than a rival's:

> For the first time in her hoydenish life Meg felt that she needed a cavalier. But it was Giles, her beloved, scapegrace companion in sports and adventures, whom she desired for this post. Why must Giles

squander his affections on July, who thought nothing of him at all . . . ?
(*T.S.F.*, p. 220)[39]

Noting Meg Yarde's straight, bold, and free demeanor as she moves unescorted through a Cambridge hall filled with men, an onlooker remarks, "She's like a lad in petticoats" (*T.S.F.*, p. 221). Further heightening the similarities of the sister to the brother is the circumstance that, with the advent of the English Civil War, *both* die in battle. After Giles was killed in the King's cause at Exeter:

> Meg had donned her brother's clothes and arms, and ridden out secretly to join the troops that fought Fairfax around Ashburton, and had been killed in the first skirmish. (*T.S.F.*, p. 470)

These minor characters in *The Shadow Flies* are large of limb and small of intellect. Their obverse is to be found in two of the story's more central characters: its heroine Julian Conybeare and her brother Christopher. Like the previously considered sibling pairs, these two exhibit both physical and temperamental likenesses. Both are dark-haired, dreamy-eyed, fair-skinned, "pretty,"[40] petite, serious, and studious. The brother's "pale . . . grave face" is "almost the spit of his sister's" (*T.S.F.*, p. 213). They are fond of each other and often, although not always, confide in each other.[41] Both are good scholars, although Julian excels her brother, both in industry and ability.[42] However, unlike her "hoydenish" friend Meg, who envies men the freedom conferred on them by their maleness (*T.S.F.*, pp. 219, 259), Julian envies them their opportunity for advanced study, an opportunity denied her because of her sex. "I would I had your chances," she tells her suitor Giles, an indolent, dull-witted Cambridge undergraduate, "Particularly as you don't use 'em" (*T.S.F.*, p. 31).

Much of the action of *The Shadow Flies* is set in Cambridge, where both Julian and her brother pursue their studies. He is a student at St. John's College; she studies independently, and attends Henry More's Tuesday afternoon "philosophy class for females."[43] While Julian and Kit are at Cambridge, each is carrying on a dangerous intrigue—she with a lover; he with a church. Both are ruined as a result.[44] Ironically, Kit's Cambridge tutor, the poet John Cleveland, is actively attempting to forestall the seduction of the young man's mind by the Catholic Church, even while he is himself simultaneously in the process of seducing the young woman's body. Cleveland's quibbles on the words "tutor" and "pupil" after he coaxes his student's sister into a first embrace are lost on Julian, who naively thinks this display of physical affection means her brother's revered teacher is willing to help her with her studies, as well (*T.S.F.*, p. 347).[45] However, although Cleveland truly cares about the development of the young man's mind, he acknowledges the young woman only as an object of carnal desire, even when she dresses in her brother's clothes (*T.S.F.*, pp. 307, 343, 439–41). This "sharing" of an older, more experienced and exploitive male by a brother and sister is highly reminiscent of the situation in *The Furnace* in which Warren is simultaneously Tommy's "friend" and Betty's paramour.

Such female/male pairs appear not only in central roles in many of Rose Macaulay's novels; they make some minor, seemingly gratuitous appearances, as well. They are always, in some manner, undifferentiated, and thus androgynous. For example, Hero Buckley, important in an ingenue role in *Going Abroad* (1934), has a brother, Giles, who serves as her male complement, but who does very little else in the novel:[46]

> A young couple came walking along the sea road towards them, damp-headed, clad in white shorts, and carrying towels. They were brother and sister. (*G. A.*, p. 15)[47]

But the most singular minor example of the "pairing" tendency occurs in *Mystery at Geneva* (1923), in which the heroine, "Henry Beechtree" (Miss Montana), has a seemingly gratuitous brother who surfaces just seven pages prior to the novel's conclusion, where he is mentioned in but a single sentence.[48]

It is possible to see in all the aforementioned sets of "twins" dual aspects of only one androgynous personality—Rose Macaulay's. Such female/male compounds appear in central roles in her fiction, as in the case of Julian and Christopher Conybeare. They also occur as minor characters, as in the case of Meg and Giles Yarde. Finally, they are evident in the consanguinity of an important character with one of lesser significance, as in the case of Miss Montana and her otherwise inexplicable brother.

The least consanguineous of Rose Macaulay's sister/brother pairs are the teenagers Barbary Deniston and Raoul Michel of the post–World War II novel *The World My Wilderness* (1950).[49] Barbary and Raoul are an unruly pair of stepsiblings who live with Barbary's mother, Helen Michel, in a villa just outside a small French Mediterranean coastal town. After the war these intractable adolescents are sent to their respective relatives in London, where they reunite and run wild in the bombed-out areas of the city. Biologically, these two are linked only by their mutual half brother, the baby Roland Michel.[50] Still, as it is with their fictional predecessors, so it is with them: Barbary and Raoul are physically, temperamentally, and spiritually alike.[51] They also are in many ways undifferentiated and androgynous, but there is more of the boy in Barbary than of the girl in Raoul. Despite frequent quarrels, these teenagers are "inseparable" (*W.W.*, p. 23). Both are "slight and small, olive and pale" (*W.W.*, p. 10). Both are "untidy" in appearance, uninterested in school, and lawless in behavior.

During the German Occupation of France both Barbary and Raoul were juvenile maquisards (W.W., p. 4); with the coming of peace they find it impossible to revert to pre–World War II mores:

> "Barbary . . . is an anarchist, like Raoul and all their maquis friends."
> "An *anarchist*?"
> "Well, they don't call it that. . . . But, actually, they seem anarchists; they are against all authority, and used to hiding bombs about the place and derailing trains. It seems have become an instinct." (W.W., pp. 21–22)

The virtually illiterate Barbary and the slightly more accomplished Raoul are both young savages. "Farouche beyond reason" is the way Raoul's grandmother characterizes their behavior (W.W., p. 17). For them—owing to the barbarism of their wartime experiences—antisocial acts have become a way of life. Both youngsters, in truth, find their spiritual home—"chez nous"—in the "wrecked waste" of bombed out London.[52]

Very often Rose Macaulay stresses the similarities of Barbary and Raoul by having them act or react in tandem, as when

> Two pairs of melancholy and apprehensive eyes envisaged that remote wilderness of cold stone. (W.W., p. 28)

Of great significance as a bond between them is a strain of apparently hereditary lawlessness that runs rampant through the ancestry of each. On the matrilineal side, Barbary is a direct descendant of the "volatile," hard-living Charles James Fox. She is also the granddaughter of a disreputable Galway peer (W.W., pp. 226–27), and the daughter of an unprincipled lady artist totally devoid of a moral sense.[53] On the patrilineal side, the young lady's ancestry is even more dubious. Although her putative father is the eminently ethical lawyer and K. C., Sir Gulliver Deniston, her natural father is the Spanish painter, Vicente Rodriguez (W.W., pp. 237–40).

These "irregularities" in Barbary's background are reflected in her physiognomy. She is an "irregular-featured elf" (W.W., p. 14), and her very name suggests the alien and uncivilized.[54]

Like Barbary, her stepbrother Raoul has a family in which the tendency toward moral turpitude seems almost a heritable trait, at least in the male line (W.W., pp. 12–13). However, there is also a strong tendency towards morality in Raoul's bloodlines. His paternal grandmother is almost noxiously "upright" (W.W., p. 5), while his late, convent-bred mother was insipidly virtuous. It is the physical build of this "girl mother" that Raoul's own physique recapitulates. Thus, his "features were neater and prettier than Barbary's" (W.W., pp. 10–11).[55] Even his name combines savagery with sagacity.[56]

In the first chapter of *The World My Wilderness* the reader is told regarding this pair that the virtually illiterate Barbary evinces

> something defensive, puzzled, wary about her, like a watchful little animal or savage. [While Raoul,] . . . two years younger, had a touch of the same expression; but he looked French, and quick, perhaps clever, nearer to civilization, as if it might one day catch hold of him and keep him, whereas the girl would surely be out of the trap and away, running uncatchable for the dark forest. (*W.W.*, p. 10)

Sexually, Barbary is also the "wilder" of the two. There is no evidence that Raoul knows anything more than the first faint flutterings of desire (*W.W.*, p. 170). Barbary, by contrast, was made violently aware of sex during wartime (*W.W.*, p. 72); she has since become thoroughly "experienced" at provoking and then fending off the unwanted attentions of unsavory men.[57]

Like Peter Margerison and Lucy Hope in *The Lee Shore*, Barbary and Raoul are sundered at the end of their story. The differing fates of this pair of "twins" as set forth in the denouement of *The World My Wilderness* vindicate the expectations set up at the novel's beginning. Raoul is last seen abjuring forever the lawless companions and pretty crimes to which he had been habituated and making a grudging but genuine capitulation to the "civilized" world of adult authority. "I shall collaborate," he announces to Barbary at their last meeting,

> That is to say; [*sic*] I shall observe the laws, go daily to school, obey my uncle and aunt, attend mass on Sundays, keep out of the way of the police. Then they will perhaps let me visit you in France next year as my stepmother has invited me. (*W.W.*, p. 228)

But, although Raoul has been "civilized" by the story's end, the same cannot be said of his stepsister, who has very likely only been tamed. In a scene Barbary does not witness, the truth about her "Spanish" ancestry is revealed, and she is wholly disclaimed by her mother's ex-husband. Her mother then resumes custody of her, vowing that Barbary will "work at painting in Paris" (*W.W.*, p. 234). However, judging from the mother's own past performance and present predilections, the daughter is most probably destined to exchange a life lived in open defiance of the law for one lived merely in wanton disregard of conventional morality.[58] This shift from an overtly criminal to a flagrantly bohemian life style can scarcely be considered a triumph for "civilization."

Rose Macaulay's last[59] and most innovative novel, *The Towers of Trebizond* (1956),[60] contains what is also her most innovative coupling of two complementary characters of kindred blood and opposite gender. The narrator/protagonist, Laurie, is paired with a second cousin and lover, Vere. Contrary to her practice of the preceding half-century, in *Trebizond* Macaulay causes these "twins" to be fully intimate with one another sexually, as well as psychically. Also contrary to her practice of the preceding half-century, in this novel Macaulay fails to ascribe like physical features—however undifferentiated—to her female/male dyad. In fact, she sedulously avoids any physical description of them whatsoever, and purposefully assigns androgynous names to them. This is because their respective genders are not meant to be revealed until the book's concluding chapter, and, long before this the readers are expected to form their own erroneous conclusions.[61] Mark Bonham Carter, editor of *The World My Wilderness* and *The Towers of Trebizond*, recalls:

> it is certainly true that her hero/heroines had to be sexually ambiguous[.] This was the only instruction she gave about the blurb or publicity material—it must not reveal the sex of the chief figure or in the case of the "The Towers of Trebizond" the narrator.[62]

The narrator, Laurie, makes use of first-person narration, representing another significant departure from Rose Macaulay's practice of half a century.[63]

Like the other "twins" in Macaulay's previous novels, cousins/lovers Laurie and Vere are linked by a strong emotional bond, and are greatly compatible, whether they are together or apart.[64] Since both of them travel extensively for different purposes,[65] since they move in different "sets," and since at least one of them—presumably Vere—is married to someone else, the opportunities they have to be together are limited. Because they are so often apart, the reader perceives Vere only infrequently, and always through Laurie's eyes. Still, Vere is ever-present in Laurie's consciousness. Whenever they are separated, each keeps a "daily journal," and posts it once a week to the other.[66] Frequently, Laurie muses on Vere and on their relationship;[67] travels long distances anticipating a reunion with Vere;[68] enjoys stolen moments with Vere.[69]

Although Laurie has what Vere unsympathetically calls a "church obsession," Vere is seemingly totally lacking in any religious tendencies. Laurie is a lapsed High Church Anglican. She has, like Rose Macaulay, a long family history of deep devotion to that faith.[70] It is the relationship with Vere that is the cause of this lapse; for, says Laurie,

> the Church met its Waterloo . . . when I took up with adultery. (*T.T.*, p. 66)

The irresolvable conflict between conscience and concupiscence; between profound spiritual yearnings and passionate fleshly desires, produces a deep psychic "discord"[71] in Laurie (*T.T.*, p. 216), who speculates incessantly regarding what T. S. Eliot termed, "The perpetual struggle of good and evil."[72] When Laurie gratuitously poses as a "celibate missionary" (*T.T.*, p. 188), the reader may readily perceive in this a kind of wishful thinking, a fantasized triumph of faith over flesh. Similarly, when Laurie is attempting to ride a camel, and has to prevent it from having "love" with other camels who roar like "the waves . . . on Dover Beach" (*T.T.*, p. 131);[73] or when Laurie is struggling to instill religion—a "moral sense" (*T.T.*, p. 240), a "conscience and sense of sin" (*T.T.*, p. 243) in a pet ape, the reader perceives that what is symbolized is the spirit straining ineffectually to govern the body.

In the concluding chapter of *Trebizond*, Laurie's "reckless anger" while driving in heavy traffic causes Vere's death in a collision with a bus. It is only when Laurie has "murdered" Vere, just as Rose Macaulay nearly "murdered" Gerald O'Donovan,[74] that the reader learns the respective sexes and marital statuses of the cousins: Laurie is a single woman; Vere was a married man with children. For ten years Laurie has been joined in an emotional and sexual union with her male cousin and counterpart (*T.T.*, pp. 272–73). Like Joanna Vallon in *The Valley Captives*, she terminates the relationship with her male "twin" by reckless behavior which inadvertently causes his death. However, whereas Joanna is mystically completed by the union of her dead brother with herself,[75] Laurie and Vere had been complete only while Vere was alive. Now Laurie is no longer part of an androgynous "whole," since she has slain her male self:

> When a companionship like ours suddenly ends, it is to lose a limb, or the faculty of sight; one is, quite simply, cut off from life and scattered adrift, *lacking the coherence and the integration of love*. (*T.T.*, pp. 273–74; emphasis added)

Laurie remains in a state of incompletion, cut off by death from her "other self," and by sin from God. But the story implies at least the possibility that she may, at some future date, be restored to The City of God by means of that Church towards which her heart has never ceased to yearn.[76]

Replete with autobiographical elements, *The Towers of Trebizond* is Rose Macaulay's attempt to relive the experience and expiation of guilt and to come to terms with the personal suffering and loss that led her home to the Church of her forebears. But the novel is also, like so many of its twenty-two predecessors, a celebration of androgyny and an artful polemic on behalf of women. Like "Abbot Daniel," its source; and like "De Eunucho" and *Orlando*, its sisters,[77] *Trebizond* proclaims the "participation" of each and every human being "in the Divine Unity."[78] "Time after time in the novels," as the *Times Literary Supplement* observed of Rose Macaulay in 1961, "she voices her dislike of people who persist in treating women differently" from "men on no other ground except that they are women."[79] As she makes a "pilgrimage" that transcends a multitude of boundaries and barriers,[80] Laurie repeatedly points out to the reader, with seeming casualness, horrifying instances of the brutal, irrational, and perennial subjugation of her sex.[81]

Two of Laurie's travelling companions are far more militant in their feminism. These are Laurie's Aunt Dorothea—"Dot"—an Anglican lay missionary, and Dr. Halide Tanpinar, an M.D. who has converted to Anglicanism from Islam. As these women journey through Moslem lands by boat, camel, and jeep, they have ample opportunity to research—but are frustrated in their plans to ameliorate—"the position of women, that sad and well-nigh universal blot on civilizations" (*T.T.*, p. 12).

Dr. Tanpinar begins her journey as a kind of adjunct to the others, "like Dr. Watson" (T.T., p. 45), but the personal failings of her traveling companions—among whom is a highly bigoted Anglican priest—and the harsh realities of rural Turkish life cause her to rediscover her own culture and to find her own voice. Ultimately, she announces to the others that she has rejoined the Islamic religion:

> I have come to see . . . that we emancipated Turkish women, if we are to lead our poor countrywomen into freedom, must do this from within. What is the use that I speak to them in the villages and tell them that I belong to the Church of England? What is that to them, when they belong to the Church of Turkey? . . . [W]e must speak to them *as Moslems, we must tell them that our religion and theirs allows these things that they think they may not do, and this way we shall awake them to ambition and to progress, and make their men ashamed to keep them down.* There is now a band of educated truly Moslem women, who will go into the backward villages and teach them along these lines. (*T.T.*, p. 261)[82]

Agreeing with Dr. Tanpinar as to ends if not means is Aunt Dot, the widow of an Anglican missionary who is herself a missionary, and whose particular gift is for discerning "the pattern and the hard core" of Christianity[83] beneath the sexist—and other—excrescences that have so plagued the women adhering to that faith over the centuries. Like Dr. Tanpinar and like Aunt Dot, Rose Macaulay loved the faith into which she was born, but that love was never blind. A 1928 letter, sent to Father Johnson when she was outside the Anglican Communion longing to be within, regrets the "folly" of those who manifest "a . . . silly, smug religiosity, attaching great importance to things which aren't the part of Christianity that matters."[84] A 1951 letter, mailed to Father Johnson when she was newly readmitted to the Church, both appreciates John Donne's genius and castigates his misogyny:

No wonder that those who sat under him in St. Paul's used to swoon with excitement and emotion. But what a bore he was about women—all that anger and hate and scorn; that eternal tendency to regard women as a peculiar section; instead of [as] ordinary human beings.[85]

While a 1955 letter, written to Father Johnson nearly five years after she felt herself to be fully "a good *civis*" of the *Civitas Dei*, poses the question:

> Fr. Harris laments that he can't find more servers. What is the reason that women mayn't serve at Mass? If they could, he would have an abundance of willing [and dextrous] helpers. . . . [86]

Macaulay goes on to answer her own question:

> there is a theory that they [women] may not handle the vessels. I wonder why. I suppose it is the oriental basis of Christianity; and one feels that St. Paul would not have liked the idea at all! On the other hand, one can imagine Our Lord saying that such distinctions were nonsense, and that [there] were neither male or female in such matters.[87]

Published in 1956, *Trebizond* develops these same ideas at far greater length:

> . . . [Father Chantry-Pigg] added, "As for women, they've got to be careful, as St. Paul told them. Wrapping their heads up is a religious tradition that goes very deep."
> "An oriental tradition," said aunt Dot.
> "Christianity," Father Chantry-Pigg reminded her, "is an oriental religion."
> "Anyhow," said aunt Dot, "Christianity doesn't derive from St. Paul. There is nothing in the Gospels about women behaving differently from men, either in church or out of it. Rather the contrary. So what a comfort for these poor women to learn that they needn't." (*T.T.*, pp. 19–20)

It was to the metaphorical "City of Trebizond,"[88] to "the pattern and the hard core" of Christianity, that Rose Macaulay returned after decades of alienation from the Anglican Church of her forebears.[89] And it was in this faith that, not too long after the publication of *Trebizond*, she died: "There is nothing in the Gospels about women behaving differently from men, either in church or out of it. Rather the contrary." For those seeking to understand Rose Macaulay's entire output of androgynous women and androgynous men this credo is, indeed, "the pattern and the hard core."

Afterword
"Those Who Establish the Virtues of Writers"

PAYING POSTHUMOUS tribute to Virginia Woolf, T. S. Eliot once wrote: "In the case of authors whose merits have been ignored or misunderstood there is sometimes a particular obligation of championship."[1] There is most certainly that obligation in the case of Rose Macaulay, whose twenty-three novels and voluminous other writings constitute an immense social and artistic legacy that we are only now beginning fully to appreciate. The obvious merits of much that she has written clamor for far greater attention from critics than they have heretofore received.

I have examined at length the many biological males in Rose Macaulay's novels who are less active, less insensitive, and less pragmatic than social custom—and literary convention—dictate. Even greater attention has been devoted to elucidating the masculine women of the novels, those powerful female presences engendered because the author herself was more active, more rational, more intellectual—and far more successful in the sphere outside the home—than the society of her day intended its women to be. Frequently, these feminine men and masculine women are merged by Macaulay into consanguineous twins. Undifferentiated in appearance, alike in behavior, and marked in their mental affinities, these androgynous pairs provide a vehicle for the exploration of the sexism and misogyny of entities both secular and religious.

From earliest childhood, Rose Macaulay readily identified with males engaged in those pursuits which she herself found congenial to physical, mental, and spiritual growth. On her ninth birthday she became "a Shelleyan," admiring for the remainder of her life "the sturdy masculine depth and width of his reading and scholarship."[2] The fantasy projection of herself as "lieutenant-commander" "Denis Carton," sailor and popular metaphysical poet,[3] derives from her admiration of men who could, like Shelley, move unencumbered by custom or costume through a wide range of experiences and achievements prohibited to the female body and denied to the female mind. Her fictional heroines protest in thought and/or action the

147

traditions encumbering females. Invariably these heroines must contend with a social order repressive in its insistence that gender determines destiny.

In the androgyny of her perceptions, in the oblique feminist polemic of her novels, and in the overt feminist satire of certain outstanding pieces of prose, Rose Macaulay is, as I have established, markedly akin to Virginia Woolf. Like "Chloe" and "Olivia" in Woolf's famous paradigm,[4] the author of *Trebizond* and the author of *Orlando* and *A Room of One's Own* shared a common vocation and a common conviction that life, as well as literature, "is impoverished beyond our counting by the doors that have been shut upon women."[5] The reader of Virginia Woolf's *Letters* and *Diary* will find countless instances in which Woolf scalds with vitriol her nearest and dearest friends and acquaintances. On several occasions she takes pot[6] shots at "poor dear Rose."[7] But, draining away the vitriol and dodging the barbs,[8] the reader of Woolf's *Diary* will also find this:

> R. M. . . . attacks authority in literature. . . . In some lights she has the beautiful eyes of all us distinguished women writers; the refinement; the clearness of cut; the patience; & humbleness.[9]

The first—and only—book-length study of the Macaulay corpus to be published in English prior to this one appeared in 1969.[10] By dealing almost exclusively with issues relating to gender, I do not seek to exclude other approaches; I wish to invite them. The possibilities for scholarship on Rose Macaulay are virtually untapped, and they are enormous: work on bibliography, linguistics, and imagery is urgently needed. The encyclopedic chronicling of historical events, religious and political conflicts, and social trends has been acknowledged, but has never been thoroughly researched. Metaphysical questionings, Utopian yearnings, satires on human fallibility, pervasive Freudian influences—these run like a rich vein of ore through Macaulay's works and will handsomely reward the critic who mines and refines them. Finally, source studies[11] and comparative studies[12] have already yielded impressive results, but there might still be much profit in pursuing these further, particularly in light of Macaulay's omnivorous reading of and extensive interaction with other writers.[13]

T. S. Eliot's tendency to sacrifice critical objectivity to literary enthusiasm was once called into question by Rose Macaulay. "In point of fact," she cautioned him, "those who establish the virtues of writers are the writers themselves, however intelligently posterity may write essays on them."[14] No literary scholar could dispute this verity. Nevertheless, marveling at the immensity of Rose Macaulay's own achievement in the years 1906–56 and at the astonishing lack of critical response to her work, I can only urge that it is high time "posterity" made a start.

Appendix A
"Staying with Sanctimonials"

Author: John Hamilton Johnson
Title: *"Liber de Miraculis":* [Third story about the Abbot Daniel by his
disciple] n.d.
Part iii. of "The Disciple's" Trilogy, concerning the Abbot Daniel—Translated from *"Liber de Miraculis"* [no page number]. (Page references in brackets [] refer to the holograph MS. The symbol † indicates Father Johnson's interpolations. N.B. He capitalizes "disciple" only sporadically, and uses variant spellings for "Scithis.")

In a book called: *"Johannes Monachus, Liber de Miraculis"* edited by P. Michael Huber O.S.B., (published by *Carl Winter*. Heidelburg 1913). [One of a series of Medieval Latin Texts, arranged by *Alfons Hilka,*] there are 42 stories, translated from Greek texts, by Johannes Monachus, a Western monk (c. 950–1050 A.D.). I found this date in Beeson's "Primer of Medieval Latin." Three of these stories are about the Abbot Daniel, of the Thebaid, written by his "Disciple," (who had lived with him in the desert), after the death of the old man, at the end of the 6th century—Here there follows an attempt to translate into English the third of these three stories, written about the Abbot Daniel, by his disciple (written when the Disciple was old, telling of things that occurred when he was, probably, very young). [1] "De Abbate Daniele et Quadam Sanctimoniali,"—"Concerning the Abbot Daniel and a Certain Religious Woman" (page 114):

The Abbot Daniel went up from Scithis, together with his Disciple, to the upper part of the Thebaid, for a memorial of the Abbot Apollonius. (I.e. they went South;—up the Nile†). [2] All the fathers came out to meet him to a distance of some seven stadia. There were about five thousand of them.

You could see them, stretching away over the sand, lying there with their faces on the ground, looking like angels of God, as they waited for him with fear, as if for Christ. Some of them spread their garments before him, others their head-coverings. It was wonderful to see how tears poured forth like streams from their eyes. [3] Then the Archimandrite, coming out from among the rest, did reverence seven times before he came up to the old man. Then, after mutual salutations, they both sat down.

Presently the Archimandrite prayed him that they might hear some word from his mouth; for the old man was no one who was prompt to speak to anybody (they had probably not uttered a word yet†).

However, when they had sat down, out of doors, in front of the Monastery, there on the sand,—for the church would not hold [4] them all, the multitude being so great,—the Abbot Daniel said to his disciple, "Write;"—"If you desire to be saved, follow along the way of poverty and silence; for it is upon these two virtues that the entire life of monks depends."

So the disciple gave the writing to a certain brother, for him to interpret it to the brethren in the Egyptian language.

When therefore the writing had been read out to the brothers and to the fathers, they all wept, [5] and took leave of the old man. For not one of them had the boldness to suggest to him that they should make a love-meal. ["Nullus enim presumpsit dicere ei, ut facerent caritatem."]

Now when the old man was come into Hermopolis,[1] [On the way back, I suppose, for the "Memorial" incident is quite finished†]. (Not even a "cup of tea" offered†—) he said to his disciple:—"Go and knock at the door of that Monastery of women, and say to the Abbess that I am here."

For there was in that place a monastery of women, which is [6] called by the name of Saint Jeremiah; and they had there about three hundred sisters. [I don't believe it. The boy was used to living in the desert in a community of two. Fifty sisters would have looked to him like hundreds. Besides, what follows does not suggest more than forty or fifty at the most.†][2]

So the disciple went, and knocked. And the sister who kept the door answered him in a soft voice, ("Subtili voce.") saying, "We give you greeting; you are welcome; what can we do for you?" And he answered her, saying, "Ask the Mother Archimandrite to come to me, for I wish to speak to her." And the door-keeper answered: "She does not ever speak [7] to anyone that is a man; but tell me what it is that you want, and I will give her your message."[3] And he said: "Tell her, 'There is a monk who wishes to speak with you.' " So she went away and gave her the message.

And the abbess (abbatissa) came, and in a gentle voice (levi voce) said to the brother: "The Mother Superior (mater major) has told me to say, 'What is it that you want?' " And the brother replied: "That you will be so kind as to let me sleep here, together with a certain old man; for it is late, lest perhaps wild beasts may make a meal of us." And the Abbess said to him: "Nobody who is a man ever comes in here;[4] for it is [8] better that you should be devoured by[5] beasts that are without, rather than by those that are within." ["Opportunius est enim ut magis devoremini ab exterioribus bestiis quam interioribus."] Then the brother said: "It is the Abbot Daniel, of Sithis"—

She had no sooner heard these words, than straightway she opened both the doors, and, rushing out, began to run to meet him, together with the whole congregation of sisters.

And they spread their veils (maforia sua) all the way from the door of the monastery to the place where the old man was. And they kept on throwing themselves at his feet, and licking the ground where it [9] was marked by his foot-prints.

And when they had come into the monastery, the chief lady (domina major) brought a flask (concam) and filled it with warm water, fragrant with sweet-smelling herbs, and, having arranged the sisters in two rows, one on one side, and the other on the other, ("statuit sorores in duos choros hinc et inde"). [Were there 150 in each chorus?†] she washed the feet of the old man and of his disciple.

Then she took a small cup, and, bringing the sisters before the old man, she took water from the flask, and poured it from the cup over their heads. After that, she poured some into her own bosom, and upon her head ("et in capud"). [10] You could see the sisters standing there, looking like stone statues, immovable and speechless. This, to be sure, was the angelic manner of their conversation ("Hec vero erat conversatio illarum angelica.")!

The old man, however, said to the Abbess: "Are the sisters afraid of us, or are they always like this?" She replied: "Thy servants, sir, are always like this;—but pray for them." And the old man said: "Tell that to my disciple; for he rises up against me just like a cat." ("Hoc discipulo meo dic, qui, sicut *gattus* insurgit contra me."[6]) [11] But there was one of them who was lying in the middle of the monastery hall, asleep. The clothes that she was wearing were torn, and she was ragged and half naked.

And the old man said; "Who is that, lying there asleep?" One of the sisters made answer: "She is a drinking woman, sir; And what to do with her we don't know." ["Hebriosa est, domine. Et quid faciamus ei, nescimus";] "We don't like to turn her out of the monastery, for we fear the judgement of God; but if we send her away from where she is, she upsets the sisters." [12] So the old man said to his disciple: "Take that flask, and pour it over her."

When this had been done, she rose up as if out of a drunken state. And the Abbess said: "All the time, sir, she is as you see her now."

Then the Abbess took the old man and brought him into the Refectory where she had supper made ready for the sisters. And she said: "Give a blessing, Father, to thy hand-maids, that they may taste a little food in thy presence. And the old man gave them a blessing. But only the Abbess, with her assistant Superior, sat down with him[7] [13] (sat down with him).[8]

And those who waited upon them set before the old man a little bowl of bean-broth, uncooked vegetables, dates, and some water.

Before the disciple they set;[9] boiled lentils, a little bread, and wine mixed with water. Before the sisters, however, they set various sorts of helpings;—fish, and wine, as much as they wanted; and they made a very good meal. And not a word did anybody speak.[10]

But when they rose up from the table, the old man said to the Abbess: [14] "What is the meaning of this that you have done? Surely we ought to have had good things to eat. You had a good meal yourselves."

The Abbess answered him saying: "You are a monk, and I had a monk's food set before you. Your disciple, on the other hand, is a monk's disciple, and before him I set a disciple's food. We, however, are novices, and we eat the food of novices.[11]

The old man said to her: "Let charity be mindful. For in fact you have given us great pleasure."[12] [15] Now when they had begun to go to rest, the Abbot Daniel said to his disciple: "Go and see where that drinking one sleeps;—the one that lies in the middle of the hall."

And the disciple went, and saw, and came back, and told him, saying: "Close by the way out into the back yard." [Et nuntiavit ei dicens: "Juxta exitum necessariorum.".].

And the old man said to his disciple: "Keep watch with me tonight."

And when all the sisters had got up from where they had been [16] sitting, he took his disciple with him, and they went down in silence to the place at the back of the house; ["et descenderunt silenter retro locum, et viderunt"] and they saw that the one who was called "the drinking one" got up and stretched out her hands to heaven, and her tears poured down like rivers. Her lips were just moving, but what she said could not be heard.[13] She kept on kneeling down, over and over again, and offering prayer and supplication to God. Then, falling flat [17] upon the ground, she adored the Majesty of God.

As often, however, as she heard one of the sisters coming down to the back-yard, ["Quando autem sentiebat quia ex sororibus aliqua descenderet ad necessaria,"] she would throw herself down upon the ground, and begin to snore. Now this was what she always did every day of her life.

And the old man said to his disciple: "Go quietly and tell the Abbess to come to me."

And he went, and told her to [18] come, and she came with her Assistant Superior [cum vicaria sua].

And all night long they saw what The Drinking One was doing.

At last the Abbess began to weep, and to say: "O what a lot of unkind things I have done to her!"

Then, when she had knocked upon a clapper, as a signal for the sisters to assemble,[14] an inquiry was made among them concerning the woman.

But the woman herself, as soon as she became aware of what was going on, went off quietly to [19] the place where the old man had been lying down, stole his walking-stick and his head-covering,[15] opened the monastery door, and, having written a note on the bar with which the door had been bolted, saying: "Pray for me, and forgive me for everything wherein I have done you wrong," went out and was seen no more.

As soon as there was day-light, they looked for her, but she was not found.

Then going to the door ["abeuntes ad portam"] they found it open, and the letter written, as has been described ["et epistolam scriptam taliter"] (and the note written just like that). [20] Then there was great lamentation throughout the whole monastery.

And the old man said: "It was on her account that I came hither; for inebriates of that sort are dear to God."[16]

Then the whole community of sisters began to make confession to the old man of all the unkind things that they had done to her, asking him to give them absolution ["querentes penitentiam ab eo"]. (One does not know what the words were in Greek†).

And when the old man had made a prayer for the sisters, he went on his way, with his disciple, back to his own cell, [21] praising and giving thanks to God, who alone knows how many he has, both of men and of women, who are his hidden servants.

[Here Father Johnson's translation ends and his commentary begins.]

I will write down a few thoughts that come into my mind concerning this story, a little further on in this notebook. [22] [no page numbers in the MS. hereafter; subsequent pagination provided by J. Passty.]

Here are a few reflections upon the foregoing artless and, to me, very interesting story.

The young brother, ("Monk's Disciple,") noticed and remembered all that he saw in the "Monastery of Women" at Ermopolis (sic.) that evening, night, and morning when he stayed there.

There are some things which he would certainly have recorded if they had taken place.[17] On the other hand there are things which, to our surprise, are entirely missing, possibly because the young man's mind was not at that time capable of grasping them. He was thinking of Monasticism as a way of life in which multitudes were escaping from the vanities and evils of the world, to devote themselves to God. How much did he [23] grasp of the Christian Faith,—the Faith set forth in the New Test[ament] and formulated in the Creeds? How much of it did these, apparently unshepherded, "Sanctimoniales" grasp of the Christian faith? In this story there is no mention of Christ at all. In the other two stories there is more Christianity,—but hardly that of the New Testament; certainly not that of later Christian piety in the West, whether Catholic or Protestant. In the story "about the Eunuch," the dying Solitary asks for, and is given Holy Communion. Her last words,—very religious, and solemnly spoken,—were about Abraham, and about Elijah and Elisha; there was no reference to the New Testament.

[24] In the long story about the stone-cutter Eulogius, Our Lord and his Blessed Mother are very prominent;—He as *the Ruler* of all things,—"Dominator," "Infans" (certainly [Here, Father Johnson has handwritten Greek characters in what appears to be a very poor hand. Dr. Thomas G. Wilkens, Department of Theology, Texas Lutheran College, suggests the most likely reading is *ho pais*, "the child."]) "The Child," foretold by the Prophets; She as "The heavenly Augusta," (The Empress). Mercy is obtained from "The Child" through *her* intercession.[18]

In none of these stories is there anything about the new Creation, in Christ, the "Second Adam" nor anything about Redemption through the atoning Sacrifice of the Cross or about the washing away of sins through the Precious Blood of Christ.

There is nothing about Our Lord's earthly life, or his teaching. Contrast [25] any one of these three stories with the teaching of the New Testament especially in S. Paul's Epistles, or the Epistles of S. John and of S. Peter or with the Epistle to the Hebrews. Contrast these stories with later, Western piety,—whether Catholic or Protestant, where there is so much emphasis upon Redemption, The Passion, The Precious Blood, Regeneration, Membership in the Mystical Body of Christ.

These things may have been there; but they do not seem to have been prominent in the mind of the Abbot Daniel's disciple.[19]

Now about the things that he would have recorded *if they had been there,* [26] when he spent a night in that "Monastery of Women."

There was no daily mass. (No doubt the Sisters went to the Parish on Sundays and great Feasts, for the "Oblation";—the Offering of the Christian Sacrifice.

There was nothing resembling "Choir Offices." The Disciple says nothing about a Chapel. There is nothing to suggest that the sisters had a chaplain to minister to them the Sacraments, or to instruct and guide them, in religious or in practical matters; e.g. as to how to deal with such an irregular and eccentric Religious as the "Hebriosa." They certainly needed a pocket-prophet;—equally certainly they lacked one.

It comes into one's mind, that where, [27] and when, the Blessed Sacrament falls into the background, the *"Memory of Him"* falls into the background too. He said, "do this *in remembrance of me."* viz. in remembrance of *His existence now,* and *for us;* not merely in remembrance of his teaching, or his example or of his passion, hundreds of years ago. Without the Mass, the Memory of Him *would have been lost* hundreds of years ago. We *"do this"* in remembrance of *Who He is,* and of the fact that He Still is, and that He is *for us* and "we believe that Thou shalt come to be Our Judge." "Judex crederis esse venturus," See all that section in the "Te Deum" "Tu Rex gloriae ——— quos pretioso sanguine redemisti" [28]. Through nearly three centuries the Holy Eucharist was falling into the background in English Protestant Christianity. Is it perhaps true to say that an adequate memory of Jesus Christ was, *pari passu*, being lost along with it?

Far away, in the West, there was already S. Benedict. And *none too soon*. He had been born three years before Justinian.

Mohammed was being born just about the time of the Disciple's sojourn with "the old man,"—the Abbot Daniel,—in the desert. These stories give us a glimpse of that African and Arabian Christian world,— the world of *desert Christianity*, which Mohammed found waiting for him.

These observations about the apparently barely-Christian Christianity of these [29] desert stories, do not apply in the same degree to some of the other stories in the *Liber de Miraculis*," which are more about Constantinople, Syria, Antioch, and perhaps Alexandria.

There follow a few remarks about the importance of saying some sort of *Divine Office*. Officium; Duty, obligation—[30] Anyone who is trying to live a religious life, ought to plan for the reading, or recitation, of some sort of *daily Office;* especially anyone who is not able to take part daily in the public services of the Church. One of the most important and fruitful practices of the Tractarians was the saying of Morning and Evening Prayer by the clergy *daily*, if possible in the Church, but, otherwise, privately, and the treating of this duty as an obligation.[20]

This is important as a daily offering of devotion to God, which should not be dependent upon mere inclination, or upon a feeling of interest in some particular part of Holy Scripture. It is [31] also important as providing an occasion when God may speak to us through *all sorts of places* in *Holy Scripture*, which we should not have been likely to select for ourselves.[21] Thus our understanding is nourished by fresh, and often quite unexpected, thoughts; whereas, if left to our own choice, we are apt to dwell upon one set of ideas that appeal to us, until those ideas lose their interest and significance through not being kept alive, by "the exercise of the reasoning and reflecting powers, increasing insight, and enlarging views." (S.T.C.)

The Order, (about the obligation to say the daily offices), occurs in the English Prayer book at the end of "Concerning the Service of the Church," in the [32] beginning of the 1662 P.B. It was through their obedience to that direction, that the tractarian clergy began to use their churches on week-days. Thus the churches were gradually *got open*. This prepared the way for week-day Masses. In many parishes, this was the only thing that the Tractarian country clergy *could* do, as an assertion of their Catholic principles, and of their own duty as Catholic priests.

The absence of the *Direction* from the American Prayer Book has caused many[22] of the American Anglican clergy to be much less familiar with the Bible and the Psalter, than we, in the C. of E., became in the early years of our ministry. [33] See again, Eph. i. 17–19——"the eyes of your understanding being enlightened," etc. and Ps. cxix. 125. "I am thy servant, O grant me understanding: that I may know thy testimonies."

It would be possible for a lay person, not bound, as the clergy are, to the saying of the Church's Offices, to arrange, out of our two offices of M. and E. Prayer, one single, very good Office, to be said daily,—all at once or in parts,—the whole of which would take less than half an hour.

Throughout *one* year, the two Morning Lessons might be read; throughout the following year, the Evening ones; and so on. Throughout *one* month, the Morning Psalms and Canticles; throughout the next month the Evening ones,—always saying the *Verite* first. Or, all The Psalms for the day of the [34] month,—morning and evening,—might be said each day. The two fixed Collects, following the Collect for the week, might be said according to the time of day.

Or if two Offices each day were desired, one of them might be from the Little Hours of the Breviary, so as to say the 119th Psalm; sometimes the parts of it that are said at *Prime* sometimes *Terce Sext* or *None;* varying according to the days of the week. If late, it might be Compline.[23]

Unintelligent people might think that such a plan would be boring, and would become perfunctory.

But anyone with a quick imagination would find that a great deal of excellent food for the mind and soul would be derived from it. [35] In the S.S.J.E. we use the Breviary Offices, (not the night office,) in the *chapels*[24] of our houses. In our public *churches,* the Prayer-Book M. and E. Prayer. For the Breviary Offices we have for more than forty years, used Fr. Trenholme's compilation:—"The Hours of Prayer." "From Lauds to Compline, (inclusive.) Compiled from the Sarum Breviary and Other Rites." (Now:) 3rd Edition, Revised. Published by A. R. Mowbray and Co. Limited. London and Oxford.

This Sarum compilation has a good many things in it,—hymns, etc.,—which are not in the Brev. Rom. Anyhow we are used to it now. I should hate *not* to say Ps. cxix daily at the Little Hours,—as the present Brev. Rom. doesn't.[25] [36].

[Johnson, John Hamilton . . .]

Liber de Miraculis: [Third story about the Abbot Daniel by his disciple].

Ams with A notes and insertions [43 pp.] nd

From the Harry Ransom Humanities Research Center, The University of Texas at Austin. Reprinted with the permission of the University of Texas and the permission of Father Superior M. Thomas Shaw, S.S.J.E.

Marginalia and other notes to Appendix A

[Marginalia too numerous and/or too copious to be included in the text are indicated by a superscript and included here. I have in almost all cases attempted to retain Father Johnson's original punctuation and other characteristics of his prose.]

1. "Et senex veniens in Ermopolion."
2. (Later.) I may be wrong; I believe they did have very large numbers, but still, this story, as it goes on, does not sound like three hundred.
3. I think the Disciple was very young—perhaps not more than 20—He was very interested and observant. He probably seldom went out into the world. He notices details and remembers it all when he is an old man.
4. Father Johnson originally translated this as "into this house," but then lined out these three words and wrote the phrase "ever comes in here; for it is" twice, perhaps because he feared his handwriting was not sufficiently legible. This was his practice passim in the manuscript. [Author's note].
5. Here Father Johnson originally wrote "the," but then lined it out. [Author's note].
6. *Dic. catus* = a male cat. (post class.)
7. "cum preposita sua" sat down with him.
8. Father Johnson's reiteration, as in n. 4. [Author's note].
9. Punctuation unclear; possibly a semicolon or comma. [Author's note].
10. The boy seldom went out; he was intensely interested, and remembered details.
11. Nos vero novite sumus, et cibum novitiorum commedimus.
12. Memor sit caritas. Vere quia; juvasti nos.
13. Here Father Johnson has written, and then lined out, the words "With many." [Author's note].
14. Here the word "she" is written and then lined out. [Author's note].
15. "no doubt so as to be able to look like a monk of the desert—"
16. The upper corner of the MS. page on which this appears seems deliberately folded downward, as though to mark the place. The corner is smudged, indicating that Macaulay must have turned directly to this page of the pamphlet quite a number of times. [Author's note].
17. There are some things which are very conspicuously absent from the Disciple's story, but which, if they had occurred, he would certainly not have failed to notice with interest, and would have remembered and recorded;—e.g. Mass, or some kind of common recitation of prayer *in a Chapel;*—or the existence of some resident, or near-by priest, responsible for ministering to, and guiding, this large community of women.
18. They do not seem to have been thinking about "Salvation" through Christ, or of Christ as "The Saviour of the world". In the Eulogius story, "Salvator" is used once, as a sort of title. "Tunc cum defecissem, abi et proieci me ad imaginem Salvatoris nostri Jesu Christi cum luctu et lacrimus dicens: 'Domine, absolve me ab hac fideiussoria; sin autem, et ego Vadem ad seculum.' "
19. There is nothing to suggest the Old Man had ever guided the boy's thoughts to doctrine of that Scriptural sort.
I can remember only one *(possible)* quotation from the New Test[ament] in these stories. Viz. (Heb. vi 10) "Non enim injustus est Deus ut obliuiseretur priorum laborum ejus." The re † in the typed copy was mine, not the editor's.
20. This brought it about that C of E clergymen became more familiar with the *Whole Bible,* and with all the Psalms, than the ordinary, busy, and not very scholarly or studious, ministers of other religious bodies. I fear that this familiarity is being lost. The rubric about the obligation is not in the American Prayer Book; and "Anglo Catholics" tend to substitute the Breviary Offices, which, however excellent, do not provide in the Day Hours the same amount of Bible-reading; and *much* of the Psalter is seldom said.
21. When we read passages that are provided in a regular course, words which

are very familiar often come to life with some fresh significance, never perceived before, when brought into contact with matters which are in our minds at the moment. This sort of light often comes from passages in which we should never have thought of looking for it.

22. Yes, *many;* but by no means *all.*

23. Besides, this is a way by which a Solitary individual may take part in the daily prayer of the Church.

24. the house-chapels

25. I think the Brev. Rom. now says Ps. cxix (Vulg. cxviii) on Sundays, and varying Psalms through the week.

Appendix B
"Woman: the Eternal Topic"

From *The Outlook*, 6 August 1921, as reprinted in *Living Age* 310 (17 September 1921): 734–36:

WOMAN: THE ETERNAL TOPIC
by Rose Macaulay

[Miss Macaulay is an English novelist whose latest book, *Dangerous Ages,* dealing mainly with the lives of a group of women, has roused much discussion.]

From *The Outlook*, 6 August
(London Conservative Literary Weekly)

There is a number of puzzling facts connected with the strange life lived by humanity and others on this perplexing and surely unusual planet. There is a vast number of questions that the inquisitive will be forever asking themselves and their neighbors, and of these only the smaller part receive any satisfying answers. Not among these last are the inquiries rising out of a remark carelessly made to me the other day by one who never inquires, but takes all for granted. "Women," she said, "are a topic. Men aren't."

It is entirely true. Man is not a topic; he is merely a sex—hardly, in fact, even a sex, for he is humanity and women are *the* Sex (in spite of their present preponderance in numbers). As a topic, woman is a hardy annual. Annual? No, a hardy monthly, seminal, daily. Women's clothes: are they too few, too short, too transparent, too tight, too cool? (Who ever discusses thus seriously the garments of men, whether they are too many, too thick, too hot, too much designed to be a lure to the other sex?) Mateless maidens, surplus women, women as a social danger, the modern girl—is she different from her grandmother? Are women becoming more (if possible) dishonest? More ill-mannered? Should they smoke in baby's face? What kind of women do men prefer? And so on, and so on, and so on.

The psychology, physiology, rights and status of woman—how far more often they are discussed than those of man. Man too, presumably, has a status, has his rights, even his psychology—and Rousseau and Tom Paine and their contemporaries used to discuss them at length at one time. But in these days women hold the field. It is possible, even probable, that there are also too many men—but newspapers do not point it out in the rather rude manner they adopt where women are concerned. And why? Merely because woman is a topic; she is interesting; it is even interesting, therefore, though deplorable, that there should be too many examples of her. She is a problem to be discussed and dealt with. "The mentality of women," people say, just as if women were Germans, who notoriously possess mentalities. People no more write of the mentality of men than they wrote during the war (we are beginning to do it a little now, owing to Silesia) of the mentality of Frenchmen.

Women are regarded in some quarters rather as a curious and interesting kind of beetle, whose habits repay investigation. Someone writes a novel about a woman, even a bad novel, and there will not be lacking critics who will say, "Here at last is the truth about woman!" (One should perhaps apologize for quoting this particular phrase, for I have been informed by the rightly indignant user of it that he only used it in a private letter of thanks for the book, and on these difficult occasions one must, as we all know, say something foolish. But still, it may stand as an example.) Any number of books about men may be written by the biographers of adolescent manhood, and no one says (or do they perhaps say it in letters of thanks to the authors?) "Here at last is the truth about man."

Why do they say it of one sex and not of the other? It is no use asking them; they do not know. They vaguely feel that woman is a topic under investigation, and man is not. We do not get up correspondences in the press during the silly seasons (all seasons are pretty silly), comparing the man of today with the man of fifty years ago; we take it for granted that the manners and habits of men slowly alter, and have always slowly altered; but that those of women should also do so seems to many people profoundly interesting. So much are women regarded as a topic, rather than merely as people, that in some circles (army messes, for instance) they are a forbidden topic. Among no feminine military organizations—Waacs, Fannies, Wrens, V.A.D.'s, or Land Armies,—was man (one believes) ever a forbidden topic.

One might think that this studying of the topic of woman came from the fact that literature and thought have, anyhow till lately, been in the main in the hands of men, and men have found themselves unable to accept women as an ordinary, and not at all out of the way, section of humanity, but have really believed them to be a kind of extra-human species. But this cannot be the only explanation, for of late years women themselves have enthusiastically weighed in with discussions of their own status and qualities.

It seems hardly fair to men, who are, after all, quite as interesting in their way, and more unusual. Why should we not now put up man as a topic? We have talked a great deal about whether women should have votes, degrees, seats in Parliament, holy orders, tobacco, and other privileges. Why not discuss now whether men should have cool muslin clothes, seats in buses, parasols, and face-powder? Why not write books and articles about them: Two well-known writers have, during the past year, written books on women—*Our Women* and *The Good Englishwoman*, they were called. It is time someone wrote corresponding works on man.

It lately came to my knowledge that a daily paper intended starting this autumn a correspondence on the New Woman, and was asking various literary people to assist in chasing this ancient hare. Will not some other paper open its columns to thoughts on the New Man? For Man is quite as new, which, however, is not saying much. Man will repay the trouble expended on his study; he is an interesting creature. All sorts of thoughts about him come into one's head directly one begins to think him over. Has he a sense of humor, of fair play? Should he wear knickerbockers in the country and display the leg to the knee, thus attracting women? Should he smoke, vote, preach in church? How can he arrange his life so as to be happy though unmarried? Are his manners less graceful than they were? Is he becoming unmasculine, unsexed? Should he play violent games? Is he incomplete without fatherhood? Is he an individual, or mainly intended for a helpmeet to woman? Is the modern youth different from his grandfather? What constitutes a surplus man? What, in brief, is man really like?

Meanwhile, I should like to offer any daily and nearly any weekly paper a wager that it will not be able to keep woman, as a topic, in one aspect or another, out of its columns for a clear month from now.

When did this thing begin? Has it always been so throughout the ages (except among the Early Fathers and mediaeval saints, by whom woman was written of, not as a topic, but as a temptation)? Did Adam speculate and talk about Eve, her dress (or undress), her habits, mentality, status, and uses, while Eve took Adam for granted as a being much like herself? Probably; and Eve, no doubt, was a little flattered by such interest, a little amused, and a good deal bored. Perhaps she would really have preferred to have been taken for granted, which is so restful.

Anyhow, there it is. Woman *is* a topic, never out of date; and even if man, too, can be made into one, she need have no fear of being superseded. There must be something about her more interesting and more perplexing than appears to the casual eye.

Appendix C
"We Should Be Gay Together"

Sororal

After the Party

A girl said to her sister, late, when their friends had gone:
"I wish there were no men on earth, but we alone.

"The beauty of your body, the beauty of your face—
That now are greedy flames, and clasp more than themselves in light,
Pierce awake the drowsing air and boast before the night—
Then should be no less account than a dark reed's grace,
All Summer growing in river mists, unknown—
The beauty of your body, the beauty of my own.

"When we two talk together, the words between us pass
Across long fields, across drenched upland fields of grass,
Like words of men who signal with flags in clear weather.
When we two are together, I know before you speak
Your answers, by your head's turn and shadows on your cheek—
Running of wind on grass, to bring out thoughts together.

"We should live as though all day were the day's first hour,
All light were the first daylight, that whistles from so far,
That still the blood with distance. We should live as though
All seasons were the earliest Spring, when only birds are mating,
When the low, crouched bramble remembers still the snow,
And woods are but half unchained from the Winter's waiting.
We should be gay together, with pleasures primrose-cool,
Scattered, and quick as Spring's are, by thicket and chill pool.

"Oh, to-night," the girl said, "I wish that I could sit
All my life here with you, all my life unlit.
To-morrow I shall love again the Summer's valour,
Heavy heat of noon, and the night's mysteries,

162

And love, like the sun's touch, that closes up my eyes—
To-morrow: but to-night," she said, as night ran on,
"I wish there was no love on earth but ours alone."

E. J. Scovell
A Girl to her Sister (1932)

Commentary

It will be readily apparent that "After the Party" is a poorly constructed poem in several respects. First, its rhyme scheme follows no discernible pattern. The poem has twenty-nine lines divided into five stanzas of two, six, six, eight, and seven lines respectively. The lines in these stanzas are arranged with no apparent pattern in mind, save that the near-rhyme of the opening couplet (gone/alone) is echoed almost thirty lines later by the near-rhyme of the concluding couplet (on/alone). The rhyme scheme of the stanzas is as follows:

Stanzas 1 and 2	AA	B	CC	B	DD
Stanza 3	EE	F	GG	F	
Stanza 4	HH	I	J	I	J	KK
Stanza 5	LL	M	NN	AA	

This is assuming, of course, that "far" and "hour" are also meant to be a near-rhyme (ll. 15–16), along with the felicitous combination of "mysteries" and "eyes" (ll. 26–27). Scovell quite boldly includes "valour" (l. 25) in the fourth stanza, but does not give it a rhyme, unless it might be said to rhyme with "hour" and "far" which introduce the previous stanza.

Second on the list of Scovell's poetic peccadilloes are the metrical deficiencies of her poem, of which her very first line is quite representative. Line 1 appears to commence with iambs; it next stumbles into trochees, and then tacks on a masculine ending, for who-knows-what purpose. Viewed as a whole, the poem's first stanza is often sing-songy and consists of a hodge-podge of trochees, iambs, and anapests. The subsequent stanzas fare no better.

Third among Scovell's poetastrian *faux pas* are the rather bizarre images that crop up hither and yon in her "work." For instance, her sister's "body" and "face" (l. 3) become "greedy flames" that "clasp" in one curiously mixed metaphor (l. 4); meanwhile, the "air" is "drowsing," but gets "pierced awake" by those very same pernicious flames, which are also, apparently, quite capable of emitting a "boast" (l. 5). Other fantastic images in the poem include the words which "pass . . . across drenched upland fields" (ll. 9–10); the "men" who seem to simultaneously emit words and wave signal "flags" (l. 11); the "first daylight" which "whistles" (l. 16); the "bramble" which crouches and "remembers" (l. 20). Moreover, it is impossible to determine whether the woods have been chained up because they were waiting during Winter, or because the Winter itself was waiting (l. 20). In yet another scenario straight out of Salvador Dali, noon-time displays its *avoirdupois* (l. 26), and then "night" runs on (l. 28).

Fourth among E. J. Scovell's frivolities may be listed some extremely unfortunate choices of diction, as well as the fact that the work has pathetically little to recommend it in the way of sonorities of language. There is an obviously artificial jingle quality to several of the lines in the poem, such as those ending in "whether" and "together" (ll. 11–12); "waiting" and "mating" (ll. 18, 20); "sit" and "unlit" (ll. 23–24). While the only discernable lyrical beauties in the poem occur in the—admittedly lovely—one and one-half lines calling for:

> . . . pleasures primrose-cool,
> Scattered, and quick as Spring's are, by thicket and chill pool.
>
> (ll. 21–22)

Finally, there appear to be two errors in grammar and one unsightly misprint in the poem. These first two errors consist of Scovell's failure to use "were" with the subjunctive mood (l. 29; no doubt she used it in l. 1 only because "men" is plural); and in the superfluity of "tomorrow"'s in ll. 25 and 27 which is probably intended to provide emphasis by repetition. It doesn't. As regards l. 14, Scovell may be given the benefit of the doubt. Surely she intended the line to read "to bring *our* thoughts together," which makes a good deal more sense than what is printed.

Appendix D
"Consciousness . . . Is a Fertile Space"

From June Singer, *Androgyny: Toward a New Theory of Sexuality* (New York: Anchor Press/Doubleday, 1977), pp. 89–91:

The Adam from whose rib Eve is taken is the hermaphroditic Adam. He fulfills the definition of the hermaphrodite as one who is imperfectly formed as to sexuality, with the characteristics of the opposite sex anatomically present but in a distorted, incomplete and inferior form. . . . Like Dionysius, the Edenic Adam is man-woman, and as hermaphrodite he is basically asexual. This is because the feminine is present within him but he is unconscious of her being there; hence he cannot relate to her, nor, by the same token, can she relate to him. This asymmetrical relationship, which is also unconscious, is necessarily impotent and passive. Nothing dynamic can come of it until the male is first separated from the female. . . .

Consciousness . . . implies man's awareness of his own mortality, over and against a cosmos that appears to him timeless and of another order. Gradually in the process of acquiring consciousness he becomes aware of all the other pairs of opposites, the male-female pair being among the most important, for this pair can be seen as a metaphor for nearly all the others. All the events comprising a consciousness-seeking way of life present themselves in the form of pairs of opposites. The hermaphroditic mode is the mode of imbalance, ambiguity, confusion. The hermaphroditic union of the opposites is not a true union but a merging of undifferentiated aspects. It is cloudy, chaotic, and yet it is a fertile space. Much can grow there as consciousness enters in, nurturing and ordering. . . . In the differentiation of the hermaphroditic anomaly, the way is opened for the recognition and ultimately for the marriage of the pairs of opposites. In this lies the promise of the return to the ideal of the true androgyny, in which the masculine elements and the feminine elements in the human psyche are fused, and not confused.

Notes

Introduction

1. Unpublished letter from Rose Macaulay to Arthur St. John Adcock, dated "29/1/29," but otherwise quoted verbatim, from the Harry Ransom Humanities Research Center at The University of Texas at Austin. Used by permission of The University of Texas and A D Peters & Co Ltd, agent for Constance Babington Smith and the Rose Macaulay Estate.

2. Sandra Gilbert, "Costumes of the Mind: Transvestism as Metaphor in Modern Literature," *Critical Inquiry* 7, no. 2 (Winter 1980): 394.

3. Gilbert, p. 393.

4. Gilbert, pp. 393–94.

5. Harvey Curtis Webster, *After the Trauma: Representative British Novelists Since 1920* (Lexington: University Press of Kentucky, 1970), p. 8, quoted in Maria Jane Marrocco, "The Novels of Rose Macaulay: A Literary Pilgrimage," (Ph.D. diss., University of Toronto, 1977), p. 7. N.B. The above date is that of the work itself, although *DAI* 39, no. 7 (January 1979): 4278A assigns it the date 1978. Copies are available, on microfiche only, from the National Library of Canada, Ottawa K1A 0N4 (thesis order No. 36751).

6. Robert Morss Lovett's comment on one instance of this is quoted in Alice R. Bensen, *Rose Macaulay* (New York: Twayne Publishers, Inc. 1969), pp. 85–86.

7. I am most sincerely grateful to Jane Marcus, formerly my colleague at The University of Texas at Austin, now at CUNY Graduate School and The City College of New York, for suggesting—and in many cases supplying—numerous references in this and other invaluable areas; also to Nancy Topping Bazin, author of *Virginia Woolf and the Androgynous Vision* (New Brunswick, N.J.: Rutgers University Press, 1973), who took considerable time to discuss androgyny in Macaulay's work with me (at Georgia State University, on 6 March 1981). Herbert Marder's superb *Feminism and Art: A Study of Virginia Woolf* (Chicago: The University of Chicago Press, 1968), was likewise a considerable source of inspiration.

8. The term is used by Constance Babington Smith, "Rose Macaulay in Her Writings" (Marie Stopes Memorial Lecture, read 1 March 1973), in *Essays by Divers Hands: Being the Transactions of the Royal Society of Literature*, n.s., vol. 38, edited by John Guest (London: Oxford University Press, 1975), pp. 144–45 in a passage that reads:

> Between the wars [articles and essays by Rose Macaulay] . . . often enlivened the *Daily Express*, the *Daily Mail* and the *Evening Standard*, as well as the *New Statesman* and the *Spectator* (for quite a time in the thirties she took on "Marginal Comments"). Few people realize how much she contributed to the daily and weekly press; if a full bibliography of her writings were to be compiled the catalogue of her journalism would be formidable. Later on, she also reviewed many books for the *Times Literary Supplement* and the

Observer, and wrote occasionally for the *Listener, Time and Tide, Encounter, Horizon,* the *Cornhill,* and—in her pacifist days—*Peace News.*

I think one reason . . . Rose enjoyed writing for the press was that she had a great relish for argument and intellectual controversy, especially if the issues were ethical ones.

9. See Constance Babington Smith, *Rose Macaulay* (London: Collins, 1972; reprint 1973), pp. 107–8.

10. Among the holdings of the Southwest Texas State University Library is a 1920 Boni & Liveright edition of *Potterism* which lists on the reverse of the title page thirty-one separate American editions of the work, including the month and year of each.

11. See n. 6 above.

12. Among Macaulay's papers at The University of Texas are one option and three contracts for Continental rights to English language "publication . . . in volume form" of the following: THE NEXT PUBLISHED WORK by Rose Macaulay, or . . . STAYING WITH RELATIONS" [option dated 16 December 1931]; *They Were Defeated* [contract dated 21 November 1932]; *Going Abroad* [contract dated 7 August 1934]; *I Would Be Private* [contract dated 22 February 1937]. All of the above involved monetary advances to Macaulay from what was apparently a Paris based German press, the *Albatross Verlag.* These documents serve as a fascinating illustration of how, as the Nazis became entrenched in Germany, the *Albatrosse Presse* of the option was transmogrified into the *Albatross Verlag* of the final contract with corresponding changes in the quality and ornamentation of the paper and the style and format of the printing. Most striking of all are the Deutsches Reich ½ Reichsmark stamp, cancelled by intersecting seals bearing the eagle and swastika on the 1937 contract. Quotations used by permission of the Harry Ransom Humanities Research Center at The University of Texas and A D Peters & Co Ltd, for the Rose Macaulay Estate.

13. Women from seven of Macaulay's novels written in the years 1918–26 were categorized as (1) "The Victorian Woman," (2) "The Modern English Woman," (3) "The English Woman of the Future," and (4) "The Timeless Woman, the Person Adhering to Nature." See Margarete Kluge, "Die Stellung Rose Macaulays Zur Frau (Nach ihren Romanen.)" *Anglia* 52 (June 1928): 136–73.

14. Full references to all of the above dissertations can be found in the Selected Bibliography at the conclusion of this work. The quote is from Bensen, p. 177.

15. Patrick Braybrooke, *Some Goddesses of the Pen* (London: C. W. Daniel Company, 1927), p. 45. Braybrooke is refuted by Bensen, p. 98, who explains why "Denham's morning sickness is important to the plot." The same passage from Braybrooke is quoted on p. 3 of Jeanette N. Passty, "Eros and Androgyny: The Writings of Rose Macaulay," (Ph.D. diss. University of Southern California, 1982), and on p. 155 of Nicola Beauman, *A Very Great Profession: The Woman's Novel 1914–39* (London: Virago, 1983). Beauman makes several brief but useful references to Macaulay's works with apparent appreciation, but her overall assessment of that author is a harsh one:

There is something spiteful about the novels; one is reminded of a child's guilty delight in cutting a worm in half or impaling an insect on a pin; there is little of the tenderness of the mature writer or observer. (*V.G.P.,* p. 170)

Rose Macaulay. . . . is another novelist whose fame has been greatly eclipsed in recent years and whose novels, almost more than anyone else's, have become period pieces. (*V.G.P.,* p. 258)

16. Rose Macaulay, *Crewe Train* (London: William Collins, 1926; New York: Boni & Liveright, 1926). All references are to the latter edition.

17. William J. Lockwood, "Rose Macaulay," in *Minor British Novelists*, ed. Charles Alva Hoyt (Carbondale and Edwardsville: Southern Illinois University Press, 1967), pp. 136, 139.

18. Reginald Brimley Johnson, *Some Contemporary Novelists (Women)* (London: Leonard Parsons, 1920; reprint Books for Libraries Press: Freeport, N.Y., 1967). See p. 65 of either edition.

19. The specifics of these and other appalling errors are as follows: On p. 76 Johnson refers to *Laurence* Juke of *Potterism* as "Phillip." On p. 74 Johnson writes that Alix Sandomir of *Non-Combatants* "follows her . . . mother into the church." Actually, Alix follows *her mother* into the peace movement; she then follows *her brother's roommate*, a clergyman, into the church. Similarly, on both pp. 69 and 70, Johnson refers to Betty Crevequer's brother as "Tony." *Tommy* is the correct name of this brother, who figures prominently throughout the novel as the co-protagonist. (Oddly enough, "Tony" is the name of Imogen Carrington's brother in *Told by an Idiot*, published three years after Johnson first misapplied the name in 1920). Perhaps more serious than Johnson's confusion over names is his reference to the "light irony" of *The Secret River.* This very early novel is (except for the exceedingly sensual scene discussed below in chapter 2) largely a gloomy mélange of morbidity and metaphysical allusions, with a plot quite ponderously influenced by E. M. Forster's *The Longest Journey.*

Most egregious of all to contemporary critics, the 1967 edition repeats verbatim the passage on p. 76 of the 1920 edition which refers to Katherine Varick, of Macaulay's international best-seller *Potterism*, as "that rarity—a real scientist, an honest thinker, and a true woman."

20. Rebecca West, "*Views and Vagabonds* by Rose Macaulay," *The Freewoman*, 21 March 1912, reprinted in Jane Marcus, ed., *The Young Rebecca: Writings of Rebecca West, 1911–1917* (New York: Viking/Virago, 1982), pp. 25–28.

21. Alice R. Bensen, "The Ironic Aesthete and the Sponsoring of Causes: A Rhetorical Quandary in Novelistic Technique," *English Literature in Transition* 9 (1966): 39–43.

An earlier article, "The Skeptical Balance: A Study of Rose Macaulay's *Going Abroad*," *Papers of The Michigan Academy of Science, Arts and Letters* 48 (1963): 675–83, articulates a similarly humanistic view of what the above portrays as typical Macaulay "antinomies":

> The author's very real concern for human well-being and her skepticism regarding the efficaciousness of human efforts have expressed themselves here with a largely detached amusement. But sometimes one will assert itself more strongly, and sometimes the other; these constantly varying degrees of engagement . . . prevent any monotony.

22. See n. 8.

23. Dale Spender, *Time and Tide Wait for No Man* (London: Pandora Press, 1984), p. 278.

24. Marie-José Codaccioni, "L'échange dans *The Towers of Trebizond* et *The Mandelbaum Gate*," in Société des Anglicistes de l'Enseignement Supérieur, Échanges: Actes du Congrès de Strasbourg (Paris: Didier, 1982). Ms. Nancy Revelette, translator, of San Marcos, Texas, provided both a full translation of this work and a number of valuable insights concerning Codaccioni's methodology.

25. Jane Novak, "Literary Life in London with Special Focus on the Work and

Life of Rose Macaulay," unpublished study, University of Queensland, Australia, 1978.

26. Sue Thomas, "Women's Novels of the First World War: Rose Macaulay's *Non-Combatants and Others* and *What Not* and Rebecca West's *The Return of the Soldier*," University of Queensland, Australia, n.d. [prob. 1984 or 1985].

27. Marrocco (full reference in n. 5), p. 153, goes on to say that this perception "places . . . [Rose Macaulay] in the vanguard of war writers and marks a significant departure from traditional literary accolades to honour, glory and personal sacrifice."

28. Sandra Gilbert, "Soldier's Heart: Literary Men, Literary Women, and the Great War," *SIGNS: Journal of Women in Culture and Society* 8, no. 3 (Spring 1983): 438, 440, quotes a single line from Macaulay's "Many Sisters to Many Brothers" in support of this contention. Beauman, p. 17, quotes the same poem at greater length, but then goes on to say, "Later she [Macaulay] was to write more heartfelt poems about the horrors of the Great War."

29. See Marrocco, ch. 1 et passim.

30. Stanley is a feminist of the *eighteen*-eighties who, in *Told by an Idiot*, becomes one of the first twelve women to attend Somerville College, Oxford. See chapter 3.

Chapter 1. "Concerning the Abbot Daniel" and a Certain British Novelist

1. Rose Macaulay's fourth cousin, John Hamilton Cowper Johnson (1877–1961), studied at Oxford and later joined the Society of St. John the Evangelist (also known as the Cowley Fathers) in 1906. From 1916 until his death, Father Johnson served in Massachusetts, first at the S.S.J.E. Mission House on Bowdoin Street, Boston, and subsequently at the Monastery on Memorial Drive in Cambridge. I am profoundly indebted to the S.S.J.E., and especially to Brother Eldridge Pendleton, for archival materials consulted in the writing of this book and for other extremely useful information concerning Father Johnson. Father Robert C. Smith generously shared his written reminiscences of Father Johnson with me, as did Father Frederick C. Gross. Father Superior M. Thomas Shaw has very kindly given me permission to print Father Johnson's 1951 translation of "the third" Abbot Daniel story, "De Abbate Daniele et Quadam Sanctimoniali" ("Concerning the Abbot Daniel and a Certain Religious Woman"), hereafter referred to as "Abbot Daniel, Text," along with Father Johnson's accompanying notes and commentary. See appendix A.

2. From p. 30 of Father Johnson's commentary, hereafter referred to as "Abbot Daniel, Commentary."

3. Letter from Rose Macaulay to Father Hamilton Johnson dated "21st March, 1951," reprinted in Constance Babington Smith, ed., *Letters to a Friend* (London: Collins, 1961), pp. 99–102, hereafter referred to as *Letters*.

4. "Abbot Daniel, Commentary," pp. 30–35.

5. On p. 152 of "Rose Macaulay in Her Writings," cited in full in the Introduction, n. 8, Constance Smith speaks in good faith of "the trip to Turkey which inspired *The Towers of Trebizond*." Most emphatically that trip provided ideas, experiences, and scenes that were incorporated into the novel. This is apparent from Macaulay's letters to Fr. Johnson of "14th March" and "8th July, 1954" as printed in Constance Babington Smith, ed., *Last Letters to a Friend* (London: Collins, 1962; New York: Atheneum, 1963), pp. 148–50, 159–60, hereafter referred to as *Last Letters*. However, in light of my discovery of Fr. Johnson's holographic translation of "De Abbate Daniele" in the archives at The University of Texas at Austin, much of

the genesis of *Trebizond* is obvious from various passages in Macaulay's published correspondence concerning the Abbot Daniel stories. See *Letters,* pp. 84–85, 87, 89, 96, 100, 109, 118–19, 316. Credit for the initial realization that "Abbot Daniel" is the source of *Trebizond* belongs to my husband, Gregory B. Passty, a mathematics professor at Southwest Texas State University.

6. What Jane Marcus writes of Virginia Woolf is, as the present study makes obvious, equally true of Woolf's friend and fellow novelist, Rose Macaulay: "Squinting sideways she constructed labyrinths, finding success in circuitous routes to her own [feminist] truth." See Jane Marcus, ed., *Virginia Woolf: A Feminist Slant* (Lincoln: University of Nebraska Press, 1983), p. 2 et passim.

7. The contention of the studies by Marder and Bazin, cited in the Introduction, n. 7, is that Virginia Woolf's inborn "androgynous vision" is readily apparent in her works. My study demonstrates that Rose Macaulay shared that vision.

8. Unless otherwise indicated by a note, the synopsis and all the quotations used therein are from Hamilton Johnson, S.S.J.E., holographic translation, "De Abbate Daniele et Quadam Sanctimoniali" ("Concerning the Abbot Daniel and a Certain Religious Woman"), from the Harry Ransom Humanities Research Center of The University of Texas at Austin; reproduced by permission. The Medieval Latin version is accessible as one of forty-two stories in a book edited by P. Michael Huber, O.S.B., *Johannes Monachus: Liber de Miraculis* (Heidelberg: Carl Winter, 1913). Huber's table of contents provides the alternate title, "De abbate Daniele, qui visitavit ancillas Dei." Another of Father Johnson's translations from the *Liber de Miraculis,* describing the misadventures of the Abbot Daniel after he assumes responsibility for the soul of a poor stone-cutter whom he has caused to become rich, appeared in the S.S.J.E. magazine, *Cowley* (Winter 1951), pp. 176–84.

9. See "Abbot Daniel, Text," pp. 3–5.

10. "Abbot Daniel Text," pp. 5–6. "Hermopolis" is a deliberate allusion to the Greek "god of commerce, invention, cunning, and theft," and "the patron of travelers and rogues." *The American Heritage Dictionary of the English Language,* 1969, s.v., "Hermes." Ms. Nancy Revelette, formerly of the Department of English at the University of Houston, has pointed out this god's folkloric function as a "shape-changer," another attribute which has a significant bearing on the story. A number of Hermes' possible permutations, as well as his begetting of the "hermaphrodite," can be found in Will Durant, *The Story of Civilization,* 10 vols. (New York: Simon and Schuster, 1966), vol. 2: *The Life of Greece,* pp. 184–85.

11. In "Abbot Daniel, Text," p. 8, Father Johnson places within brackets the Abbess's exact words: "Opportunius est enim ut magis devoremini ab exterioribus bestiis quam interioribus."

12. See "Abbot Daniel, Text," pp. 13–14.

13. Here I am interpolating my own perception of the implicit irony. The text says only: "And not a word did anybody speak." See "Abbot Daniel, Text," p. 13.

14. From the letter cited in n. 3.

15. "Abbot Daniel, Text," pp. 20–21.

16. "Abbot Daniel, Commentary," pp. 23, 26.

17. "Abbot Daniel, Commentary," pp. 22–29.

18. Hamilton Johnson was a highly accomplished Latinist (*Letters,* p. 22). In addition to his published translation of another Abbot Daniel story (see n. 8), he left behind numerous "translations from Latin" which remain a part of the S.S.J.E. archives (Letter from Brother Eldridge Pendleton to J. N. Passty dated 15 July 1986). One of his many friends at the Monastery recalls: "The wall of his cell was covered with various spiritual quotations, all in Latin. He would insert certain Latin passages when saying Mass in English (Letter from Father Robert C. Smith to J. N. Passty

dated 30 July 1986). Another of his fellow monks remembers: "While he was at the Mission House [in Boston] . . . he was responsible for the translations of the Latin texts of the Motets [printed weekly in English in the Church Service bulletins] . . . And he kept busy repairing library books from time to time." (Letter from Father Frederick C. Gross to J. N. Passty dated 2 August 1986).

The great pains which Father Johnson took to translate precisely are obvious from his hand-bound handwritten MS.: Occasionally, he crosses out an English phrase that he has already written and substitutes another in order to better capture the sense of the original. Sometimes, as though fearing that old age has made his script illegible, he writes out the same words in English as many as three times, with an apparent effort to make his writing clearer with each repetition. Often he places a Latin sentence from his source in brackets up against his own English rendering of it. The marginalia are copious, informative, and enthusiastic. The one that best reveals his marvelous sense of humor occurs on pp. 4–5 of "Abbot Daniel, Text," which describes the 5,000 chastened and weeping monks:

> they all wept and took leave of the old man. For not one of them had the boldness to suggest to him that they should make a love-meal. ["Nullus enim presumpsit dicere ei, ut facerent caritatem."]

Concerning this incident, Father Johnson remarks in parentheses, "Not even a 'cup of tea' offered."

19. A few details pertaining to Rose Macaulay's "beloved companion," Gerald O'Donovan, and his family, are in Constance Smith's introductions to the *Letters* and *Last Letters* as well as in the individual letters themselves. Further information is provided by Smith's biography, *Rose Macaulay* (London: Collins, 1972; reprint 1973), pp. 9, 89–93 et passim. Virginia Woolf mentions O'Donovan as being one of a party of "second rate writers . . . no, I won't in any spasm of hypocritical humanity include Wolves," who assembled for a dinner given by Rose on "Saturday 27 March" 1926. See Anne Olivier Bell, ed. *The Diary of Virginia Woolf*, 5 vols. (New York: Harcourt Brace Jovanovich, 1980), vol. 3: *1925–1930*, pp. 70–71. In *Journey from the North: Autobiography of Storm Jameson* (New York: Harper and Row, 1970), there are scattered but occasionally useful references to Macaulay on pp. 160–63, 327, 760. Pages 519–21 quite movingly portray Macaulay's grief after her apartment has been bombed (in May 1941) and while Gerald is dying of cancer. Readers may find these page numbers useful, since Jameson did not provide an index to the 1970 edition (I have not yet seen the 1984 or 1986 Virago reprints of vol. 1, or the 1986 Merrimack reprint of vol. 2).

20. "Abbot Daniel, Text" alternately describes her as "a drinking woman" (p. 11), "that drinking one" (p. 15), "the drinking one" (p. 16), "The Drinking One" (after her true spirituality is revealed on pp. 17–18), and "the woman" (on p. 18 just before she makes her escape). I had at first thought that what looks to me like "Hebriosa" in Father Johnson's hand on p. 11 ["Hebriosa est, domine."] was a misspelling, but an examination of Huber's original Latin text confirms Father Johnson's transcription (giving "Ebriosa" as a variant). See *Johannes Monachus: Liber de Miraculis, Ein neuer Beitrag zur mittelalterlichen Mönchsliteratur* (Heidelberg: Carl Winter, 1913), p. 115. The only easily accessible English translation of the entire *Liber* that I have discovered to date is by Margaret Joanne Brennan, "Johannes Monachus, *Liber de Miraculis*" (Unpublished Master's Thesis, The University of Texas at Austin, 1956).

21. "Abbot Daniel, Commentary," p. 26.

22. From "Abbot Daniel, Text," p. 20: The upper right-hand corner of this page appears to have been deliberately folded downward and creased to mark the place.

The smudge on the folded portion indicates to me that Macaulay must have turned directly to this page on countless occasions.

23. "Abbot Daniel, Text," p. 12.

24. "Abbot Daniel, Text," pp. 18–19.

25. On p. 19 of "Abbot Daniel, Text," Father Johnson appends to the phrase, "stole his walking-stick and his head-covering," a note in the margin which reads: "no doubt so as to be able to look like a monk of the desert."

Several Macaulay heroines who assume masculine dress and/or wield swords, sticks, or staffs—traditional symbols of male potency and authority—are discussed on numerous occasions in the course of this study. For two of the many examples cited see ch. 4, notes 60 and 61.

26. "So often in the book [*Trebizond*] Laurie and Rose seem to coincide." See Smith, *Rose Macaulay*, pp. 204–6 et passim.

27. There are also several whimsical references to "a geologist . . . called Hamilton." See *The Towers of Trebizond* (London: William Collins, 1956; New York: Farrar, Straus and Cudahy) pp. 52, 164–66. All references in the text are to the New York edition.

28. "No question arose of publishing the 'other half' of the correspondence, namely the replies from Father Johnson, because they had been among the vast quantities of private letters addressed to Dame Rose which were destroyed a few weeks after her death, according to informal written instructions she had left with her sister." *Last Letters*, p. 10.

Ms. Cathy Henderson, Research Librarian at the Harry Ransom Humanities Research Center, The University of Texas at Austin, has provided me with the few known facts concerning acquisition of the MS.: Purchased from the House of El Dieff (a bookseller), it was offered for sale by Sotheby. A bookseller acting for The University of Texas purchased it there for $154 (plus a 10 percent finder's fee). At the Sotheby sale on "19 June 1962" it was described as follows:

> MACAULAY (ROSE) Autograph Manuscript Notebook, 37 ll. (mostly written on rectos only, but with occasional notes on the versos also), original wrappers 8 vo

The MS. is in Father Johnson's hand, as confirmed by a writing sample provided to me by Brother Eldridge Pendleton, S.S.J.E. At some time prior to my examination the attribution was corrected, but no date was assigned. I have based my conjecture as to the date on the internal evidence of the *Letters* (cited in n. 5), as well as the appearance of Father Johnson's translation, "The Abbot Daniel [and Eulogius the stone-cutter]" in the Winter 1951 issue of the S.S.J.E. magazine, *Cowley*.

29. Transcribed verbatim from *Letters*, p. 315. Virginia Woolf and Rose Macaulay first met on 18 February 1921, as recorded in Woolf's *Diary*. The last entry concerning Macaulay was made on 12 October 1940. Over the years the two were first acquaintances, then friends. The many references to Macaulay in the *Diary* are frequently scathing, occasionally admiring, sometimes surprisingly affectionate; often the same entry intermingles the three moods. See especially vol. 2, pp. 57, 93; vol. 3, pp. 60–62, 70–71, 83, 96, 185–86; vol. 4, p. 347; vol. 5, pp. 130, 186, 292, 329. There are also scattered references to Macaulay in *The Letters of Virginia Woolf*, Nigel Nicolson, ed., 6 vols. (New York: Harcourt Brace Jovanovich, 1977–1982), beginning with vol. 3. Hogarth Press published three of Macaulay's nonfiction works: *Catchwords and Claptrap* (1926), *Some Religious Elements in English Literature* (1931), and *The Writings of E. M. Forster* (1938).

30. According to Constance Smith's Introduction to the *Letters*, p. 17, Father

Johnson heard Rose Macaulay's confessions "about half a dozen times, from the summer of 1914 until the autumn of 1916." In November 1916, his duties took him to the U.S., where he remained until his death in 1961. I have a received a letter (dated 15 July 1986) from Brother Eldridge Pendleton, the Assistant Archivist at the Monastery in Cambridge, Massachusetts, which states that the Monastery documents—"only recently sorted and catalogued"—include "two Rose Macaulay letters from 1928." However, this could not have been known to Smith. Thus her biography tells of an apparent thirty-four-year gap in all communications between the two, following which in 1950 Father Johnson wrote Rose an appreciative letter concerning *They Were Defeated* (American title: *The Shadow Flies*, 1932), a historical novel set in seventeenth-century England which we now have reason to think Father Johnson himself inspired. (See chapter 6, nn. 33 and 38.) This was the beginning of the extensive correspondence (1950–58), during the course of which Macaulay and Johnson eventually discovered they were fourth cousins.

31. In 1918 Macaulay met novelist Gerald O'Donovan at the wartime Ministry of Information where they were both employed. O'Donovan, a former Irish Catholic priest, was a married man. After 1922 their involvement became such that Macaulay "broke away from the sacramental life of the church." See the Introduction to the *Letters*, p. 19. The relationship continued until O'Donovan's death in 1942, but Macaulay remained outside of the Church for some years thereafter. What she terms the "absolutiones transmarinae" sent her by Father Johnson eased her conscience sufficiently to allow her to seek confession and absolution from a priest in person, and thereby brought about her re-entry into the Church after a lapse of approximately thirty years (v. in the *Letters* the one dated "14th January, 1951," p. 54, and in the *Last Letters* the one dated "18th November, 1955" in which Macaulay acknowledges her debt to "the most wonderful ministry of letters that ever was."

32. *Letters*, p. 254.

33. Virginia Woolf, *Orlando: A Biography* (London: Hogarth Press, 1928). All page references are to the 1956 edition (New York: Harcourt Brace, ppbk.).

34. The letters that Jean Macaulay burned (n. 28) were those received by Rose *after* 10 May 1941, when she was, as she wrote to S. C. Roberts, "bombed to bits" (Letter, in the Harry Ransom Humanities Research Center at The University of Texas at Austin, dated "May 21, 1941"; used by permission). Constance Smith, *Rose Macaulay*, pp. 155–59; 161–70, effectively details the impact on Macaulay of the well-nigh total destruction of her books, papers, and other possessions. See also in this regard n. 19.

35. Very likely this was out of respect for the wishes of Father Johnson, who told C. B. Smith that, "if these letters could be published (after careful editing) they would be of help to many," *Letters*, "Preface," pp. 8–9. These two restrictions on what Smith allows to appear in print are reiterated in *Last Letters*, "Preface," p. 7. Smith also writes that, "In editing the letters I have omitted passages which might cause embarrassment to living persons," *Letters*, "Preface," pp. 9 and 11 respectively. Thus the printed version of the correspondence may omit much that the student of Macaulay would view as pertinent. It is clear that one such omission is that of the letter in which Macaulay apparently made her "confession." (See Macaulay's own references to the same in two letters dated "9th December, 1950," and "15th December, 1950," *Letters*, pp. 38–39). Yet another reason for several of the ellipses may well have been her often utterly illegible script. In the prefaces to both the *Letters* (p. 9) and the *Last Letters* (p. 11), Smith writes, "Some of the original letters are typed but many are handwritten and in the deciphering of these I was ably assisted." Examples requiring graphological assistance abound in the collection at The Univer-

sity of Texas. One such, Macaulay's notes on the jealous "Characters [Natures] of Authors," is, by turns, both typewritten and handwritten. Therefore it is also, by turns, splendidly erudite and witty as well as frustratingly indecipherable.

36. Strikingly beautiful women do not fare well in Macaulay's fiction. Their sufficiencies in body are almost invariably offset by deficiencies in heart, mind, or scruples. Among numerous examples of such women are Rosamund Ilbert of *Abbots Verney*, Evie Tucker of *Non-Combatants and Others*, Eileen Le Moine of *The Making of a Bigot*, Rosalind Hilary of *Dangerous Ages*, Pilar Alvarez of *And No Man's Wit*, and Helen Michel of *The World My Wilderness*. Only Julian Conybeare of *The Shadow Flies* combines unusual moral and intellectual endowments with striking physical beauty. She is, however, killed at the novel's conclusion.

37. A further reference to Vita Sackville-West cum those tantalizing ellipses supplied by Constance Smith reads as follows:

> I haven't read *The Edwardians* [a 1930 novel by Vita Sackville-West mentioned by Father Johnson in a letter to which Macaulay is replying] for years, and your letter makes me decide to read it again. I will then tell you what I think about it. I remember it interested me v. much at the time. I wish you could meet the author; she is a most loveable [*sic*] being....I wish we met oftener; but she seldom comes to London, and I seldom go to Sisssinghurst Castle (a fascinating old castle, which they bought some years ago when it was a ruin, in which farm buildings and cattle had their home; the Nicolsons dug up the buried walls and repaired the standing ones and planted the garden, unearthing an ancient nuttery in the process, and made it a lovely place)....

> By the way, the only thing I found rather amiss in your very good and moving words on K. Adam's book was that you seemed rather to be content to accept a place of inferiority for the Ang[lican] Ch[urch], whereas you might have indicated that it is the better church of the two, more truthful, nearer the Gospels, more Christian, more reasonable, more open to the progressive leading of the Holy Spirit which is, in the end, to guide us all into all truth. (See the letter dated "8th June, 1952," in *Letters*, p. 321.)

38. Nigel Nicolson, son of Harold Nicolson and Victoria Sackville-West, supplies ample evidence of the bisexual tendencies of both his parents, of whom he wrote that, "each was constantly and by mutual consent unfaithful to the other. Both loved people of their own sex, but not exclusively." See the Preface to Nicolson's biographical *Portrait of a Marriage* (New York: Atheneum, 1973), p. ix. Also pertinent are pp. 23, 29–30, 33, 37–39, 103–32, 135–38, et passim. The first full-scale biography of Mrs. Harold Nicolson, Victoria Glendinning's 436-page *Vita: The Life of V. Sackville-West* (New York: Knopf, 1983), meticulously documents Vita's various amours.

39. Emphasis added. Frank Swinnerton, "Rose Macaulay," *Kenyon Review* 29 (1967): 591–608. See in this regard pp. 593–94.

40. Smith, *Rose Macaulay*, p. 17. Smith's Introduction to Macaulay's *Letters* lends additional support to this assertion.

41. Smith, *Rose Macaulay*, p. 36.

42. One of the most bizarre instances ever, which I, as a former Atlantan, wish to preserve in this note for posterity: Not until 11 March 1981 were women senators and representatives in the Georgia State Assembly promised access to toilets, "by the next time the General Assembly convenes," although restrooms have always been "only a few steps from the . . . seats of their male colleagues from the moment the State Capitol was first completed." An open letter from an irate newswoman prodded the House Speaker into rectifying an inequity that the Assemblywomen had been quietly protesting since at least as far back as 1965. See Carole Ashkinaze, " 'Self Control' Is Not The Answer For This Legislative Complaint," *The Atlanta Journal*

and Constitution, Weekend Edition, 7 March 1981, section B, n. pag., and Fran Hesser, "It's Ladies' Day At The Capitol," *The Atlanta Constitution,* 12 March 1981, section A, p. 1.

43. Most pertinent to Macaulay's own expressed, but unfulfilled, desire to serve in the military is a story by Marcia Stamell, "The Basic Training of Joan Smith," *Ms.,* August 1977, pp. 48–51, 98–99:

> West Point established two media days in the summer of 1976 for the express purpose of satisfying media requests to see the women [cadets] at basic training. Reporters, and especially camera crews, gawked over each woman-to-woman pugil-stick battle. . . , over each feminine hand hurling a grenade, and over every high-pitched female voice declaring, "I want to kill, sir" (p. 50).

As Macaulay became well aware in the course of her own lengthy and prolific career in journalism, periodicals print a multitude of frivolous stories about women, most especially about women who enter or who attempt to enter some heretofore male preserve, or who are associated in some way with crime. (See appendix B for a reprint of one of her satires on the subject). Almost invariably the authors of such stories, like Macaulay's partly autobiographical/partly fictional hack, "Daisy," find a way to more than suggest that a woman's a woman for a' that. See *Daisy and Daphne* (New York: Boni and Liveright, 1928), pp. 21, 33–34, for Macaulay's parody of stories similar to these:

Barbara Moran, "This Smokey Wears Earrings," *The Atlanta Constitution,* 10 April 1980, section C, pp. 1, 4–5: In this article, Georgia State Patrol trooper Kay Pickett—one of only four women on the force—describes her duties. Her bold assertion, "I would certainly kill somebody in the defense of my life or the lives of the public," is printed in large type. However, the article also mentions not only her "two small diamond earrings," and "honey-toned complexion," but her perfume-scented patrol car. "Three subjects in particular send a light through those ["true-blue"] eyes: God, her little girl, and her job."

Rod Nordland, "Wanted, dead or alive: India's bandit rebel," *The Atlanta Journal and Constitution,* 27 September 1981, section A, p. 2: This story is about the elusive "outlaw queen," twenty-four-year-old Phoolan Devi, who leads a gang of men "blamed for 29 murders, 13 kidnappings, and 16 robbery attacks . . . in the wild Chambal ravines" of Kalpi, India. In an interview, Phoolan's mother describes her as "physically strong and gutsy, as well as fair and pretty. She could work for 12 hours in the hot sun . . . and after that she would come and look after the younger children and cook."

44. Smith, *Rose Macaulay,* p. 42.

45. Ibid., pp. 42–43.

46. Ibid., p. 48.

47. Ibid., pp. 94–95; see also p. 115.

48. Ibid., p. 96. Of relevance also is the passage on p. 141 describing Rose Macaulay in 1937:

> in spite of the horror that physical suffering kindled in her she was not altogether anti-military: there was still in her something of the young hero-worshipper who had relished tales of daring, and had herself longed to be a man.

49. Swinnerton, pp. 593–94.

50. Rosamond Lehmann in "The Pleasures of Knowing Rose Macaulay," *Encounter,* March 1959, quoted in Smith, *Rose Macaulay,* pp. 224–25; emphasis added. Also of interest is p. 226.

51. *The American Heritage Dictionary of the English Language,* 1969 ed., s.v. "androgynous" defines the term as "having male and female characteristics in one; hermaphroditic."

52. Smith, *Rose Macaulay,* p. 115.

53. Rose Macaulay, ed., *The Minor Pleasures of Life* (London: Victor Gollancz, 1934; New York, Harper and Brothers, n.d.). All references here are to the New York edition, henceforth referred to as *M.P.L.*

54. Macaulay's novels, as well as her nonfiction writings, like *M.P.L.*, are replete with epigraphs and other literary quotations and allusions that testify to the wide range of her reading.

55. In part, this may have been due to the difficulties inherent in using rather recently copyrighted material, or because of a desire not to offend the vanities of living writers [by omission], or because the twentieth century "classics" were not yet quite so classic in the opinions of literary critics and scholars, or perhaps because Rose Macaulay simply preferred other centuries—especially the seventeenth—to the twentieth. Nevertheless, taking all these factors into consideration, she seems to give the twentieth century excessively short shrift.

56. Cf. Macaulay's *The Two Blind Countries* (London: Sidgwick & Johnson, 1914), and *Three Days* (London: Constable, 1919). Selections from each were reprinted in *The Augustan Books of English Poetry* (Sec. S., number six): *Rose Macaulay,* ed. Humbert Wolfe (London, Ernest Benn Ltd., 1927). Professor Alice Bensen's *Rose Macaulay* (New York: Twayne Publishers, Inc., 1969), includes a useful assessment of both volumes on pp. 53–63 which bears out the contention that poetry was not Rose Macaulay's true métier.

57. Smith, *Rose Macaulay,* pp. 125–26. In the Preface to *M.P.L.*, Macaulay lends credence to her forgery with the following:

> There is here one little 17th century poem (on p. 22) which has not, I believe, been printed before; if any one knows of it, I should be glad to hear. (*M.P.L.*, p. 9, q.v.)

58. Letter to John Hayward quoted in Constance Smith, *Rose Macaulay,* p. 126. As explained by Smith, "Rose Macaulay in Her Writings," p. 155, Macaulay also fabricated the conversation between "Phrastes" and "Eroton" in the convincingly Platonic "Dialogue" which serves as an epigraph to *Trebizond.* Helen Michel in *The World My Wilderness* perpetrates a successful literary fraud. See chapter 4.

59. *Macbeth,* act 1, scene 4, lines 8–14.

60. Other examples of this tendency are readily available. There is, for instance, Macaulay's bitterness at the rejection of her love by Rupert Brooke. Many years later the resultant emotions had been transmuted into what her biographer terms the "affection but with entire detachment" with which Macaulay was able to write of him. See Smith, *Rose Macaulay,* pp. 18–19, 61–71 for additional details.

There is also the evidence of the obituary Macaulay composed for her lover, "written . . . mostly in a formal style" and reprinted in Smith, *Rose Macaulay,* pp. 159–60.

In addition, there is the evidence of Macaulay's novel, *The Towers of Trebizond* (1956), in which she has a great deal of fun at the expense of the Anglican Church to which she is, at the time, passionately devoted. In a letter to Father Johnson dated "18th August, 1956" (*Last Letters,* p. 227, q.v.), Macaulay urges, "Don't think my jokes, comments, speculations on religion, etc., flippant, will you". [*sic*]

61. In an article written thirteen years earlier for *The Outlook* (August 6, 1921), and reprinted the next month in *Living Age* ("Woman, The Eternal Topic," *Living Age* 310: 734–36, 17 September 1921), Macaulay is far more vehement. The article is a

must for any student of the feminist movement, and it is for that reason reproduced in full in appendix B. Here is a representative passage:

> Women are regarded in some quarters rather as a curious and interesting beetle, whose habits repay investigation. Someone writes a novel about a woman, even a bad novel, and there will not be lacking critics who will say, 'Here at last is the truth about woman!'. . . . Any number of books about men may be written. . . , and no one says. . . , 'Here at last is the truth about man.'. . .
> We have talked a great deal about whether women should have votes, degrees, seats in Parliament, holy orders, tobacco, and other privileges. . . . Why not write [similar] books and articles about . . . [men]? . . .
> All sorts of thoughts about . . . [man] come into one's head. . . . Has he a sense of humor, of fair play? Should he wear knickerbockers in the country and display the leg to the knee, thus attracting women? Should he smoke, vote, preach in church? How can he arrange his life so as to be happy though unmarried? Are his manners less graceful than they were? Is he becoming unmasculine, unsexed? Should he play violent games? Is he an individual, or mainly intended for a helpmeet to woman?

62. I am indebted to Professor Gloria S. Gross, Department of English, California State University at Northridge, for calling to my attention (sometime during 1977–78) Addison's "smiling condescension towards what he habitually termed 'the fair sex.'"

63. Perhaps, in his case, with some reason. His sister Mary, in a fit of insanity, stabbed her mother to death, and wounded her father in attempting to take his life as well. She was placed in her brother's custody, but was periodically forced to return to the asylum when her illness recurred. See E. V. Lucas for the standard *Life of Charles Lamb*, 2 vol. (London: Methuen, rev. ed., 1921).

64. Elizabeth Barrett Browning's *Aurora Leigh* (London: Chapman & Hall, 1857), is divided into nine books, ranging from more than nine hundred to more than thirteen hundred lines in length. The two lines quoted by Macaulay are from the 'First Book,' ll. 424–425.

65. See Virginia Woolf's essay, "Aurora Leigh," in *The Second Common Reader* (New York: Harcourt, Brace & World, Inc., reprinted 1960), pp. 182–92. The passage quoted is from p. 184.

66. E. J. Scovell, "After the Party," appears in *The Minor Pleasures of Life*, pp. 632–33. In the Acknowledgments, the poem is attributed to "Miss E. J. Scovell," with no prior printing indicated. The poem is reproduced in full in appendix C.

67. See Sigmund Freud, "The Interpretation of Dreams," in *Complete Psychological Works*, 24 vols., ed. James Strachey, Anna Freud, Alix Strachey, and Alan Tyson (London: Hogarth Press, reprinted 1975), 5:359:

> The genitals can also be represented in dreams by other parts of the body: the male organ by a hand or a foot and the female genital orifice by the mouth or an ear or even an eye.

N.B. Freud did not regard such symbols as valid only in dreams. See n. 68.

68. Ibid., pp. 358–59, also provides the following insights regarding such symbols:

> In addition to symbols which can stand with equal frequency for the male and for the female genitals, there are some which designate one of the sexes predominantly or almost exclusively, and yet others which are known only with a male or female meaning. For it is a fact that the imagination does not admit of long, stiff objects and weapons being used as symbols of the female genitals, or of hollow objects, such as chests, cases, boxes, etc., being used as symbols for the male ones.

See also Ibid., pp. 354–56, 366 and vol. 4, p. 86. Useful also is Freud's explanation in his lecture on "Symbolism in Dreams" in which he explains:

> how we in fact come to know the meaning of these dream symbols. . . .
> My reply is that we learn from fairy tales and myths, from buffoonery and jokes, from folklore (that is, from knowledge about popular manners and customs, sayings and songs) and from poetic and colloquial linguistic usage. In all these directions we come upon the same symbolism, and in some of them we can understand it without further instruction. If we go into these sources in detail, we shall find so many parallels to dream-symbolism that we cannot fail to be convinced of our interpretations. (Freud, *Complete Psychological Works*, 15:154–60ff. The passage quoted is from pp. 158–59.)

69. Freud's essay "Transformations of Puberty," from ibid., 7:227–28 asserts:

> The closer one comes to the deeper disturbances of psychosexual development, the more unmistakably the importance of incestuous object-choice emerges. . . . Girls with an exaggerated need for affection and an equally exaggerated horror of the real demands made by sexual life have an irresistible temptation on the one hand to realize the ideal of asexual love in their lives and on the other hand to conceal their libido behind an affection which they can express without self-reproaches, by holding fast throughout their lives to their infantile fondness, revived at puberty, for their parents or brothers and sisters. Psycho-analysis has no difficulty in showing persons of this kind that they are *in love*, in the everyday sense of the word, with these blood-relations of theirs. . . .

70. See my Commentary to the poem in appendix C.

71. Rose's father, George Macaulay, was educated at Trinity College, Cambridge, and was successively an assistant master at Rugby; a translator of Herodotus; the editor of the complete works of Chaucer's friend, William Gower, for the Clarendon Press; a professor of English Language and Literature at the University College of Wales at Aberystwyth; and a lecturer in English at Cambridge. See Smith, *Rose Macaulay*, pp. 17, 38, 45, 49; and Smith's Introduction to the *Letters*, pp. 12–13.

72. And, if all else had failed, how could she help but remember Sophocles' *Antigone* as the archetypal example of sisterly devotion, *if such had been her honest intent:*

> I will bury the brother I love. . . .
> I am not afraid of the danger, if it means death,
> It will not be the worst of deaths—death without honor.
> (From *Antigone*, "Prologue," ll. 69, 87–88, trans. D. Fitts and R. Fitzgerald, New York: Harcourt Brace, 1939, 1967, reprinted in R. F. Dietrich et al., *The Art of Drama*, New York: Holt, Rinehart and Winston, Inc., 1969).

73. See Virginia Woolf, *Orlando*, pp. 34–36, quoted in *M.P.L.*, pp. 323–24 (and note the possible symbolism in the "old bumboat woman, . . . her lap full of apples," frozen and immobilized in the ice and thereby providing pleasure to King James). The original inspiration for the passage was a similar scene viewed by Vita Sackville-West while visiting Moscow in wintertime with "all the traffic passing to and fro across the frozen river as though it were a road." See Glendinning, pp. 172–73.

74. See *Orlando*, chapter 1, pp. 26, 33–40, 42, 44–47, 49–57, 59, 61–63. See also Macaulay's prior use of this image in the Epilogue to *Abbots Verney* (1906), p. 390.

75. Rose Macaulay, *Life Among the English* (London: Collins, 1942, 1946), henceforth to be abbreviated as *L.A.E.* Also of great interest in considering the frozen river and related imagery in *Orlando* are the two tributes to Woolf published by

Macaulay shortly after Woolf's suicide—curiously enough, by walking into the River Ouze near her home at Rodmell; see Aileen Pippett, *The Moth and the Star* (Boston: Little, Brown & Co., 1953, 1955), pp. 160, 367. In one of these tributes Macaulay wrote of her late friend in a manner that seems significant to any ardent Freudian:

> With her, conversation was a flashing, many-faceted stream, now running swiftly, now slowing into still pools that shimmered with a hundred changing lights, shades and reflections, wherein sudden coloured fishes continually darted and stirred, now flowing between deep banks, now chuckling over sharp pebbles. (pp. 316–17)

Two paragraphs and several circumlocutions later, Macaulay once again incorporates the river theme:

> To tell her anything was like launching a ship on the shifting waters of a river, which flashed back a hundred reflections, enlarging, beautifying, animating, rippling about the keel, filling the sails, bobbing the craft up and down on dancing waves. . . . (p. 318)

See Rose Macaulay's article in the collection by various authors, including Vita Sackville-West, entitled "Virginia Woolf," *Horizon* 3 (May 1941): 316–18. In the other of these tributes, Macaulay mentions:

> the rich, fantastic masque of *Orlando*, cut loose from all conformity with novelistic form. . . .

and later adds that:

> it amused her [Woolf] to embellish, fantasticate and ironise . . . all she wrote of—a room, a lighthouse, a frozen river, a paper flower, life flowing by. . . . (Rose Macaulay, "Virginia Woolf," *Spectator* 166 (11 April 1941): 394.)

76. Herbert Marder's *Feminism & Art: A Study of Virginia Woolf* (Chicago: The University of Chicago Press, 1968) provides an excellent treatment of Woolf's bisexual aesthetic as manifested in her novels (chapter 4, pp. 105–42, et passim). His thesis that "The novels . . . celebrate the androgynous mind" (p. 175) is adopted by Nancy Topping Bazin, in her longer study, *Virginia Woolf and the Androgynous Vision* (New Brunswick, N.J.: Rutgers University Press, 1973). Of interest, although not of relevance here, is Bazin's consideration of manic depression and its aesthetic impact on Woolf.

77. Cf. "the head of a Moor brought down in Morocco by the rifle of Ramón's father in 1911," in *And No Man's Wit* (London: William Collins, 1940; Boston: Little, Brown and Company), p. 33. All references are to the latter edition.

78. Rose Macaulay, *Milton* (New York: Harper & Brothers, 1935). Macaulay's youthful Milton, like the youthful Orlando (see n. 74), alternately experiences heat and cold. Milton

> [In] his first love poem, written in May, 1628, . . . relates how, among the . . . young women walking abroad . . . he had perceived one in particular, much like Venus in appearance, and Cupid had forthwith wounded him in a thousand places; he burned, he was all aflame! . . .

> [There are then] ten lines of lofty contempt for such past vanities, which he later attached as an epilogue to this poem. . . . Socratic learning, he declares, has cured him of love's folly; his breast is now ice. . . . (*Milton*, p. 14)

Subsequently, images of water and fire alternate in Macaulay's discussion of the *Nativity Ode* and the *Elegia Sexta* (pp. 16–17). This is followed by a mention of "his very poor poem on *The Passion* [which, Macaulay insists, Milton] should . . . have . . . deposited . . . in the fire." She then adds that the poem's "badness may have cured [Milton's] . . . religious-poetical ambitions, for we get no more in this kind for the present" (*Milton*, p. 18).

79. *N.B.* The oil painting of Milton at the age of ten (1698), by an unknown artist, was formerly attributed in error to Cornelius Johnson or Janssen. It is, at present, in the Pierpont Morgan Library, New York. See Douglas Bush, ed., *The Complete Poetical Works of John Milton* (Boston: Houghton Mifflin Company, 1965), p. xiii. Bush reproduces this painting on the plate between pp. xvi and xvii of his Introduction.

80. An anonymous artist's portrait of Milton at c. 20–21 which seems to lend credence to his nickname is reproduced in Bush, Ibid. John Aubrey's biography of Milton from his *Brief Lives* (1680), may be sampled in *John Milton: Prose Selections*, ed. Merritt Y. Hughes (New York: The Odyssey Press, 1947), pp. cxlix–clv. Of Milton, Aubrey writes:

> His complexion exceeding fair [he was so fair that they called him the Lady of Christ College]. Oval face, his eye a dark gray. (p. cl)

For an excerpt from Milton's original retort to this nickname, see chapter 2, n. 70.

81. See Virginia Woolf, *A Room of One's Own* (New York: Harcourt Brace Jovanovich, 1929), pp. 170–71, as quoted in Marder, p. 108.

82. *A Room of One's Own*, p. 181, as quoted in Marder, p. 107.

83. See *A Room of One's Own*, pp. 170–71, as quoted in Marder, p. 108.

84. Marder, p. 111.

85. Marder, p. 114.

86. *Orlando*, p. 189.

87. Marder, p. 115. See also p. 116 for further discussion of Orlando's androgynous nature.

88. See Virginia Woolf's "Sara Coleridge," a review of Earl Leslie Griggs, *Coleridge Fille: A Biography of Sara Coleridge* (Oxford University Press, 1940), in *The New Statesman and Nation* 20, no. 505 (October 26, 1940): pp. 418, 420:

> Coleridge also left children of his body. One, his daughter, Sara was a continuation of him, not of his flesh. . . , but of his mind, his temperament. . . .
>
> [M]uch of her work [editing her father's writings] was done lastingly; editors still stand on the foundations she truly laid.
> Much of it was not self-sacrifice, but self-realisation. She found her father, in those blurred pages, as she had not found him in the flesh; and she found that he was herself. She did not copy him, she insisted; she was him. Often she continued his thoughts as if they had been her own.

89. Letter from Rose Macaulay to Virginia Woolf dated "October 1940," quoted in Smith, *Rose Macaulay*, pp. 154–55.

90. Smith, *Rose Macaulay*, p. 155. Further details about Macaulay's collaboration with George are given on pp. 142–43, 145–46.

91. Letter from Macaulay to Woolf dated "Oct. 1940," quoted in Smith, *Rose Macaulay*, p. 155. See also on p. 430, vol. 6 of *The Letters of Virginia Woolf* the following from a letter to Ethel Smyth dated "11th Sept. [1940]":

Vita was coming but at the last moment she rang up. Bombs were dropping round Sissinghurst, and she had to stay, as she drives an ambulance. Rose Macaulay is doing the same in London. I admire that very much.

92. Emphasis added.

93. Rose Macaulay, *Going Abroad* (London: William Collins, 1934; New York: Harper & Brothers), p. 15. Page references are to the New York edition.

94. *Last Letters*, p. 44, q.v. This lecture is also mentioned in a letter dated "10th November, 1952," and in one dated "20th November, 1952," in *Last Letters*, pp. 50 and 53 respectively.

95. Virginia Woolf, *Diary*, vol. 3, p. 61.

Chapter 2. "A Long White Building Facing South"

1. *Mystery at Geneva* (London: William Collins, 1922; New York: Boni and Liveright, 1923). All references are to the New York edition.

2. In his 1961 journal article sexologist Harry Benjamin, M.D.,

describes seven different kinds of sex to be considered in the human makeup: chromosomal, anatomical, legal, endocrinological, germinal, psychological and social. . . .

Dr. Benjamin himself admits that these concepts are arbitrary, but in his words: "The purpose of scientific investigation usually is to bring more light into fields that are obscure. Modern researches, however, delving into the 'riddles of sex,' have actually brought more obscurity, more complexity. What sex really is, has become an increasingly difficult question to answer." (Quoted in *Christine Jorgensen: A Personal Autobiography* [New York: Bantam Books, 1968], pp. 188–89.)

3. Imogen Carrington is discussed at length in chapter 4.

4. *The Secret River* (London: John Murray, 1909).

5. The only characters of any importance in the entire corpus who could even begin to vie with him for this distinction are sisters-in-law Rosalind Hilary and Nan Hilary *(Dangerous Ages);* and Helen Michel *(The World My Wilderness).* Nan is discussed passim in chapter 3; Helen is considered in chapter 4. Rosalind is the "painted" "psycho-analyst" who appears in *D.A.*, pp. 101–2 et passim. All three women are far more cerebral than Michael.

6. The ten "parts" of the novel serve the same function as chapters. Each is headed by a thematically appropriate epigraph or epigraphs.

7. Cf. a passage written nineteen years later by Virginia Woolf:

"Haunted!" she cried, suddenly pressing the accelerator. "Haunted! ever since I was a child. There flies the wild goose. It flies past the window out to sea. . . . Always it flies fast out to sea and always I fling after it words like nets . . . which shrivel as I've seen nets shrivel drawn on deck with only sea-weed in them." (*Orlando* [New York: Harcourt Brace, 1928, 1956], p. 313.)

8. *S.R.*, pp. 12–13, 15–16.

9. A portion of the lengthy epigraph to "part 2" reads:

Now he who is not newly initiated or who has become corrupted, does not easily rise out of this world to the sight of true beauty in the other; he looks only at her earthly namesake. (Plato, quoted in *S.R.*, p. 17; see also pp. 27, 111).

10. E. M. Forster, *The Longest Journey* (New York: Vintage Books, [1907] 1962, ppbk.), p. 310. The indebtedness of Macaulay's early novels to the novels of E. M. Forster is considerable, and warrants further study. See, e.g., Philip Rizzo's "Rose Macaulay: A Critical Survey," pp. 14–18, 21–22, 24–25, 27.

11. Philip Rizzo sees this as "the inviolate rose of Yeats" (Rizzo, p. 12), but a more immediate progenitor is probably Forster's "mystic rose" episode in *The Longest Journey,* pp. 293, 298, 302.

Perhaps a future study will gather up and examine the great quantity of "roses" to be found in certain early novels in which Macaulay did some extensive—and sometimes self-revelatory—punning on her own name. See, e.g., *V.C.,* pp. 20–21.

12. *S.R.,* pp. 3, 5, 9. Cf. the "Sasha" passage from Woolf's *Orlando,* p. 37:

> He called her a melon, a pineapple, an olive tree, an emerald, and a fox in the snow all in the space of three seconds; he did not know whether he had heard her, tasted her, seen her, or all three together.

13. Michael is able to pierce the "veil" between this world and the unseen world. The best written speculations on "spirit" versus "form" in all the early writings are to be found in *The Lee Shore* (1912), pp. 55–59, in a chapter ironically titled "The Complete Shopper." Numerous otherworldly "veils" that flutter through Macaulay's volumes of poetry, *Two Blind Countries* (1914), and *Three Days* (1919), reveal her persistent Platonic preoccupations.

14. In *Mystery At Geneva* (1922), pp. 39–40, and elsewhere in her writings, Macaulay rails against the imprecision of this adjective, but no other seems to suit here.

15. Cf. T. S. Eliot's *The Waste Land,* III, lines 293–99.

16. *Non-Combatants and Others* (London: Hodder and Stoughton, 1916; *What Not* (London: Constable, 1918). Appropriately enough, since it satirizes excessive government regulation of the lives of private citizens, publication of *What Not* was delayed from November 1918 to March 1919 because of government interference. See the Author's "Note" on p. xi.

17. *Non-Combatants,* p. 60.

18. See Ibid., pp. 60, 62, and also 115–16:

> Alix wasn't really altogether what he wanted. She was too nervy. Some nerve in him which had been badly jarred by the long ugliness of those months in France winced from contact with nervous people. Besides, he suspected her of feeling the same shrinking from him: she so hated the war and all its products. However, they had always amused each other; she was clever, and nice to look at; he remembered vaguely that he had been a little in love with her once, before the war. If the war hadn't come just then, he might have become a great deal in love with her. Before the war one had wanted a rather different sort of person . . . ; more of a companion to discuss things with; more of a stimulant, perhaps, and less of a rest. He remembered that they had discussed painting a great deal; he didn't want to discuss painting now. . . .

If for "painting" one substitutes "writing," this passage can be perceived as revealingly autobiographical, as can Basil's rejection of Alix (pp. 213–15), cited in Smith, *Rose Macaulay,* pp. 70–71.

19. See *N.-C.,* pp. 98, 104, 112, 116, 213.

20. In Christopher Hassell, *Rupert Brooke: A Biography* (London: Faber and Faber, 1964; New York: Harcourt, Brace & World, 1964; identical pagination in both editions), Macaulay is mentioned by name on pp. 134, 171. She is also, in my opinion, one of the "others not identified" regarding Rupert and another "unidenti-

fied" woman over her teacup in the photo of Brooke at a picnic facing p. 225. (Cf. the bottom photo, facing p. 49, of Smith's 1972/73 biography.) The purest speculation on my part also compels me to suggest that the ornate headpiece worn by the woman seated immediately next to Brooke provides the inspiration for Evie Tucker's profession ("she trimmed hats," *N.-C.*, p. 45). Even purer speculation compels me to wonder why, in none of the photos of Rose as an adult in the biography, is she shown standing unsupported and upright. (See, e.g., her unexplained walking stick or cane in the bottom photo facing p. 177.) Several of the novels feature a number of personae who limp and/or use a stick for support when walking. There are two such individuals in *The Valley Captives;* two in *Views and Vagabonds;* one in *Staying with Relations;* two in *Orphan Island.* Needless to say, Alix Sandomir in *N.-C.* also limps and uses a cane (pp. 4–5, 115, 142, 155).

21. See, for only one of many examples in the novels, *The Towers of Trebizond* (London: Collins, 1956; New York: Farrar, Straus and Cudahy, 1957), pp. 216 et passim. All references are to the latter edition. These conflicting feelings were a cause of the "nervous breakdown" she experienced in 1919. See Smith, *Rose Macaulay,* pp. 91–93.

22. Perhaps by no great coincidence, "to nick" in British slang means "to steal." Years later, in *The Towers of Trebizond* (1956), Macaulay's partly autobiographical heroine, Laurie, confesses to having been "a thief" insofar as she had robbed her lover's wife of "his love, mental and physical" (*T.T.,* p. 273).

23. I am indebted to Ms. Dorothy Esther Cady, formerly of the Department of English, University of Southern California, for supplying this term (during a conversation that occurred sometime during 1977–78) and suggesting this line of reasoning.

24. The mystery novels of Dorothy Leigh Sayers Fleming (1883–1957), M.A., (Oxon.), Hon.D.Litt. (Durham), remain perennial favorites. In addition to her great success in the field of detective fiction, Ms. Sayers had impressive credentials as a religious playwright, and was an accomplished medieval scholar whose published translations include *Tristan in Brittany, The Song of Roland,* and (the posthumously completed) Dante's *Divine Comedy.* From 1939 until 1945 she was President of the Modern Language Association. See Janet Hitchman, *Such a Strange Lady: A Biography of Dorothy L. Sayers* (New York: Avon Books, 1975), pp. 68, et passim.

25. See Hitchman, pp. 63–67.

26. Smith, "Rose Macaulay in her Writings," p. 143.

27. *The Valley Captives* (London: John Murray, 1911; New York: Henry Holt and Company). Page references are to the latter edition.

28. "John," the female co-protagonist in *V.C.,* is discussed in chapter 3.

29. See Smith, *Rose Macaulay,* pp. 61, 63–64.

30. Ibid., p. 63.

31. *V.C.,* p. 7; see also *V.C.,* p. 6, and n. 32.

32. The locale of the novel is probably that of Aberystwyth, Wales, where Macaulay's father was Professor of English Language and Literature at the University College of Wales during 1901–5. See Smith, *Rose Macaulay,* pp. 44–47, 49.

33. Cf. *V.C.,* p. 44, to Smith, *Rose Macaulay,* p. 47. A paragraph on *V.C.,* p. 332, written after all the novel's passion has been spent, serves as a tentative retraction of the preceding story. This paragraph briefly raises the supposition that the major premise of the main plot—the "tainting" of the victimized Vallons by the victimizing Bodgers—may have been merely the Vallons' own *folie à deux.*

34. Cf. Smith, *Rose Macaulay,* p. 47.

35. Woolf's conception of "the androgynous mind" is discussed at length in chapter 1. (See e.g. n. 82 and the accompanying text.)

36. See Smith, *Rose Macaulay*, pp. 24, 28, 45, 59, et passim.

37. See also *V.C.*, pp. 116–17.

38. See also *V.C.*, p. 90. The "feather-bed" is an allusion to *The Antiplatonick* of John Cleveland (1613–1658), which serves as an epigraph to *The Shadow Flies*, part 3.

39. For more on Oliver Vallon's blind intransigence as a parent see *V.C.*, p. 27.

40. Tudor's habitual voyeurism vis-à-vis his large and handsome stepbrother's sex life is unconvincingly described by the narrator as merely an attempt by Tudor to annoy Philip. This explanation has a false ring, since in every other conflict of their lives, Philip is invariably the provocateur. On one occasion, Tudor's presence at their tryst is said to cause a girlfriend of Philip's to become "excited." Tudor perceives this as threatening. (*V.C.*, pp. 130, 132, 134).

41. *V.C.*, pp. 187–89, et passim.

42. This is his stepsister's description (*V.C.*, p. 210).

43. Rizzo, "Rose Macaulay: A Critical Survey," p. 11; see also p. 10.

44. See Smith, *Rose Macaulay*, chapter 5.

45. Ten years later Macaulay, who was then living with her widowed mother in Beaconsfield, published *Dangerous Ages* (1921), which Macaulay's biographer explains

> may be regarded as an indirect but heartfelt protest against "living at home". In it an ageing [*sic*] widow, "Mrs. Hilary", a "muddled bigot" in the eyes of her children, is held up to scorn and ridicule. When [Rose's mother] Grace Macaulay read the book in manuscript she recognized the portrait of herself and was deeply hurt. To [her daughter] Margaret she confided her distress, and she begged her to persuade Rose to tone "Mrs. Hilary" down. But the portrait remains a cruel one. Possibly however Rose [*sic*] was trying to make some sort of amends when she dedicated the book "To my mother, Driving gaily through the adventurous middle years.". . . Something of Rose herself can be seen in one of the daughters in *Dangerous Ages* ("Nan") who, finding her mother unbearably trying, oscillates between sparring with her and making extravagant gestures of reconciliation. (Smith, *Rose Macaulay*, p. 98.)

46. OE. *blod* = blood + OE. *wen* = expectation. Many of the characters in *V.C.* have names that were deliberately chosen for their singularly appropriate meanings. For example, the young lady who renounces her worldly goods and social status to marry a wandering preacher is named "Dorothy Wynne" from Gk. *Dorothea*, "gift of God" and OE. *wynn*, "joy," "delight," "pleasure."

47. *N.B.* It is Blodwen's father, a Calvinistic Methodist minister named *Morris* Hughes (after the morris dance, which is performed around a Maypole), and Blodwen's uncle, *Hughey* Hughes, who torture and castrate Laurie Rennel.

48. See, e.g., *V.C.*, pp. 199, 204, 229.

49. *V.C.*, pp. 230–31, 233. See also the "Rose-trees, broken from their supports" on p. 199. Sharp-bladed objects are also noticeably present in the story, sometimes in conjunction with "fingers," *V.C.*, pp. 92, 319, 36.

50. *V.C.*, pp. 315–16, 227, 336.

51. "In the summer of 1910," notes Constance Smith, "he [Brooke] had toured the New Forest by horse-drawn caravan, campaigning for Fabianism with his friend Dudley Ward" (*Rose Macaulay*, p. 63).

52. See *V.C.*, p. 36. The "donkey cart" appears not only in *V.C.*, but in subsequent novels as well. In *Views and Vagabonds* (1912),

> Tom and Betty Crevequer. . . . Though of gentle birth, . . . lead an extremely happy-go-lucky life of picaresque poverty. . . . and enter and leave this novel in a gypsy cart. (Alice Bensen, "The Ironic Aesthete . . . ," *ELIT* 9 (1966): 41).

In the interim of its use by the Crevequers, the cart is driven about by the novel's hero, Benjamin Bunter, and his girl cousin, Cecil. In *The Lee Shore* (1912), Peter Margerison is last seen as a homeless vagabond roaming Italy in a donkey cart. Still later, the story of Alix Sandomir in *Non-Combatants* (1916), opens with a woodland scene in which Alix dismisses the model she has been painting and drives off through the trees in a small donkey cart (*N.-C.*, pp. 3–5).

53. Contributing to this interpretation is the oft-iterated contrast in the novel of Laurie's pale and trembling weakness with the preacher's virile strength. (*V.C.*, pp. 316–18, et passim.) Thus, although the two rivals for Dorothy's love are contemporaries, Rennel *seems* like the much older man. Additionally, there is the insistence by Dorothy on receiving not just Laurie's forgiveness, but his *permission* to "find happiness" (*V.C.*, pp. 317–18), as though he were more a guardian than a cast-off suitor. And cf. the following:

> His [Rupert Brooke's] was the initial influence which caused the axis of her [Macaulay's] life, previously centered on family and home, to start gradually to shift towards independence. (Smith, *Rose Macaulay*, p. 61)

> It was so splendid that he [Lloyd Evans] should go [as a tramping preacher] and so disturbing. Never before had he so intensely forced on her [Dorothy] the vision that was his characteristic gift to her of roads making for the open. (*V.C.*, pp. 176–77)

54. *The Lee Shore* (London: Hodder and Stoughton, 1912).
55. See also *V.C.*, p. 114.
I am indebted to Professor Richard John Dunn, Department of English, University of Washington at Seattle, for pointing out this probable derivation (in a conversation during August 1977).
56. See Smith, *Rose Macaulay*, pp. 59–60. If the character of Peter Margerison was, as Smith believes, inspired by that of Macaulay's father, her compassionate treatment of him here is in striking contrast to her harsh treatment of him in *V.C.* However, there is no less striking a contrast in Nan's love-hate relationship with her mother (see above, n. 45, and *Dangerous Ages*, pp. 222–23, 227–28), or in Daisy Simpson's alternating shame at, and love for, her lower-middle-class mother (*Daisy and Daphne*, pp. 112–16, et passim).
57. See especially *L.S.*, chapter 1.
58. *L.S.*, pp. 21, 91, 305, et passim.
59. A similar phrase is used concerning Laurie Rennel, *V.C.*, p. 55. See also *V.C.*, pp. 101, 166–67.
60. Cf. Tudor Vallon: "anything that pleased his eyes pleased the most essential part of him," *V.C.*, p. 47. See also *V.C.*, p. 133.
61. *L.S.*, pp. 8–9, explains:

> Peter's mother had made two marriages, the first being with Urquhart's father, Urquhart being already in existence at the time; the second with Mr. Margerison, a clergyman, who was also already father of one son, and became Peter's father later.

62. *L.S.*, p. 283; see also pp. 281, 300–301.
63. On *L.S.*, p. 277, Rodney tells Peter,

> "So your emptiness found pleasure in his fullness, your poverty in his riches, your weakness in his strength, and you loved him."

64. For example, the love triangle in *S.R.* is foreshadowed by Michael's stated intention to consume five cups of tea containing three lumps of sugar each (*S.R.*,

p. 15). The love triangle in *L.S.* is revealed in the scene in which Lucy serves Peter "tea, with three lumps in it," while making references to "we three" (*L.S.*, pp. 152–53).

65. This is particularly true of the passages describing their grammar school days, when, for example, Peter dislocates his shoulder and Urquhart insists on being the one to "put it in." This expression—or variants of it—is used several times within a very few pages. Other such images may be found in chapters 1 and ff. One striking phallic image occurs toward the story's end, when Peter, now an itinerant embroidery vendor in Italy, meets Livio, "a vivacious and beautiful youth," to whom he presents "two black and snake-like cigars," *L.S.*, p. 287. Similar suggestions can be found in *S.R.*, part 1.

66. *Orphan Island* (London: William Collins, 1924, 1961; New York: Boni and Liveright, 1925). All references are to the latter edition.

67. *O.I.*, pp. 244, 252.

68. See n. 32.

69. *Milton*, p. 9; see also pp. 15–16.

70. The "retort" to which Macaulay is referring (but does not footnote) reads in part as follows:

> Some of late called me "the Lady." But why do I seem to them too little of a man? . . . It is, I suppose, because I have never brought myself to toss off great bumpers like a prize-fighter, or because my hand has never grown horny with driving the plough, or because I was never a farm hand at seven or laid myself down full length in the midday sun; or last perhaps because I never showed my virility in the way these brothellers do. But I wish they could leave playing the ass as readily as I the woman. . . . (from *Prolusion VI* (1628) in *Complete Prose Works of John Milton*, ed. Douglas Bush et al., Vol. 1, New Haven and London: Yale University Press, 1953, 1970).

71. *The Shadow Flies* (New York: Harper and Brothers, 1932); British title, *They Were Defeated* (London: William Collins, 1932, 1960). The latter is now available in paperback (New York: Oxford University Press, 1986) with an Introduction by Susan Howatch. All references are to the Harper and Brothers edition.

72. The novel both begins and ends on a "pagan" note. In chapter 1 Robert Herrick, Vicar of Dean Prior, is celebrating Mass in a church filled with

> harvest decorations . . . the vicar had himself conceived the notion of bringing the rejoicings of harvest home and the hock-cart into the church itself, and carrying on the good old pagan custom of decking the altars of Ceres with the fruits of the earth. . . . the vicar climbed into the pulpit, and stood, a burly, Roman-headed figure, among the corn and barley-sheaves, and apples. . . . (*T.S.F.*, pp. 3, 5)

While, in the book's final sentence, after the Civil War has caused the death or exile of all of the story's principal characters—including Herrick—he remains a symbol of the continuity of Nature:

> Slowly he walked . . . across the meadows . . . ; and he seemed to have already put on immortality, for he might have been some sturdy sylvan god in that serene pastoral landskip, passing on his way to eat and drink with his friends. (*T.S.F.*, p. 476)

73. The better selections from *Two Blind Countries* (1914), and *Three Days* (1919), were reprinted in *The Augustan Books of English Poetry* (Second Series, Number Six): *ROSE MACAULAY* (1927).

74. *I Would Be Private* (London: Collins, 1937; New York: Harper and Brothers). All references are to the latter edition.

75. See P. N. Furbank, *E. M. Forster* (New York: Harcourt Brace Jovanovich, 1978), vol. 2, passim.

76. Forster's homosexuality did not become a matter of record until the publication of Furbank's biography.

77. The novels influenced by Forster include *S.R.*, *L.S.*, *V.& V.*, and there may well be others, e.g. *Potterism*. See n. 10.

78. Smith, *Rose Macaulay*, p. 103.

79. Papagayo—(Sp.) "parrot; talker, chatterer"—is an ironic name for the island in view of the aforementioned goal.

80. Despite their carping at McBrown's wife and numerous babies, Charles and Francis take an active part in providing Mrs. McBrown and the quints with a refuge when they need one, *W.B.P.*, pp. 236–41, et passim. Likewise, certain of the young men's political and aesthetic ideals are quite admirably motivated, *W.B.P.*, part 2, chapter 14.

81. Furbank, *E. M. Forster*, vol. 2, p. 165.

82. Furbank, vol. 2, pp. 182–83, 205.

83. Furbank, vol. 2, pp. 172–73.

84. See, e.g., Furbank, vol. 1, pp. 191–92, and vol. 2, p. 169.

85. This is the motto of Forster's *Howards End* (1910), which is elucidated in chapter 22 of that novel, q.v. See also Furbank, vol. 1, pp. 188–90, et passim.

86. On one of their walks together there are several phallic and at least two oral images of note. Most striking of the former is the "stone pedestal on which a naked boy bestrid a dolphin." See *W.B.P.*, pp. 189ff. See also the last meeting in which Charles experiences very tender feelings for Ronald and asks if he has considered leaving his wife. Through much of this scene Ronald "had nails in his mouth," which he then exchanges for his pipe, *W.B.P.*, pp. 291ff.

87. *W.B.P.*, pp. 99ff., 195, 213, et passim.

88. On *W.B.P.*, pp. 301–2, when Ronald explains to Charles that it has never entered his mind to leave his wife, Charles muses about marriage, "It must be an extraordinary queer tie to feel." The narrator then interpolates: "To Ronald it seemed natural enough."

89. Although Forster did not like her *Writings of E. M. Forster* (1938), this affection was mutual. See Furbank, vol. 2, pp. 282, 283n., 289. There are several references to Forster in Macaulay's *Letters* and *Last Letters*.

90. See *Howards End*, chapters 6 and 41.

91. I have here extrapolated an idea found in Rizzo, "Rose Macaulay: A Critical Survey," p. 21:

> It is Forster's *A Room With A View* which provides the thesis and the types of conflict presented in *Views and Vagabonds*. Each of the characters has a "view," which is made to appear absurd because sinful or sinful because absurd, and each is an object of satire to the degree he deviates from the line of virtue established by Forster. . . .

Chapter 3. "Femme coupée en morceaux"

1. Agatha Christie, *Murder in Mesopotamia* (New York: Dell Publishing Co., Inc., 1935, reprinted December 1979), pp. 193–94. See also p. 113. Androgynous characters in Christie's own fiction include "womanish" Mr. Satterthwaite and "man-of-the-world" Miss Wills in *Murder in Three Acts* (New York: Popular Library, 1934, 1961), pp. 12–13, et passim.

2. *Crewe Train* (London: Collins, 1926; New York: Boni and Liveright). All references are to the latter edition.

3. *Told by an Idiot* (London: Collins, 1923; New York: Boni and Liveright, 1924). All references are to the latter edition.

4. Cf. Gloria Steinem, "The Trouble with Rich Women," *Ms.*, 14, no. 12 (June 1986): 42:

> Most of my wealthy classmates conformed in the same way the rest of us did: by marrying a man who had the profession we wanted but thought we could not have.

5. From Henrik Ibsen, *A Doll's House* (1879), act 3, reprinted in *Eleven Plays of Henrik Ibsen*, introd. H. L. Mencken (n.p.: Modern Library/Random House, n.d.), p. 73.

6. Ibid., act 1, p. 13. See in this regard Jane Flanders, "The Fallen Woman in Fiction" (Department of English, University of Pittsburgh), paper delivered at " 'A Fabric of Our Own Making': Southern Scholars on Women" Conference, Georgia State University, 6 March, 1981, p. 8:

> Just as a man "owned" a wife, from ancient times the virgin daughter was regarded as a father's property to be disposed of at his will.

7. *The Valley Captives* (London: John Murray, 1911; New York: Henry Holt and Company). All references are to the latter edition.

8. Macaulay's penchant for symbolic garb was exhibited in fact, as well as in fiction. After an "academic fiasco" at Somerville College in 1903, she attended a "going-down party" dressed as a "worm." See Constance B. Smith, *Rose Macaulay*, pp. 43–44.

9. See *V.C.*, pp. 180–81, 184–86, 305–6.

10. The word was perhaps suggested to Macaulay by a passage in *Jane Eyre:*

> "You are no ruin, sir—no lightning-struck tree: you are green and vigorous. Plants will grow about your roots, whether you ask them or not, because they take delight in your bountiful shadow; and as they grow they will lean towards you, and wind round you, because your strength offers them so safe a prop."
> Again he smiled: I gave him comfort. (See Charlotte Brontë, *Jane Eyre*, reprinted in Sandra Gilbert and Susan Gubar, Eds., *The Norton Anthology of Literature by Women: The Tradition in English* (New York: W. W. Norton & Company, 1985), chapter 37, p. 728.)

11. Lloyd Evans is Macaulay's surrogate for Rupert Brooke. See chapter 2.

12. Their relationship seems much like that of Adam and Eve in *Paradise Lost*, 4: 295–99; 8: 48–53, 537–46, q.v.

13. Yet more immobile—and at least equally vitriolic—is attractive but obese Pilar Alvarez in *And No Man's Wit* (1940), who compulsively gorges herself on chocolates and sews doll clothes for the statues of saints for want of other outlets.

14. Her given name, "Joanna," is used only once, on *V.C.*, p. 13. She is thereafter invariably called "John" for the remainder of the novel. Very likely admiration for St. Joan of Arc inspired the names or nicknames of various women characters, especially in the early novels. Thus, Alix Sandomir of *Non-Combatants* is addressed as "Joanna" (*N.-C.*, p. 59), Imogen Carrington of *Told by an Idiot* is called "Jean" and "Jennie" by various relatives (*T.b.I.*, pp. 166–67), and, in *Going Abroad*, Hero Buckley is called "Joe" by her father and is said to resemble "St. John the Baptist"; additionally, she encounters a lady named "Jeanne Joseph." See *Going Abroad* (London: William Collins, 1934; New York: Harper and Brothers), pp. 30, 294–95. All page references are to the latter edition.

15. Nan and Gerda vie for the title of "sportsman" in *Dangerous Ages* (London: William Collins, 1921; New York: Boni and Liveright), pp. 151, 159, 165. All page references are to the latter edition.

16. Cf. the description of a photograph of a Neapolitan family by Maria Montessori, *Pedagogical Anthropology* (New York: n.n., 1913), pp. 266–67, quoted in Rita Kramer, *Maria Montessori: A Biography* (New York: G. P. Putnam's Sons, 1977), p. 101:

> The man, or rather the beardless youth who is just beginning to feel himself a man, and therefore hopes for independence, holds his head proudly level; but the very pretty woman seated beside him holds her head gracefully inclined forward. For that matter, this is woman's characteristically *graceful* attitude. She never naturally assumes, nor does the artist ever attribute to her the proud and lofty attitude of the level head. But this graceful pose is in reality nothing else than the pose of slavery. The woman who is beginning to struggle, the woman who begins to perceive the mysterious and potent voice of human conflict, and enters upon the infinite world of modern progress, raises up her head—and beauty is enhanced, rather than taken away, by this attitude which today has begun to be assumed by all humanity: by the laborer, since the socialistic propaganda, and by woman in her feministic aspirations for liberty.

17. During World War I, Macaulay left an uncongenial career in hospital nursing for a far more "unladylike" stint as a farm laborer. See Constance Smith, *Rose Macaulay*, pp. 78–80.

18. Oliver's cousin, Vincent Carter, likewise takes up the cause of the experientially starved Vallon children:

> Everybody . . . ought to be given his chance to find his way into life—life as he, individually, can live it so as to be most alive. (See *V.C.*, p. 6, et passim.)

19. On *V.C.*, p. 132, Tudor

> Saw Philip Bodger and Blodwen Hughes, the minister's daughter. They were sheltering from the rain in a cart-shed. Philip, astride on a shaft, had the girl on his knee.

20. The "flint" and the "feather bed" (*V.C.*, pp. 119–20, 307) are allusions to John Cleveland's "The Antiplatonick," several lines of which serve as an epigraph to, and set the theme for, part 3 of Macaulay's seventeenth-century historical novel *The Shadow Flies* (1932). A complete text of the poem appears in Hugh Kenner, ed., *Seventeenth Century Poetry: The Schools of Donne and Jonson* (New York: Holt, Rinehart and Winston, Inc., 1964), pp. 415–16.

21. See *V.C.*, p. 332. See also pp. 307, 330–31.

22. Rhea and Saturn (Gk. Ops and Cronos) were sister and brother Titans whose union produced—among numerous other beings—Jupiter (Gk. Zeus), "called the father of gods and men." See *Bulfinch's Mythology: The Greek and Roman Fables Illustrated*, compiled by Bryan Holme (New York: The Viking Press, 1979, reprinted 1980), pp. 16, 34, 166. See also Will Durant, *The Story of Civilization*, 10 vols. (New York: Simon and Schuster, 1966); vol. 2: *The Life of Greece*, pp. 99, 102, 121.

23. The novel was awarded the Femina-Vie Heureuse Prize in 1922. On May 31, 1928, Virginia Woolf referred to this in her *Diary*, vol. 3, p. 185 (See also p. 186):

> Rose Macaulay says "Yes I won the prize"—rather peevishly. I think at once that she is jealous, & test whatever else she says with a view to finding out whether she is or not. . . . This [jealousy] shows through a dozen little phrases, as we're talking of America, articles &

c: she is jealous of me; anxious to compare us: but I may imagine it: & it shows my own jealousy no doubt, as suspicions always do. One can't know them if one hadn't got them.

24. Constance Smith uses the phrase "sexually ambiguous." See her *Rose Macaulay*, pp. 17, 205, 231.

25. Michael's oral gratifications in *S.R.*, pp. 15–16—blowing a whistle and consuming cigarettes and various sweets—are paralleled by Neville's climbing up a beech tree and whistling with the birds and her delight in "bread and marmalade" in *D.A.*, pp. 12–13.

26. Macaulay's love of nautical adventure doubtless influenced this choice of verb. See *OED*, s.v. "Swarm" and cf. Imogen's use of the word in portraying the adventures of "Wilfrid"—a male surrogate for herself in *T.b.I.*, p. 193.

27. *D.A.*, pp. 85, 109. Cf. in *T.b.I.*, pp. 61–62, Amy Garden's refusal to educate her daughter equally with her son, discussed on p. 86 of this study.

28. See *D.A.*, chapter 11.

29. See also *D.A.*, pp. 35, 79.

30. See *D.A.*, pp. 34–35, 46, 75–81.

31. The "latch-key" in Pamela's hand symbolizes her present sexual relationship with Frances, just as the "latch-key" in Gerda's hand symbolizes her future sexual relationship with Barry Briscoe, *D.A.*, p. 132. (See Freud on "The symbolism of locks and keys" in *The Interpretation of Dreams, Complete Psychological Works*, vol. 5, p. 354.) Subsequently, the "key" is transmuted from physical to metaphysical symbol, *D.A.*, p. 242.

32. "Pap" is infant food. This is appropriate, since Pamela and Frances are perpetually mothering one another. However, the word also means "teat or nipple," which is singularly appropriate in light of their lesbian relationship.

33. *D.A.*, p. 75, emphasis added. Cf. the use of the word in *Genesis* 4:1.

34. Constance Smith, *Rose Macaulay*, mentions Nancy Willetts in connection with Jean Macaulay on pp. 72n., 77–78, 151, 189, and 189n., but never suggests the obvious. That Pamela and Frances are involved in an "affair" in *D.A.* is noted briefly and disapprovingly by Philip Rizzo in *Rose Macaulay*, pp. 51, 53.

35. These women have, in some ways, never outgrown their undergraduate days at Oxford, *D.A.*, pp. 75–78, and are said to be incapable of "leaving the past behind." Cf. Sigmund Freud's essay on "Transformations of Puberty" in his *Complete Psychological Works*, vol. 7, p. 208, where he suggests:

> Every pathological disorder of sexual life is rightly to be regarded as an inhibition in development.

See also Ibid., p. 229:

> Dessoir [1894] has justly remarked upon the regularity with which adolescent boys and girls form sentimental friendships with others of their own sex. . . . Where inversion is not regarded as a crime it will be found that it answers fully to the sexual inclinations of no small number of people.

36. Cf. what George Gissing observed in 1893 in *The Odd Women* (New York: W. W. Norton & Company, reprinted 1971), p. 37, where he causes Rhoda Nunn to remark "that there are half a million more women than men in this unhappy country of ours. . . . So many *odd* women—no making a pair with them."

37. Whether Gerda is twenty or twenty-one is somewhat ambiguous. Cf. *D.A.*, p. 16 with pp. 72–73, 124.

38. See also *D.A.*, pp. 147, 149, 153.

39. Gerda's brother Kay faints in *D.A.*, p. 159.

40. Isie Rickaby's wanderings, lost, alone, and hysterical, through the Guatemalan jungle come close to equaling these. See *Staying with Relations*, (London: William Collins, 1930; New York: Horace Liveright), pp. 117–34. All references are to the London edition.

41. As Gerda is compared to Phoebus Apollo because there are no female equivalents in Greek mythology, so Isie in *S. Rel.*, p. 312, balances herself on her surfboard "like Phaeton holding the reins of his rushing chariot."

42. *Mystery at Geneva: An Improbable Tale of Singular Happenings* (London: William Collins, 1922; New York: Boni and Liveright, 1923). All page references are to the latter edition.

43. *N.B.*, at least one edition (New York: Boni and Liveright, Feb. 1923, 248 pp.), bears instead the subtitle "An Improbable Tale of *Sinister* Happenings" (emphasis added).

44. Alice Bensen, *Rose Macaulay*, p. 81.

45. The exploitation of women by the press also looms large in *Daisy and Daphne*, passim. It is satirized briefly in *Orphan Island* (p. 81); it helped to provoke Macaulay's essay "Woman: The Eternal Topic" which is printed in full as appendix B; and it is manifest in chapter 2 of Virginia Woolf's *A Room of One's Own* (New York: Harcourt Brace Jovanovich, 1929, 1957, 1981), p. 33: "The most transient visitor to this planet . . . who picked up this [news]paper could not fail to be aware . . . that England is under the rule of a patriarchy." See also chapter 1, n. 43.

46. The paper by Flanders (n. 6) makes this point quite convincingly; likewise applicable is Sally Bingham, "The Truth About Growing Up Rich," *Ms.* 14, No. 12 (June 1986): 48–50, 82–83:

> Wealthy men have always influenced the course of this nation's history. Wealthy women have, at best, worked behind the scenes. We share our loneliness, our sense of helplessness, and our alienation from the male establishment with all our sisters.

47. Alix, who yearns to go off to war in *Non-Combatants* but is sickened by the deaths and injuries that war produces, epitomizes such women. In *The Shadow Flies*, tomboyish Meg dons her dead brother's armor and is quickly killed. There is no indication that she succeeds in killing—or even injuring—anyone else. The "maquisarde" Barbary in *The World My Wilderness* lures the Nazi soldier who raped her to his death and acquiesces in the deliberate drowning of her Collaborationist stepfather, but the only violent act she herself commits is the shooting of a Scottish farmer with her slingshot. Of the more feminine of Rose Macaulay's heroines, Flora Smith inflicts gratuitous injury on random jungle plants and a hummingbird in *Orphan Island* and is compared to Rosamond's cruelly masculine scientist brother William. Only one heroine, the very feminine Clare Potter of *Potterism*, commits willful murder, and there is considerable and unresolved ambiguity about just how willful that murder is.

48. The name of Franchi's castle is, for one familiar with Byron's "The Prisoner of Chillon," a useful clue to solving the *Mystery at Geneva*. The Swiss patriot Bonnivard was immured in a place where "Lake Leman lies by Chillon's walls" (l. 107), and the kidnapped delegates are immured in Franchi's "Chateau Leman" on Lake Geneva.

49. There is no mention of his having done so in either the *Letters* or *Last Letters*.

50. See chapter 1. A letter to Father Johnson dated "23rd February, 1951" in

Letters, pp. 84–87 acknowledges the receipt of two Abbot Daniel stories, (Titled in the Latin original "De Miranda Sanctitate Danielis Abbatis," and "De Eunucho,") translations of chapters 27 and 28 of the *Liber de Miraculis*.

51. Father Johnson's no doubt beautiful rendering of this story most likely did not survive the posthumous destruction of Macaulay's papers, described in chapter 1. At present, I am relying on the translation titled "About a Eunuch," in Margaret Joanne Brennan, "Johannes Monachus, *Liber de Miraculis*," unpublished Master's Thesis, The University of Texas at Austin, August 1956. All page numbers preceded by "D.E." refer to the Brennan text; all words in quotation marks are transcribed from her work verbatim, with the exception of the title.

52. See the letter of "23rd February, 1951," cited in n. 50. There is no mention of Rose actually reading the Latin version in any of the published correspondence. However, she was certainly capable of doing so. In a letter dated "1st March, 1951," she tells of how her father "grounded us in Latin," *Letters*, p. 89. Numerous instances in that letter and throughout the published correspondence attest to her expertise in that language.

53. See the letters dated "23rd February, 1951" and "12th March, 1951" in *Letters*, pp. 84–85, 95–96.

54. Brennan translates this word as "small biscuits" on p. 149 of her text. In a note to p. 85 of the *Letters*, Smith writes that the word means "Literally, 'biscuits'." Father Johnson apparently translated *paximatia* as "toasted crusts," for which Macaulay praises him as "ingenious" in *Letters*, p. 85; while on pp. 95–96 of the same she writes:

> I lunched at a Cypriot restaurant the other day, and talked to a waiter about *paximatia*; as you said, it is toasted bread, and has caraway seeds, and is popular at Easter.

55. Full reference in n. 3.

56. Seemingly, every generation of Women's Rights activists regards some preceding generation as more militant than its own. Cf. to the passage quoted in the text this one by Dale Spender writing in the 1980s about the feminists of the 1920s:

> Great strength and great joy can be derived from the knowledge that a little over fifty years ago, many women felt much the same about male power as many women do today. They saw similar problems, sought similar solutions, engaged in similar debates—and encountered similar strategies of male resistance. To know about their existence is to confirm and validate much of our own.
>
> And to learn of their 'erasure' is to be better informed. Knowledge, too, can be power, and when we know that the presence of these women, and their activities, in the records of the past, would gravely challenge the concept of 'normal' society—and 'normal' women— we know why such women must go [from historical records], if male power is to stay. (See *Time and Tide Wait for No Man* (London: Pandora Press, 1984), p. 2).

57. Similarly, in writing of the 1920s era in which Macaulay published *T.b.I.*, Spender demonstrates how

> priorities for many women voters in 1983 were much the same as those of women voters in 1920. . . .
>
> What has changed is that . . . far from improving the gains made by our foremothers we have let some of them slip from our grasp. (See *Time and Tide*, p. 13, et passim.)

58. Two recent and fascinating feminist studies of the Hebrew Scriptures deserve mention here. One, by a biblical scholar at the University of California at Davis, uses extensive philological and Scriptural evidence to support a more accurate translation

of the Hebrew words describing Eve (Gen. 2:18b). The words *ᶜezer kᵉnegdô* mean that our primordial mother was intended by God as "a power *equal* to" man rather than as "a helper fit for him." R. David Freedman, "Woman, A Power Equal to Man," *Biblical Archaeology Review*, 9, no. 1 (January/February 1983): 56–58.

Another equally erudite but far lengthier study demonstrates that the biblical "matriarchs were learned, wise women. . . . with spiritual influence and worldly position." See Savina J. Teubal, *Sarah the Priestess: The First Matriarch of Genesis* (Athens, Ohio: Swallow Press/Ohio University Press, 1984).

59. He is a den-man, i.e., one who belongs in a cave, like an animal or a primitive man. The name "Croft"—1) "A small enclosed field or pasture near a house"; 2) "A small farm"—is equally indicative of his provincialism. *American Heritage Dictionary*, 1969 edition, s.v. "croft."

60. Stanley's—and Macaulay's—ardent feminist convictions are very much in evidence on *T.b.I.*, p. 235 q.v., which reads in part:

> To her the denial of representation in the governing body of her country on grounds of sex was not so much an injustice as a piece of inexplicable lunacy, as if all persons measuring, say, below five foot eight, had been denied votes.

See also Dale Spender, passim, for an account of the admirable and informed involvement of British women in the political process subsequent to their winning of the franchise.

61. Flavia Alaya, *William Sharp—"Fiona Macleod": 1855–1905* (Cambridge: Harvard University Press, 1970), p. 11. See also p. 12.

Chapter 4. "That Outrageous Power of Inflaming"

1. Dorothy L. Sayers, *The Unpleasantness at the Bellona Club* (New York: Avon Books, 1928, 1963), p. 172.

2. *Dangerous Ages* (London: William Collins, 1921; New York: Boni and Liveright). All page references are to the latter edition.

3. Sayers's own love involvements—and her masculine mannerisms—are chronicled in Janet Hitchman, *Such a Strange Lady: A Biography of Dorothy L. Sayers* (New York: Avon Books, 1975, 1976).

4. Significantly, the lives and/or potentials of all these women have been adversely affected in some way, generally to the advantage of a brother (in the case of Lady Dormer); a husband (in the case of Sheila Fentiman); or a lover (in the cases of Ann Dorland, Naomi Rushworth, Marjorie Phelps, and "three [nameless] women"). See *U.B.C.*, pp. 14–15, 48–56, 127, 150, 171–72, 186, et passim.

5. *Told by an Idiot* (London: William Collins, 1923; New York: Boni and Liveright, 1924). References are to the latter edition.

6. Like Macaulay's real-life lover, Gerald O'Donovan, this man, "Francis Jayne," has more than one child by his wife. Rome Garden witnesses his stabbing and death (*T.b.I.*, pp. 121–22). Mr. Jayne's feminine name and brutal fate put him in a class with other mutilated men—Laurie Rennel, Basil Doye, Nicky Chester, Denis O'Neill, Daniel O'Malley—who represent Gerald O'Donovan, Rupert Brooke, or George Macauley.

7. Alice Bensen, *Rose Macaulay*, p. 82, notes that Imogen is "a recollection of the author's childhood." See also pp. 83–84.

8. See, in this order, *T.b.I.*, pp. 211, 253, 163–64, 248, 268, 219–20, 251–52, 224.

9. Women who do not do so are subject to at least the *implied* threat of rape in *O.I.*, p. 288, *C.T.*, p. 205, and *T.T.*, p. 20. See also *W.W.*, pp. 60–62 for one of at least

five instances in the book pertaining to sexual harassment and/or violence towards women. The discussion of *M.G.* in chapter 3 is likewise relevant to this issue.

10. Letter dated "10th November, 1952" in *Last Letters*, p. 50. See also chapter 1, p. 40.

11. In young adulthood her admirations are bisexual. See *T.b.I.*, pp. 301–3.

12. See also *T.b.I.*, pp. 328, 333–34.

13. *T.b.I.*, pp. 83, 105–6, 122–24.

14. See, e.g., *T.b.I.*, pp. 140–41.

15. See also *T.b.I.*, p. 212.

16. Constance Smith, *Rose Macaulay*, pp. 78–79.

17. After Clare Potter confesses to giving Oliver Hobart a fatal push downstairs, the Anglican deacon who has counseled her writes in his journal:

> That she had truly repeated what had passed between her and Hobart I believed. But whether she had pushed him, or whether he lost his own balance, seemed to me still an open question. (*Potterism*, p. 187)

18. *Orphan Island* (London: William Collins, 1924, 1961; New York: Boni and Liveright, 1925), pp. 79, 267, 291, 311, et passim. All references are to the latter edition.

19. Writing of Denham Dobie's cartographical proclivity, Alice Bensen in *Rose Macaulay*, p. 98, states that Macaulay herself "was a great collector" of maps. Of Imogen Bensen writes, p. 91, "She is one aspect of the girlhood of her . . . creator."

20. See also *O.I.*, pp. 142, 154–55, 195–96, 208.

21. See also *O.I.*, pp. 34–35.

22. Cf. Catherine Grey, who is "excited" by and "in love with" Claudia Cradock in *Staying with Relations*, pp. 49, 88. Catherine experiences this love while she is strolling about with a stick, i.e., a "light cane," in her hand, p. 87 (also p. 97 of the 1930 New York edition).

23. See also *O.I.*, pp. 43–44.

24. It is only after Miss Smith is deposed that "THE NAME OF THIS ISLAND IS HEREBY CHANGED FROM SMITH ISLAND TO ORPHAN ISLAND" by the rebellious populace, *O.I.*, p. 282.

25. Discussed in chapter 1.

26. Flanders has a footnote here which reads as follows:

> This is a central argument in L. C. Knights, *Drama and Society in the Age of Johnson* (New York: 1968; first published 1937); see also R. H. Tawney, *Religion and the Rise of Capitalism* (New York: New American Library, 1947; first published 1922).

27. Jane Flanders, "The Fallen Woman in Fiction," pp. 10–11. See above, chapter 3, n. 6, regarding this paper.

28. *O.I.*, p. 65, reveals the Anglocentric nature of the islanders' conceptions:

> Of course, we know, for we have always been taught so here, that Great Britain, the country from which we originally emigrated, . . . is the world's hub, peculiarly chosen by the Deity as the centre of His beneficent purposes towards His universe.

This attitude is explored in Richard D. Altick, *Victorian People and Ideas* (New York: W. W. Norton & Company, Inc., 1973), pp. 188–89, q.v.

29. *O.I.*, p. 219; see also p. 220.

30. David Thomson, *England in the Nineteenth Century (1815–1914)* (Baltimore: Penguin Books, 1950, reprinted 1963), p. 188, recalls:

In 1918 the Representation of the People Act gave the vote to women over thirty who were householders or wives of householders. They numbered some 8,500,000.

See also *T.b.I.*, pp. 331–32.

31. See *O.I.*, pp. 60–61, 63–66, et passim.

32. "So Miss Smith consented to become (as she thought) Mrs. O'Malley, and they were married according to the Scottish rite, before two witnesses. . . ." (*O.I.*, p. 27).

33. *O.I.*, pp. 68, 91–92, 94–95, 170.

34. See n. 24.

35. *O.I.*, p. 98.

36. *O.I.*, pp. 62–63.

37. In *C.T.*, pp. 81–82, Catherine is said to carry her politics "ardently like a sword." Her M. P. husband Tim is merely her "chorus."

38. Cf. *Exodus* 7:8–13, and 17:5–13; *Numbers* 17:5–10 and 20:8–11. A more recent instance is in J. R. R. Tolkien's *The Two Towers: Being the Second Part of The Lord of the Rings* (Boston: Houghton Mifflin Company, 1965), p. 189:

> He raised his hand, and spoke slowly in a clear cold voice. "Saruman, your staff is broken." There was a crack, and the staff split asunder in Saruman's hand, and the head of it fell down at Gandalf's feet. "Go!" said Gandalf. With a cry Saruman fell back and crawled away. . . . The spell of Saruman was broken. . . .

39. *O.I.*, pp. 182–84, et passim.

40. This is written very much in the style of Queen Victoria. See, e.g., Elizabeth Longford, *Queen Victoria: Born to Succeed* (New York: Harper & Row, 1964, ppbk.), pp. 328–29, et passim.

41. *O.I.*, pp. 186, 243. See also chapter 2, pp. 55–57.

42. Evelyn has *five* grown children in all (Macaulay's error). Cf. to Evelyn and Audrey (*C.T.*, p. 277), Smith's *Rose Macaulay*, p. 96:

> Gerald [O'Donovan] once remarked . . . that Rose had a brain like a man's, and that this was one of the things about her which particularly attracted him.

43. The latter was still Violet Keppel at the time. See Victoria Glendinning, *Vita: The Life of V. Sackville-West* (New York: Knopf, 1983), p. 91.

44. Robert M. Lovett, *The History of the Novel in England* (New York: Houghton Mifflin Company, 1932), p. 253, quoted in Robert Kuehn, "The Pleasures of Rose Macaulay," p. 181.

45. *Crewe Train*, pp. 14–15, 33.

46. *Crewe Train*, pp. 22–23. Verney Ruth of *Abbots Verney*, Peter Margerison of *The Lee Shore*, and Raoul Michel of *The World My Wilderness* each bear a remarkable resemblance to their respective mothers. Stanley Croft of *Told by an Idiot*, Julian Conybeare of *The Shadow Flies*, the Grig sisters of *I Would Be Private*, and Barbary Deniston of *The World My Wilderness* all have much in common with their respective fathers.

47. Cf. Rose Macaulay's "Problems of a Woman's Life," pp. 233–38 of the New York edition in the collection of essays titled *A Casual Commentary* (London: Methuen, 1925; New York: Boni and Liveright, 1926) in which she ironically advises women beset with domestic chores:

Do *not* keep house. Let the house, or flat, go unkept. Let it go to the devil, and see what happens when it has gone there. At the worst, a house unkept cannot be so distressing as a life unlived.

48. There are other similarities between the fictional Denham and the factual Vita Sackville-West and their respective spouses. Cf. Glendinning, op. cit., pp. 91–93 with pp. 173–83 of this study or with *Crewe Train* passim.

49. It is very likely that Macaulay herself regularly indulged in the sailing of toy boats, at least in her youth. *The Secret River,* pp. 39–41, and *The Furnace,* p. 228ff., contain similar episodes which may derive, like this one, from the scene which concludes chapter 33 of E. M. Forster's *The Longest Journey* (New York: Vintage/Random House, 1962 edition), p. 293.

50. Cf. Virginia Woolf, *Orlando,* chapter 1, pp. 37–38.

51. See pp. 14–15 of the Introduction.

52. *N.B.* This is Macaulay's spelling, for which there is a precedent in the *OED*.

53. Kuehn, *The Pleasures of Rose Macaulay,* p. 188. A Freudian interpretation would equate the "sea" which Denham leaves on her first exploration of the cave, and to the proximity of which she returns when she is pregnant (*C.T.,* p. 298), with "amniotic fluid"; would compare the "slimy . . . tunnel" through which she crawls with the "birth canal"; and would also accord to the "rock steps," the two chambers of the cave, the cottage, and other such images in *C.T.,* chapter 9, their standard Freudian equivalents. See Freud's *The Interpretation of Dreams* in *The Complete Psychological Works,* vol. 5, pp. 354–55, 400–401, 365, et passim.

54. Kuehn, Ibid.

55. The exception is Pamela Hilary of *Dangerous Ages,* whose lesbian life style is discussed in chapter 3, pp. 73–74.

56. Original title, *Keeping Up Appearances* (London: William Collins, 1928). American title, *Daisy and Daphne* (New York: Boni and Liveright, 1928). All page references are to the New York edition.

57. Constance Smith reports that, in childhood, Macaulay frequently played at having "twelve or thirteen children." *Rose Macaulay,* p. 35.

58. Smith, Ibid., pp. 159, 185, 200–201, et passim.

59. As demonstrated by her "reefer coat," *Daisy and Daphne,* p. 196.

60. In contrast, "Daisy had no stick with her," *D. & D.,* p. 54. Especially in the early novels, characters leaning on sticks for support or wielding them in self-defense are numerous. Just a few out of many examples are Daphne Oliver, in *The Making of a Bigot,* p. 87; Alix Sandomir in *Non-Combatants,* p. 5; and Imogen Carrington, of *Told by an Idiot,* p. 251. See above in this chapter, notes 22 and 38 and chapter 2, n. 19. Macaulay herself leans on a stick in Constance Smith's *Rose Macaulay,* photograph facing p. 176. So great a proliferation of sticks prods me to recommend that an article examining in detail Macaulay's use of these symbols would be desirable.

61. In *D. & D.,* pp. 250–51, Charles is depicted as "dead asleep after his orgy"—he has devoured an entire pot of jam—with "his head hanging outside" his bed, his face smeared with strawberry jam, and "a small empty pot" at his side. Coming upon this scene in Charles's bedroom, Cary picks up Charles's "cricket bat" and goes off to defend the household.

Similar Freudian symbols occur in *The Valley Captives,* where Laurie's castration is symbolized by, among other things, a broken tree branch. See *V.C.,* pp. 199ff. See also Laurie's "wobbling" "candle" on *V.C.,* p. 229.

Another notable castration symbol occurs when Peter Conolly pulls Charles Thinkwell's tooth—and subsequently marries the girl they have both been courting—in *Orphan Island,* pp. 259–60.

One of the rare phallic images in the novels which is *not immediately* also an image of sexual impotence is that of Nicky Chester who "stabbed into the soft, damp earth with his stick," in *What Not*, p. 148, during a tryst with the woman he later marries. However, Chester is symbolically castrated elsewhere in the novel, as explained in chapter 2, p. 45.

Cf. Sigmund Freud, *Interpretation of Dreams, Complete Psychological Works*, vol. 4, p. 186; vol. 5, p. 387n., pp. 366–67, et passim.

62. Kluge, "Die Stellung Rose Macaulays Zur Frau," p. 137.

63. Freud, *On Dreams, Complete Psychological Works*, vol. 5, p. 682. Cary confesses to Daisy that she has been reading "a book about dreams" by "A man called Frood," *D. & D.*, p. 195.

64. *Staying with Relations* (London: William Collins, 1930; New York: Horace Liveright). All references are to the London edition.

65. *N.B.* Belle, Claudia's stepmother, has made a similar marriage, *S. Rel.*, pp. 11–12, and the result is a family with five children.

66. *I Would Be Private* (London: William Collins, 1937; New York: Harper and Brothers). All references are to the latter edition.

67. Win's father and his second wife have four children, *W.B.P.*, p. 141. Constance Smith records that, in her childhood Macaulay, with four of her brothers and sisters, made up a group to which they and their mother continually referred as "the five." A sixth child, Eleanor, remained ostracized and unwanted, while a seventh, Gertrude, died at the age of three. *Rose Macaulay*, pp. 24–35.

68. *W.B.P.*, pp. 61–64, presents in jest the sort of adventures that *S.Rel.* portrays in earnest.

69. Her "flop hat, umbrella size," *W.B.P.*, p. 43, is also suggestive of an Arab male's *kaffiyeh*.

70. Gert applies this term ironically to Señor Monte, but it is equally applicable—in its ironic sense—to her.

71. Señor Monte has failed to divorce a wife he left in Venezuela. He marries Gert Grig in an Anglican ceremony on Papagayo Island. Elderly Mr. Grig has left a wife in England and, under an assumed name, has married a second wife on Papagayo Island. They are pillars of the local Anglican Church. Meanwhile, back in London, Mr. Grig's first wife, believing he is dead, marries a widower named Mr. Purdie, but it is not clear if the ceremony is a religious or a civil one.

72. Her sexually troubled sister Linda watches while she does so, *W.B.P.*, pp. 259–61. See also what is possibly Linda's symbolic castration of Dorothea on pp. 178–79.

73. Cf. *Orphan Island*, p. 24, and *The World My Wilderness*, pp. 91–92.

74. *T.b.I.*, pp. 251–52.

75. See *Non-Combatants*, pp. 29, 32–33, et passim, and *The World My Wilderness*, pp. 16, 218, et passim.

76. Margarete Kluge's terms for such a woman in "Die Stellung Rose Macaulays Zur Frau," p. 137, are "Die zeitlose Frau, der naturhafte Mensch."

77. See *M.B.*, p. 95.

78. "Una is eternal and sublime; . . ." *T.b.I.*, p. 126. See also Kluge, Ibid.

79. I.e., the three homosexuals discussed in chapter 2, pp. 60–63.

80. Cf. Rosamond's susceptibility to the charms of a "fallen" naval man in *O.I.*, pp. 43–44.

81. *W.B.P.*, pp. 176, 235, 150–51, 244, 129, 238.

82. "Louie" Robinson of *Views and Vagabonds* works in a mill, but she has left her job by chapter 3 of the novel to marry Benjamin Bunter. There is, moreover, nothing noticeably masculine about her, other than her nickname.

83. Arthur Conan Doyle, "A Scandal in Bohemia," in *The Complete Original Illustrated Sherlock Holmes* (Secaucus, New Jersey: Castle Books, 1976), pp. 15–16, 23–25. Cf. also the nameless lady "avenger" in "The Adventure of Charles Augustus Milverton," pp. 547–48, 550, and the "tall, graceful, and queenly" lady bicyclist in "The Adventure of the Solitary Cyclist," pp. 495ff.

84. *The World My Wilderness* (London: Collins, 1950; Boston: Little, Brown and Company). All references are to the latter edition.

85. Doyle, "Bohemia," p. 16.

86. See n. 42.

87. See also *W.W.*, p. 30.

88. See chapter 2, p. 43.

89. *Going Abroad* (London: William Collins, 1934; New York: Harper and Brothers). All references are to the latter edition.

90. See also *G.A.*, p. 294.

91. Macaulay herself perpetrated such a literary fraud, as explained in chapter 1, pp. 28–30, and notes 57 and 58.

92. Fish and fishing are important Christian symbols in *The Towers of Trebizond*, q.v.

93. *W.W.*, pp. 3, 5–7, 12–13.

94. Flanders, "The Fallen Woman," p. 11.

95. *Don Juan*, canto 1, stanza 63, ll. 7–8, quoted in *W.W.*, p. 237.

96. A catering to English parochialism—not evident in the novels in other than amatory matters—seems to be operating here. Likewise, the sexual transgressions of Betty Crevequer of *The Furnace* are possible because she is half Italian; while those of Eileen Le Moine of *The Making of a Bigot*, Alix Sandomir of *Non-Combatants*, and Helen Michel's daughter Barbary are understandable because they are half "Irish, and a little Hungarian" (*M.B.*, p. 91); half Polish; and half Spanish, respectively. Other instances can also be cited.

97. Statements regarding Fox quoted in this chapter have been derived from the article by Arthur Aspinall in *The New Encyclopedia Britannica, Macropaedia*, vol. 7, 15th edition, 1980, pp. 578–79, s.v. "Fox, Charles James."

98. Cf. Aspinall, Ibid., with *W.W.*, p. 192.

99. See also *W.W.*, pp. 187–88.

100. Aspinall, Ibid.

101. Aspinall, Ibid.

102. See this chapter, p. 109.

103. Aspinall, Ibid.

104. Emphasis added. See *W.W.*, pp. 5, 12, et passim.

105. Cf. chapter 1, p. 39 re Macaulay's recapitulation of Byron in a female descendant and her desire to recapitulate Coleridge in like fashion.

Chapter 5. "To Flirt with the Waiters in Restaurants"

1. Maria Jane Marrocco, "The Novels of Rose Macaulay—A Literary Pilgrimage." Unpublished Ph.D. diss., University of Toronto, 1978, p. 12.

2. Marrocco, p. 25.

3. *Abbots Verney* (London: John Murray, 1906).

4. *The Furnace* (London: John Murray, 1907).

5. *Views and Vagabonds* (London: John Murray, 1912; New York: Henry Holt and Company). All page references are to the New York edition.

In "The Ironic Aesthete . . . ," *English Literature in Transition* 9 (1966): 42, Alice

R. Bensen sees the Crevequer siblings as so securely joined to one another as to preclude the possibility of a genuine romantic involvement for Betty in *V. & V.*:

> The renunciation scene [between Betty Crevequer and Benjamin Bunter] is only sketched; Betty would not have been actually available in any relation other than that of a comrade— *she is too closely linked to her brother.* . . . (emphasis added)

6. *The Valley Captives* (London: John Murray, 1911; New York: Henry Holt and Company). All references are to the New York edition.

7. John is sturdy, square-jawed, laconic, calm, unimaginative, aggressive and brave when confronted with danger. Her chief interest in life is "practical farming." Teddy is slight, frail, weak, verbal, creative, high-strung, nervous, artistically inclined, and—generally—timid and retiring in the face of real or imagined peril. He is a frustrated artist.

Their stepsiblings, Cissie and Phil Bodger, are mutually complementary only insofar as they exhibit the stereotyped feminine and masculine mannerisms appropriate to their respective sexes. However, in other ways, they appear undifferentiated from one another.

8. This is evident in passages like the following:

> [Although a considerable distance now separated them,] John was very near to him somehow today—nearer than she had been for many weeks, perhaps for years. She was as near as when they had been children together, and had stood close in mutual alliance for self-defence and mutual comradeship for adventure. (See *V.C.*, pp. 281–282, 295–297.)

9. John deliberately attempts to kill her stepsister and herself in a carriage "accident." In an uncharacteristic act of heroism, Teddy jumps in front of the horse, grabs the reins, and saves his sisters' lives at the cost of his own. Symbolically, John's living blood then drips onto Teddy's battered and dead flesh. She twice accuses herself, "I've killed Teddy." See *V.C.*, pp. 305–307, 333–34.

10. See appendix D.

11. In *A Room of One's Own*, pp. 170–71, Woolf speculates:

> whether there are two sexes in the mind corresponding to the two sexes in the body. . . . If one is a man, still the woman part of the brain must have effect; and a woman also must have intercourse with the man in her. Coleridge perhaps meant this when he said that a great mind is androgynous. It is when this fusion takes place that the mind is fully fertilized and uses all its faculties. Perhaps a mind that is purely masculine cannot create, any more than a mind that is purely feminine. (Quoted in Herbert Marder's excellent *Feminism and Art*, p. 108, q.v.)

12. The novel was awarded first prize in a £1000 competition held by the publishing firm of Hodder and Stoughton. See Alice R. Bensen, *Rose Macaulay*, pp. 39–40, and p. 171, n. 11. See also Constance B. Smith, *Rose Macaulay* (1973 ed.), pp. 58–59. The newspaper headline cited by Smith—"YOUNG LADY NOVELIST WINS £1000 PRIZE"—was probably inaccurate. Insofar as I can decipher a partly illegible and not-too-clearly worded unpublished letter from Macaulay to Sidney Castle Roberts dated 4 August 1912 (in the Harry Ransom Humanities Research Center at The University of Texas at Austin) Macaulay's share of the prize money was apparently £600.

13. The Crevequer siblings exhibit a similar kind of "e.s.p." See *The Furnace*, p. 133.

14. If such, in fact, they truly are. See chapter 2, pp. 52–55, for an entirely different view of Peter's character and sexual orientation.

15. Most appropriately, in light of its theme, *What Not* (London: Constable, 1918), was ready for publication in November 1918, but the need to revise it in compliance with "one of the laws of the realm" delayed its appearance until March 1919. See *W.N.*, p. xi, n.

16. The idea may not seem so implausible to governments as it doubtless does to *What Not*'s readers. In February 1981, the Venezuelan government announced the creation of a cabinet level "Ministerio de Estado para el Desarrollo de la Inteligencia" ("Ministry of State for the Development of Intelligence") for the purpose of upgrading the intellects of the country's citizens, so that one of them might someday win a Nobel Prize.

17. See chapter 3, note 14, for Macaulay's use of this name and some of its variants.

18. The use of Macaulay's lover's first name for this hopelessly retarded man is yet another aspect of the revenge fantasy in this novel. See chapter 2, pp. 45–46, for a discussion of the "cathartic" aspects of *What Not*.

19. That the extremely able Chester will make a comeback is strongly implied at *W.N.*'s conclusion, pp. 230, 232, 235.

20. His private as well as his public actions demonstrate his phobia. For example, in boyhood Chester had experienced a strong desire to take his mentally feeble siblings "out into a wood and lose them" (*W.N.*, p. 186). Even on his honeymoon in Italy, Chester is capable of needless cruelty to a feeble-minded beggar (*W.N.*, p. 185).

21. See, for example, *W.N.*, pp. 162–63:

> What was it, . . . this quite disproportionate desire for companionship with . . . one person out of all the world of people and things, which . . . so perverted and wrenched from its bearings the mind of a man like Nicholas Chester . . . ?

22. *Potterism* (London: William Collins, 1920, 1950; New York: Boni and Liveright, 1920, 1921). *N.B.* At the time the section about this novel was originally written, the 1950 Collins edition provided page references. However, that same edition could not be retrieved when revisions were made and additional references were added. For this reason, part, chapter, and section numbers will be given in addition to page numbers with all references to the 1920 Boni and Liveright edition (specified as "B. & L., 1920"). All other page references in the text are to the 1950 Collins edition employed in writing the original draft of this chapter.

23. The action of *Potterism* is narrated from several different perspectives. Characters describe in turn what they know of the death of Oliver Hobart and the romance of Hobart's wife, Jane, with Arthur Gideon. In its conception the novel is highly reminiscent of Robert Browning's *The Ring and the Book*.

An unpublished letter written by Macaulay to a friend named Nora in 1920 asks concerning *Potterism:*

> Did you like the mystery part? That was for my brother, who said[,] "For goodness sake write a book in which they stop talking & commit a murder or something." Stop talking they didn't . . . but I did manage a kind of semi-murder, of which I am rather proud.

(The month in which this letter was written and the surname of Nora are still to be ascertained. Quoted by permission of the Harry Ransom Humanities Research Center at The University of Texas at Austin and A D Peters & Co Ltd.)

24. On "Tuesday 10 August," 1920, Virginia Woolf wrote (*Diary*, vol. 2, p. 57): " 'Potterism'—by R. Macaulay, a don's book, hard-headed, masculine, atmosphere of lecture room, not interesting to me—"

And, at some time late in October 1920, Woolf also described the novel scathingly to Hope Mirrlees (*Letters,* vol. 6, p. 497): "Poor dear Rose, judging from her works, is a Eunuch—thats [*sic*] what I dislike about Potterism [*sic*]. She has no parts. And surely she must be the daughter of a don?"

25. See *Potterism* ("B. & L., 1920"), part II, chapter I, section 1, pp. 47–48; part IV, chapter I, section 5, pp. 133–36, et passim.

26. In *A Room of One's Own,* pp. 120–21, Virginia Woolf mourns the waste of Charlotte Brontë's genius "in solitary visions over distant fields." Woolf also deplores "the isolated life of the semi-outcast" imposed on George Eliot, while, "At the same time," as Woolf points out,

> on the other side of Europe, there was a young man living freely with, this gipsy or with that great lady; going to the wars; picking up unhindered and uncensored all that varied experience of human life which served him so splendidly later when he came to write his books. Had Tolstoi lived at the Priory in seclusion with a married lady "cut off from what is called the world," however edifying the moral lesson, he could scarcely, I thought, have written *War and Peace. (A Room of One's Own,* pp. 122–23, quoted in Marder, op. cit., p. 70).

27. A subsequent Macaulay heroine, Daisy Simpson of *Daisy and Daphne* (1928), supports herself in part by writing

> periodic articles on one or another of those absorbing problems that beset editorial minds concerning the female sex and young persons, as, should women simultaneously rear young and work for their living . . . ? (See *D. & D.,* pp. 18–19, 86–88.)

Happily for Jane, she is assisted in the arduous task of combining homemaking and a career by a most unobtrusive pair of female servants (*P.,* p. 123). For a brief, representative discussion of this perennial dilemma see "The Superwoman Squeeze," *Newsweek* (May 19, 1980). A more recent and far more thorough treatment is Barbara J. Berg, *The Crisis of the Working Mother: Resolving the Conflict Between Family and Work* (New York: Summit Books, 1986).

28. However, in fairness to the young man, the reader should note his genuine concern for Jane's career plans immediately after the announcement of her engagement to Oliver Hobart (*P.,* p. 69). As with Jim Hilary in Macaulay's next novel, *Dangerous Ages,* Johnny's initial concern for his sister's career dissipates after she becomes a wife and a mother.

29. Johnny is a member of the adoring coterie of sycophantic young literary men who perpetually surround the chief editor of the *Weekly Fact.* Appropriately, this editor's name is "Peacock" (*P.,* pp. 65, 226, 235).

30. By the time Jane's novel appears, Johnny's is in its "second impression" (*P.,* p. 248).

31. Alice R. Bensen, *Rose Macaulay,* pp. 69, 71, 74–75. Whether she is studying chemical reactions or human interactions, Katherine doesn't seek to *alter* the phenomena she observes, but only to describe them as objectively and accurately as she can. For Katherine, human nature is "interesting, like other curious branches of study," but far more complex than a science like chemistry. This is because so many variables govern human behavior, and often these variables are unknown to the very people they most directly influence. See *P.,* pp. 147, et passim.

In her striving for absolute objectivity, as well as in her secret passion for Arthur Gideon, Katherine Varick is a self-portrait of Rose Macaulay.

32. The description is Arthur Gideon's. Gideon is, like Jane and Johnny, a member of the "Anti-Potter League" while at Oxford.

33. *P.,* p. 40, describes how

> In intervals of [wartime] office work and social life, Jane was writing odds and ends, and planning the books she meant to write after the war. She hadn't settled her line yet. Articles on social and industrial questions for the papers, she hoped, for one thing; she had plenty to say on this head. Short stories. Poems. Then, perhaps, a novel.

See also *P.*, p. 90, re Jane's impressive mental and elocutionary capabilities.

34. *Potterism* ("B. & L., 1920"), part I, chapter IV, section 3, p. 37.

35. Macaulay was also a temporary civil servant during the First World War. See Constance Smith, *Rose Macaulay*, pp. 83, 89, 91, 93. And cf. Sandra Gilbert's article, "Soldier's Heart," cited in the Introduction, note 28.

36. Emphasis added. See also *P.*, pp. 69, 72–74, 76–77, 88. Having made this and other similarly cynical observations about Jane, Arthur will succumb to love for her in his turn.

> I began to see . . . where Hobart came in. Jane wrote cleverly, clearly, and concisely—better than Johnny did. But, in these days of overcrowded competent journalism—*well it is not unwise to marry an editor of standing. It gives you a better place in the queue.* (*P.*, p. 83; emphasis added)

Jane's personal and professional relationships to Hobart and Gideon parallel Macaulay's involvement with Gerald O'Donovan, who became both her lover and her editor (Smith, *Rose Macaulay*, pp. 96–97). There is considerable self-parody in Macaulay's depiction of Jane's surrender to commercialism. As Macaulay writes in the "Letter to Nora" (cited in n. 23):

> Yes, the world is full of Potters—but, not being Gideon, &, in fact, being really one myself, I don't much mind—at least I do mind, but resignedly & without rancour. . . .

Alice Walker's Mr. Sweet Little, who "had been ambitious as a boy," and "wanted to be a doctor or lawyer or sailor," epitomizes the wasted career potential of those who can advance by none of the means adopted by the archetypal Jane. See "To Hell with Dying," in *In Love and Trouble: Stories of Black Women* (New York: Harcourt Brace Jovanovich, 1973), pp. 129–38.

37. *P.*, pp. 225, 242–43.

38. Arthur is in Russia, pursuing "truth" when he dies in a futile attempt to rescue a Russian Jewish family from a mob. His death—brought about jointly by two warring Russian factions (*P.*, pp. 254–55)—has parallels in the "accidental" deaths of Julian Conybeare in *The Shadow Flies*, and of Vere in *The Towers of Trebizond*. See pp. 144, 207 n.44.

39. The twins are depicted as being comparable to animals or small children in their excessive greed for recognition, achievement, and enjoyment. *P.*, pp. 13, 16, 28, 44, 74.

40. See n. 30.

41. Cf. Gloria Steinem, "The Trouble with Rich Women," *Ms.* 14, no. 12 (June 1986); 43:

> Most of the wealthy . . . [women] I heard so much about . . . turned out to be conduits for passing power to children, especially to sons and sons-in-law. . . . "If General Motors is going to pass through your womb," as one widow explained it, "they make damn sure you can't grab it on the way through."

42. When Jane has shifted onto Arthur many of her own ambitions, there is an ironic echo of this last sentence in Jane's thoughts about "her brilliant Arthur, who had his world in his hand to play with" (*P.*, p. 244).

43. Hobart is exceedingly handsome, cool, poised, graceful, and well-groomed, with a "second-rate" mind and a "flair" for the inaccuracies of popular journalism. By contrast, Gideon is dark, unattractive, graceless, and ill-mannered, excessively nervous and brilliant, with an absolute passion for observing, recording, and transmitting objective "truth."

44. Cf. Gerda's attempt to comprehend why men are attracted to prostitutes in *Dangerous Ages* (New York: Boni and Liveright, 1921), pp. 131–32.

45. *P.*, pp. 216–17. After Clare has been courted and jilted by Oliver Hobart, who marries Jane instead, Clare gives Hobart a shove that sends him down a steep flight of stairs to his death. Clare mourns hysterically for six weeks, confesses abjectly, and, a few months thereafter, "was beginning to fall in love with a young naval officer" (*P.*, p. 221).

46. Cf. Virginia Woolf's similarly mistaken view of Macaulay, quoted in n. 24.

47. George Bernard Shaw expatiated on "the life force" in several of his plays, most notably *Man and Superman* (1904).

48. Likewise, Eddy Oliver, in *The Making of a Bigot* (1914), can spend time alone with the "fallen" violinist Eileen Le Moine. However, Eddy's fiancée, Molly Bellairs, "cannot meet" Eileen, even when well-chaperoned, for fear of damage to her own reputation. "Your young man's got to be careful of you," Molly's aunt warns her. See *M.B.*, pp. 218–27.

49. See, for example, *P.*, p. 215, about the kind of girl who is expected to get engaged to Johnny, and the girl of the other kind whom "No one thought Johnny would marry."

50. *P.*, p. 185; emphasis added. For additional evidence of the all-too-obvious linkage of Jane's romantic life with her professional life see n. 36.

51. Arthur Gideon has a sudden perception of both

> Mother and daughter. It was very queer to me. That wordy, willowy fool, and the sturdy, hard-headed girl in the [speaker's] chair, with her crisp, gripping mind. Yet there was something....They both loved success. (*P.*, p. 90)

Chapter 6. "The Pattern and the Hard Core"

1. Chapter 3 discusses Ibsen's *A Doll's House* and its influence on *Told by an Idiot*.

2. See *Medea* in *Euripides: Plays*, trans. A. S. Way (New York: Dutton, reprint 1966), vol. 1, p. 43. The irony of this passage is sublime, since Medea herself possesses great supernatural powers, and yet is utterly helpless to preserve her own marriage when her husband decides to terminate it.

3. Ibid.

4. "Problems of a Woman's Life," in *A Casual Commentary* (London: Methuen, 1925; New York: Boni and Liveright, 1926), pp. 235–36. All references are to the New York edition.

5. Milton proclaims Adam and Eve, our archetypal first parents,

> Not equal, as their sex not equal seemed;
> For contemplation he and valor formed,
> For softness she and sweet attractive grace;
> He for God only, she for God in him.
>
> (*Paradise Lost*, 4.296–99)

Like Euripides, Milton acknowledges woman's inherent intellect and reason; however, he suggests that she should forget she was ever born with these attributes so as to provide Nature with more nurture and her husband with a more seductive object for his affections. Thus, when Eve perceives her husband "Ent'ring on studious thoughts abstruse," she goes off to tend the plants in

> Her nursery; they at her coming sprung,
> and touched by her fair tendence gladlier grew.
> Yet went she not as not with such discourse
> Delighted, or not capable her ear
> Of what was high: such pleasure she reserved,
> Adam relating, she sole auditress;
> Her husband the relater she preferred
> Before the Angel, and of him to ask
> Chose rather; he, she knew, would intermix
> Grateful digressions, and solve high dispute
> with conjugal caresses; from his lip
> Not words alone pleased her.
>
> (*Paradise Lost*, 8.46–57)

Misogynist inconsistencies in *Paradise Lost* are brilliantly pilloried in chapter 2 of Mary Wollstonecraft's *A Vindication of the Rights of Woman* (1742), reprinted in Sandra M. Gilbert and Susan Gubar, *The Norton Anthology of Literature by Women* (New York: W. W. Norton, 1985), pp. 143–145. Milton's view of women is examined passim in Jean H. Hagstrum, *Sex and Sensibility: Ideal and Erotic Love from Milton to Mozart* (Chicago: The University of Chicago Press, 1980). See especially p. 36 n.24. Rose Macaulay's obvious distaste for the misogyny of that view is dealt with in a lengthy and stimulating passage in Marrocco, "The Novels of Rose Macaulay," pp. 28–29 n.25. There are also discussions of Macaulay and Milton in chapters 1 and 2.

  6. This work is discussed at length in chapter 1.

  7. Alice Munro, "The Office," from the collection *Dance of the Happy Shades* (1968), reprinted in Michael Timko, ed., *Thirty-eight Short Stories: An Introductory Anthology*, second edition (New York: Knopf, 1979), pp. 395–406. The passage quoted is from p. 396.

  8. Ibid. See also p. 397.

  9. See chapter 5, pp. 118–27.

  10. *Dangerous Ages* (London: William Collins, 1921; New York: Boni and Liveright). All references are to the New York edition.

  11. See Maria Marrocco, pp. 27–29, who writes:

> *Dangerous Ages* is without a doubt Rose Macaulay's most extensive treatment of the problem of the ambiguous role of women. . . .
>
> Neville represents one facet of the limitations of being a woman, namely the inability to combine the physical satisfactions of marriage and child rearing with the intellectual achievements of . . . a . . . career.

A note to p. 28 goes on to make the point that "other limitations and frustrations" of women "are often referred to in the fiction," as well as in the nonfiction.

  12. Neville herself thinks that her involvements in marriage and children have caused her brain to "atrophy" (*D.A.*, p. 55).

  13. His comment apropos his own niece is symptomatic of this attitude:

> "Gerda," he remarked, "is a prettier *thing* every time I see her." (*D.A.*, p. 116; emphasis added)

14. Seven times in four pages, some form of the word "envy" is used in discussing Neville's feelings, "particularly" vis-à-vis Rodney (*D.A.*, pp. 14–15, 18–19). Maria Marrocco pp. 27–29, explains that Neville is "jealous" of Rodney with reference to some of the same passages quoted in this study.

15. There are, for example, her thoughts about her husband's political work:

> And his work Neville felt that she too could have done. . . . Neville at times thought that she too would stand for *parliament* one day. *A foolish, childish game it was, and probably really therefore more in her line than solid work.* (*D.A.*, p. 58; emphasis added; see also p. 19)

Likewise, thinking of her son's success in his studies Neville recalls that in her own days as a student

> she had worked . . . with pleasure and interest, and taken examinations with easy triumph. As Kay did now at Cambridge, only more so, because *she had been cleverer than Kay.* (*D.A.*, p. 55; emphasis added)

And, with the memory of how "She had easily and with brilliance passed her medical examinations long ago" ever-present in her mind, there is her "bitterness" at her brother "Jim's telling me how I shall never be a doctor," and her determination, "in the face of growing doubt, to prove Jim wrong yet" (*D.A.*, pp. 15, 113).

16. In *The Valley Captives* (1911), dedicated "To My Father," Oliver Vallon, the protagonists' father, attempts to force totally inappropriate careers on his children, largely on the basis of sexual stereotypes (*V.C.*, pp. 20–21, 26–27, et passim). See also chapter 1, pp. 26–27.

17. In *Crewe Train* (1926), discussed in chapter 4, love and pregnancy trap the strongly individualistic Denham Dobie into the role of suburban housewife and mother:

> Because she loved Arnold, she would go and live again as he lived . . . she would bear his child, tend and rear it, become a wife and a mother instead of a free person, be tangled in a thousand industries and cares. . . . (*C.T.*, p. 312)

18. In *Eight Cousins, or The Aunt Hill* (1875; New York: Dell ppbk. reprint 1986), Louisa May Alcott makes a muted but sustained protest against the inhibitory dress, unwholesome drugs and diets, and inane schooling that so undermined the young women of her day (as deliberately contrasted with the young men).

19. Chapter 5 provides some details of these romances.

20. In Jane's view of their respective professional merits,

> "Mother's merely commonplace; she's not even a byword—quite. I admire Dad more. Dad anyhow gets there. His stuff sells." (*P.*, p. 14)

21. The term *pis-aller* is not used by Macaulay in *D.A.*, but it is certainly applicable to Neville's unresolved life crisis. For discussions of Macaulay's purpose in using the term in her earliest fiction see Philip Rizzo, "Rose Macaulay," pp. 6–7, 11, 18, 31, and Robert Kuehn, "The Pleasures of Rose Macaulay," pp. 17–18.

22. For a more recent look at what psychologists call the "empty-nest syndrome," see Laurie Lucas, "Hatching a New Life in the Empty Nest," *Prevention*, Sept. 1980, pp. 166–170.

23. *D.A.*, pp. 31–32, 115, et passim. Both Mr. and Mrs. Hilary were suggested to Macaulay by her own parents. The novel is dedicated to Macaulay's mother, who

recognized herself in Mrs. Hilary and bitterly resented it. See Constance B. Smith, *Rose Macaulay* (1973 ed.), p. 98. It is also useful, when considering the influence of role models on Neville, to remember her intellectually gifted "Grandmama," with whom Neville enjoys a special closeness. As a wife, "Grandmama" immersed herself in her clergyman husband's pastoral concerns. As a widow, she has made an unpaid career of parish work for the past twenty years.

24. On *D.A.*, p. 111, Mrs. Hilary wonders,

> To have produced Jim—wasn't that enough to have lived for? Mrs. Hilary was one of those mothers who apply the Magnificat to their own cases. She always felt a bond of human sympathy between herself and that lady called the Virgin Mary, whom she thought over-estimated. (*D.A.*, p. 111)

25. After her nervous breakdown, Neville asks herself,

> "Why do I want to work and do something? Other wives and mothers don't....Or do they, only they don't know it, because they don't analyse [themselves]? I believe they do, lots of them." (*D.A.*, p. 185)

26. Gerda wins philanthropist Barry Briscoe's heart in part by working as a volunteer (and most inept) secretary-typist in his office. Barry had been courting Gerda's Aunt Nan, a free-spirited lady novelist with a successful career of her own. This love triangle is expounded upon in chapter 3, pp. 74–75.

27. *Journey from the North: Autobiography of Storm Jameson* (New York: Harper and Row, 1970), pp. 787–88. The remainder of the paragraph is intended by Jameson as a description of her own personal plight:

> She cannot be writer and woman in the way a male writer can be also husband and father. The demands made on her as a woman are destructive in a particularly disintegrating way— if she consents to them. And if she does not consent, if she cheats...a sharp grain of guilt lodges itself in her, guilt, self-condemnation, regret, which may get smaller, but never dissolves.

28. Alice R. Bensen, *Rose Macaulay*, p. 82.

29. When Mt. Vesuvius erupts—symbolic of the "crucible" or "furnace" by means of which life crises test one's ultimate values—only Betty's tie to her brother proves to be "gold" (*T.F.*, p. 175). All other individuals, her lover included, are perceived as "shadows" (*T.F.*, pp. 177–79, 181, 183).

30. These are, respectively, Tommy Ashe and Basil Doye. The latter is modeled on Macaulay's long-time friend, the poet Rupert Brooke. See Constance B. Smith, *Rose Macaulay*, pp. 70–71.

31. See *N.-C.*, pp. 15, 157–58, 164–65.

32. There are also "triplets" of this sort in *The Shadow Flies* and *The World My Wilderness*. See nn. 44 and 51.

33. I am deeply indebted to Brother Eldridge Pendleton, to Father Superior M. Thomas Shaw, and to the Society of Saint John the Evangelist for providing me with the texts of two heretofore unknown and uncatalogued letters written to Father Hamilton Johnson by Rose Macaulay on [14 or] 15 April 192[8?] and 19 July 1928. In both Macaulay expresses a wish to "come and see" her former—and future—confessor in Boston. In the 15 April letter she describes herself as "tremendously proud that you like my books," while in the 19 July letter she writes:

It was a great pleasure to get your letter. I am so very glad that you like "Daisy & Daphne" (called here "Keeping Up Appearances", but my American publishers thought D. & D. more "human," & they like things to be human).

All page references are to the American (Boni & Liveright) edition of *D. & D.*

34. Ironically, all the other principal characters in *D. & D.*—including, unbeknownst to Daisy, her own fiancé—are likewise leading double lives. However, Daisy is the only one to suffer public exposure and humiliation.

35. Appropriately enough, Macaulay chose as epigraphs to this novel Oliver Wendell Holmes's "Three Johns" from *The Aristocrat of the Breakfast-Table,* and the following from W. D. Howells:

We all have twenty different characters—more characters than gowns—and put them on or take them off just as often.

36. See chapter 1, n. 43.

37. See "Problems of a Woman's Life" (cited in n. 4), pp. 233, 236–38.

38. Macaulay's tendency to disclaim or downplay an overwhelming concern into a seeming disinterest is found not only in the several instances cited in chapter 1, but in the mental "black-out" she wrote that she'd had concerning receipt of the "Abbot Daniel" story which became the source of *Trebizond* (*Letters,* "8th April, 1951," and "24th April, 1951"). This tendency is also exemplified by comparing what she says in the "Foreword" to *The Shadow Flies* (1932), a historical novel set in the seventeenth century and meticulously researched in every detail, with what she writes to Father Johnson only a few years before. In the former she explains how she has

done my best to make no person in this novel use in conversation any words, phrases, or idioms that were not demonstrably used at the time [in the seventeenth century] in which they lived. . . .

While previously in the letter she had asserted

Yes, I love Pepys. But I would never dare to write a historical novel—it would need too much hard work & research to do it properly. Most writers don't do it properly, of course. (Unpublished letter dated "April [14 or] 15, 192[8?]" cited in n. 33)

Father Johnson's apparent suggestion that Macaulay should write a historical novel set in the seventeenth century may very well have ultimately resulted in *T.S.F.* A "Mr. Cowley" (perhaps the poet Abraham Cowley, 1618–67, but also the name of Father Johnson's Anglo-Catholic monastic order) fleetingly intervenes on *T.S.F.*, p. 402, to encourage Kit Conybeare in his Catholicism, but also to thwart the Jesuit priest "who would have spirited him off to a seminary."

39. The American title of *They Were Defeated* (London: William Collins, 1932, 1960, 1969) is *The Shadow Flies* (New York: Harper and Brothers, 1932). All references are to the New York edition in which see also pp. 221–26.

40. *T.S.F.,* pp. 178, 180. 343. See also p. 439.

41. *T.S.F.,* pp. 167–68, 310–11, 317, 342, 388.

42. *T.S.F.,* pp. 30, 48, 254, 316.

43. *T.S.F.,* pp. 283–84.

44. The love affair with John Cleveland destroys Julian's reputation, and she herself is accidentally killed by her angry older brother Francis, a Puritan and a lawyer, as he attempts to assault the man who wronged her. Kit's conversion to

Catholicism terminates his Cambridge career, and he becomes an exile in Paris "hanging on to the beggared English court" (*T.S.F.*, pp. 471–72, et passim).

45. Solely because she is a woman, Cleveland disparages her genius as a poet. English-born Anne Bradstreet (1612–72), author of "the first volume of poems written by a resident in the New World," sardonically depicts her own similar dilemma in "The Prologue," stanzas 5–7, reprinted in Nina Baym, et al., eds., *The Norton Anthology of American Literature*, second edition, Shorter (New York: W. W. Norton, 1986), p. 39. See also chapter 4 of Virginia Woolf's *A Room of One's Own* which reprints and expounds the lament of Lady Winchelsea (1661–1720):

> Alas! A woman that attempts the pen,
> Such a presumptuous creature is esteemed,
> The fault can by no virtue be redeemed.

46. *Going Abroad* (London: William Collins, 1934; New York: Harper and Brothers). All references are to the New York edition.

Giles departs for a tour of Spain on p. 106 and does not rejoin the action until it is virtually over, 199 pages later, on p. 305.

47. The pair also acts in tandem on *G.A.*, p. 17:

> The young brother and sister caught up their towels and sped from the terrace down into the road, and into the Irun omnibus, . . .

48. The following is the *only* reference to "Henry's" brother in the entire novel:

> In her loafing, idle and poor, about London, with her idle and poor brother and her Irish journalist lover, bitterness had grown more bitter. (*M.G.*, p. 242)

By comparison, the scant attention paid to the Irish journalist lover, shot in a Belfast riot, seems voluminous indeed (*M.G.*, pp. 242–44, 246–47).

Mystery at Geneva (London: William Collins, 1922; New York: Boni and Liveright, 1923). All references are to the New York edition.

49. *The World My Wilderness* (London: Collins, 1950; Boston: Little, Brown and Company). All references are to the Boston edition.

50. Maurice Michel, Raoul's widowed French father, married Helen Deniston, Barbary's divorced mother. The baby Roland is the product of that marriage. During the Occupation, "Papa" Maurice sheltered refugees from the Nazi terror, but he also transacted business with the Germans. Eventually, he was drowned by the maquis for "collaborating" with the enemies of France.

51. Barbary also has a "civilized" (half) brother, Richie Deniston, who acts toward her in the role of protector and counselor (*W.W.*, pp. 28–29, 38–40).

52. *W.W.*, pp. 48–57, 70, 173, et passim.

53. English statesman Charles James Fox (1749–1806) was a noted profligate until midway through the fifth decade of his life. Macaulay makes him a putative ancestor of Barbary's mother Helen Michel. For a discussion of Helen herself, see the concluding section of chapter 4.

54. The dissolution of civilization by savagery is a theme that permeates the book. Rose Macaulay, who describes Barbary as "an untaught savage" (*W.W.*, p. 82), is acutely alive to the allusiveness of her heroine's name. See *W.W.*, pp. 141, 242–44, et passim.

55. See also *W.W.*, pp. 6, 220.

56. *Raoul* is a French form of *Rudolph* (O. G., "famous wolf"), or *Ralph* (O. E., "wolf-counsellor").

57. *W.W.*, pp. 56–58, 70–74, 119, 177.

58. Such a fate is predicted for Barbary by Raoul's grandmother as she—symbolically!—sits "clicking her needles" and "netting" (*W.W.*, chapter 1, p. 14, et passim). See also *W.W.*, p. 201, and chapter 33.

59. At the time of her death, Rose Macaulay had begun work on another novel. Her notes are included as an appendix to Constance Smith's edition of Macaulay's letters to Jean Macaulay, *Letters to a Sister* (1964) and are discussed by Smith in *Rose Macaulay*, pp. 210–11.

60. Father Hamilton Johnson's English rendering of "De Abbate Daniele et Quadam Sanctimoniali," the sixth-century work that inspired *Trebizond*, is discussed at length in chapter 1 and reprinted as appendix A through the kindness of Father Superior M. Thomas Shaw, S.S.J.E. and the Harry Ransom Humanities Research Center at The University of Texas at Austin, where it is currently preserved.

61. Since Laurie travels freely and alone on camelback through some of the more primitive regions of the world, and since Vere prefers to be lapped in luxury, it is easy to assume (wrongly) that Laurie is the male of the pair.

62. Mark Bonham Carter, now Baron Bonham-Carter of Yarnbury, letter to Jeanette Passty dated "29th April, 1983." Used by permission.

63. All of her other fiction, without exception, employs third-person narrative.

64. *T.T.*, pp. 91, 184–85, 268–70.

65. Laurie paints "water-colour sketches to illustrate travel books: (*T.T.*, p. 10), while Vere tends "to lead a sportive life of pleasures and palaces, yachts and private planes, villas in France and castles in Italy" (*T.T.*, p. 269).

66. *T.T.*, pp. 91, 132, 137, 153, 157.

67. *T.T.*, pp. 66, 102, 116, 216.

68. *T.T.*, pp. 159, 170, 211.

69. T.T., pp. 116, 181, 183–85, 227–28, 239, 266, et passim.

70. *T.T.*, pp. 4–5ff. Cf. in "The Path to Home," *Times Literary Supplement*, 3 November 1961, p. 788, a number of passages in this vein:

> Rose Macaulay was bound to the Church of England by ties of heredity, of education, and of natural affinity, a threefold cord too strong for breaking. It is impossible to better her own description [in the *Letters*] of her position:
>
> You know I have always felt Anglican. I mean, I have been an *Anglo* agnostic; and even were I an atheist should be an *Anglo*-atheist. . . . For years I scarcely entered a church. . . ; but still I was an Anglo-non-church-goer. . . . I suppose this attitude would emerge in what I wrote. . . ; it is in the blood and bones, at deeper levels than brain or will.

71. Details of this spiritual conflict are revealed not only in Smith's biography and editions of the *Letters* and *Last Letters*, but in the *TLS* review of the *Letters* cited in n. 70 and in two other articles on the same. "*Rose Macaulay:* Letters to a Priest," *The Observer*, Sunday, 8 October 1961, pp. 21, 34, is outstanding in its use of excerpts and photos; "NOT FOR BURNING: [Review of] *Letters to a Friend*," *Time* 79, no. 11, (16 March 1962): 88 is far less favorable:

> Numerous notable literary lights were scandalized when *Letters to a Friend* was published in England last October. Said author Rebecca West: "It made me want to vomit." But according to Editor Babington-Smith, Father Johnson and Rose Macaulay's spinster sister, Jean, felt that the letters might be "of inestimable value and help to many." . . .
>
> It is difficult to see how. Their religious element is mostly discussion of erudite Anglican minutiae and spiritual snobbisms that are more likely to chill the unconverted than warm them.

This review also mentions briefly the "somewhat sexless quality" of Macaulay's "leading characters" as well as her "tendency to" assign them "first names that were appropriate to either man or woman."

72. This and four other lines from T. S. Eliot's *"The Rock" (Chorus I)*, is quoted by Macaulay on *T.T.*, p. 151.

Note also that in the very same letter in which she acknowledges receiving the third "Abbot Daniel" story from Father Johnson, Macaulay goes on to muse not only on "the Byzantine period," but on "the great 19th cent. [*sic*] novelists, such as George Eliot, whose chief characters are at perpetual war with themselves." In the same letter Macaulay also observes, "What one misses in most novels is a sense of right and wrong and the conflict between them" (Letter dated "21st March, 1951," in *Letters*, pp. 99–102).

73. Matthew Arnold's "Dover Beach," which depicts the "Sea of Faith. . . . / Retreating. . . ." is quite appropriately mentioned in this passage about the camel, since a recurrent theme of the novel is the conflict of the spirit with the flesh. Also appropriately, the camel is a female (*T.T.*, p. 131)—a clue to Laurie's sex. Another possible clue occurs a few chapters later when Laurie "spent the night . . . in a [n archaeological] digging with a large-size female statue" (*T.T.*, p. 207).

74. In 1939 she was apparently at fault in an automobile accident that nearly cost Gerald O'Donovan his life. Details are in Smith, *Rose Macaulay*, pp. 149–51. That Macaulay was tortured by guilt over this accident for the remainder of her life is attested to not only by Smith, but by Macaulay's contemporary, Naomi Mitchison (in a letter to Jeanette Passty dated 9 September 1985), who recalls how intensely "guilty for the car crash" Rose felt right up to the time of her own death in 1958.

75. See chapter 3, pp. 70–71.

76. Calling the novel "strongly autobiographical," Codaccioni, "L'échange dans *The Towers of Trebizond*. . . ," goes on to say that "Rose Macaulay . . . gets rid of Vere, and in this way, allows for the eventual return of Laurie to the bosom of the Anglican Church" (pp. 277–78). The English translation of this and all other citations to Codaccioni is courtesy of Ms. Nancy Revelette.

77. The indebtedness of Macaulay's *Trebizond* to "Abbot Daniel" and the affinities of much of her work, especially *Trebizond*, to Woolf's *Orlando*, are detailed in chapter 1 and also mentioned briefly in the Introduction. The similarities of *Mystery at Geneva* with "De Eunucho" are discussed in chapter 3, pp. 79–80.

78. Codaccioni, p. 279.

79. *TLS* article cited in full in n. 70. It is unfortunate that the anonymous writer of what otherwise seems a very fine review errs in saying that Macaulay wrote of St. Paul: "What a bore he was about women—all that anger and hate and scorn." Actually, Macaulay was *accusing John Donne* of the above *when he preached at St. Paul's Cathedral*. See the letter dated "14th January, 1951" in *Letters*, pp. 53–54.

80. Codaccioni, p. 271, et passim.

81. The letter dated "8th July, 1954" (*Last Letters*, pp. 159–60) tells of what Macaulay herself saw while traveling in Turkey and later expanded into sights and scenes in the novel which won her the James Tait Black Memorial Prize:

> Women [are] still muffled up to the eyes and mouths. . . . Women are being ill-treated, having been looked on as slaves for centuries; they walk while the man rides the donkey; they stay at home while the men eat out in cafés and restaurants; they are pushed aside in the scramble for tram seats (as I found—I never once got a seat) and almost pushed into the sea in the stampede for getting on to a boat. A shipwreck among Turks would be a poor time for women; none of them would ever get on to one of the boats. Nor have they (quite) souls. Nor may they eat with men: not even the Consul's wife in her own house when her husband has Turks to lunch. . . .

82. Emphasis added. Scholars with an interest in Islamic women will find a veritable gold mine in the "Special Issue: Women and Islam," *Women's Studies International Forum*, 5, no. 2 (1982), guest ed. Professor Azizah al-Hibri, Department of Philosophy, Washington University, St. Louis, Mo. I am greatly indebted to Professor al-Hibri for preprints of her work and for kind encouragement of mine.

Essential readings for students of "Islamic Herstory" also include:

Azizah al-Hibri, *Women and Islam* (Elmsford, New York: Pergamon Press, 1982).

Fatima Mernissi, *Beyond the Veil: Male-Female Dynamics in a Modern Muslim Society* (Bloomington: Indiana University Press, rev. ed., 1987).

Naila Minai, *Women in Islam: Tradition and Transition in the Middle East* (New York: Seaview/Harper & Row, 1981).

83. See *T.T.*, pp. 274–77.

84. Unpublished letter dated 19 July 1928. See n. 33.

85. See nn. 79 and 70.

86. Letter dated "17th December, 1955," in *Last Letters*, pp. 215–16.

87. Ibid.

88. Cf. St. Augustine, "The glorious city of God is my theme in this work . . . ," in *De Civitate Dei*, trans. Marcus Dods, reprinted in part as St. Augustine, *On the Two Cities: Selections from THE CITY OF GOD*, ed. F. W. Strothman (New York: Frederick Ungar Publishing Co., 1965), p. 1. Cf. also Edmund Spenser, *The Faerie Queene*, book 1, canto 10, stanzas 55–58 for a description of "The Citty of the Greate King. . . . / The New Hierusalem, that God has built." And cf. as well "the city. . . . the heavenly Jerusalem" described with assorted scriptural allusions in John Bunyan, *The Pilgrim's Progress*, ed. Catharine Stimpson, with an Afterword by F. R. Leavis (New York: Signet/New American Library, 1964), pp. 141–48.

After her return to the Anglican Church Macaulay writes in a letter dated "1st March, 1951," in *Letters*, p. 88: "having been re-admitted into the freedom of this *Civitas Dei*, I should like to behave like a good *civis*, so far as I can. . . ."

See also Codaccioni, p. 274.

89. See Constance Smith, *Rose Macaulay*, pp. 192–203 and see n. 70.

Afterword "Those Who Establish the Virtues of Writers"

1. T. S. Eliot, "Virginia Woolf," *Horizon: A Review of Literature and Art*, 3, no. 17 (May 1941): 313.

2. Rose Macaulay, Unpublished Letter to John Lehmann dated "20 Sept. '47" at the Harry Ransom Humanities Research Center, The University of Texas, Austin. Quoted by permission of The University of Texas and A D Peters & Co Ltd.

3. See chapter 4, n. 8.

4. See Virginia Woolf, *A Room of One's Own* (New York: Harcourt Brace Jovanovich, 1929, 1981), pp. 82–84:

> "Chloe liked Olivia," I read. And then it struck me how immense a change was there. Chloe liked Olivia perhaps for the first time in literature. Cleopatra did not like Octavia. And how completely *Anthony and Cleopatra* would have been altered had she done so. . . .
>
> Also, I continued, looking down at the page again, it is becoming evident that women, like men, have other interests besides the perennial interests of domesticity. "Chloe liked Olivia. They shared a laboratory together. . . ."

5. Woolf, p. 83.

6. See the entry dated "Saturday 27 March" in Virginia Woolf's *Diary*, vol. 3, pp. 70–71.

7. See the letter to Hope Mirrlees dated "end October 1920" in Virginia Woolf, *Letters,* vol. 6, p. 497.

8. Virginia Woolf's sarcasms at Macaulay's expense seem unrestrained and virulent in a letter to Vanessa Bell dated "Saturday May 25th [1928]" (*Letters,* vol. 3, p. 501). Yet on the very same page on which she excoriates Macaulay as, among other things, "a spindle shanked withered virgin," Woolf also mentions that she "had Rose Macaulay to dine alone." I am indebted to Jane Marcus for a discussion at The University of Texas at Austin, during Spring 1985, confirming my perception that, however much Woolf may have ridiculed Macaulay during the twenty-year period in which they knew each other, "Rose," as Marcus expresses it, "was essential to Virginia." Gloria G. Fromm convincingly demonstrates how "Rose Macaulay exercised more of an influence on Virginia Woolf than anyone has thought to suspect," in "Re-inscribing *The Years:* Virginia Woolf, Rose Macaulay and the Critics," *Journal of Modern Literature* 13, no. 2 (July 1986): 289–306.

9. See in Woolf's *Diary,* vol. 3, pp. 60–62, the entries for "Tuesday 23 February" and "Wednesday 24 February."

10. Alice R. Bensen's praiseworthy *Rose Macaulay* is discussed in the Introduction as part of a detailed survey of the scholarship to date.

11. The discovery of "De Abbate Daniele," the sixth-century source of *Trebizond,* is explained in chapter 1, but this by no means precludes other, similar discoveries; Macaulay was an extremely allusive writer.

12. Codaccioni's comparative study of novels by Macaulay and Muriel Spark will seem like strange fare to British and American scholars accustomed to the use of secondary sources. Nevertheless, it is a stimulating and perceptive article. (Full reference given in Introduction, n. 23).

13. See, for example, the section on E. M. Forster which concludes chapter 2.

14. See "Miss West, Mr. Eliot, and Mr. Parsons," Rose Macaulay's letter to the *Spectator* 149 (22 October 1932): 534–35, from which the epigraph to this study is taken.

Select Bibliography

I. Books by Rose Macaulay

References to Macaulay's writings are to the edition first listed, unless an asterisk denotes use of a subsequent edition.

NOVELS (IN CHRONOLOGICAL ORDER)

Abbots Verney. London: John Murray, 1906.

The Furnace. London: John Murray, 1907.

The Secret River. London: John Murray, 1909.

The Valley Captives. London: John Murray; *New York: Henry Holt and Company, 1911.

Views and Vagabonds. London: John Murray; *New York: Henry Holt and Company, 1912.

The Lee Shore. London: Hodder and Stoughton, 1912.

The Making of a Bigot. London: Hodder and Stoughton, 1914.

Non-Combatants and Others. London: Hodder and Stoughton, 1916.

What Not: A Prophetic Comedy. London: Constable, 1918.

Potterism: A Tragi-Farcical Tract. London: William Collins, 1920, *1950; New York: Boni and Liveright, 1920–21. Reprint. Darby, Pa.: Arden Library, 1978.

Dangerous Ages. London: William Collins; *New York: Boni and Liveright, 1921. Reprint. ppbk. New York: Carroll & Graf, 1986.

Mystery at Geneva. London: William Collins, 1922. *New York: Boni and Liveright, 1923.

Told by an Idiot. London: William Collins, 1923. *New York: Boni and Liveright, 1924. Reprints. Darby, Pa.: Arden Library, 1978; New York: Virago/Doubleday ppbk., 1983.

Orphan Island. London: William Collins, 1924, 1961. *New York: Boni and Liveright, 1925. Reprint. St. Clair, Mich.: Scholarly Press, Inc., 1971.

Crewe Train. London: William Collins; *New York: Boni and Liveright, 1926. Reprint. New York: Carroll & Graf, 1986.

Keeping Up Appearances. London: William Collins; American title, *Daisy and Daphne.* New York: Boni and Liveright, 1928.

Staying with Relations. London: William Collins Sons and Company, Ltd., 1930; Reprint. 1969 with an Introduction by Elizabeth Bowen. New York: Horace Liveright, 1930.

They Were Defeated. London: William Collins, 1932, 1960. American title, *The

213

Shadow Flies. New York: Harper and Brothers, 1932. American title Reprint. St. Clair, Mich.: Scholarly Press, Inc. 1972. British title Reprint. New York: Oxford University Press, 1986, paperback with an Introduction by Susan Howatch.

Going Abroad. London: William Collins; *New York: Harper and Brothers, 1934.

I Would Be Private. London: William Collins; *New York: Harper and Brothers, 1937.

And No Man's Wit. London: William Collins; *Boston: Little, Brown and Company, 1940.

The World My Wilderness. London: Collins; *Boston: Little, Brown and Company, 1950.

The Towers of Trebizond. London: William Collins, 1956. *New York: Farrar, Straus and Cudahy, 1956, 1957. New York edition still in print; also available in ppbk.

POETRY (IN CHRONOLOGICAL ORDER)

The Two Blind Countries. London: Sidgwick and Jackson, 1914.

Three Days. London: Constable, 1919.

Rose Macaulay. In *The Augustan Books of English Poetry.* 2d series, no. 6. Selections reprinted from the above two works, edited and with an Introduction by Humbert Wolfe. London: Ernest Benn, Ltd., 1927.

ESSAYS, LITERARY CRITICISM (IN CHRONOLOGICAL ORDER)

A Casual Commentary. London: Methuen, 1925. *New York: Boni and Liveright, 1926.

Catchwords and Claptrap. London: Hogarth Press, 1926.

Some Religious Elements in English Literature. London: Hogarth Press; New York: Harcourt, Brace, 1931. Reprints. Westport, Conn.: Greenwood Press, 1972 and St. Clair, Mich.: Scholarly Press, Inc., 1972.

Milton. London: Duckworth, 1934. *New York: Harper and Brothers, 1935. Reprint. New York: Haskell, 1974.

Personal Pleasures. London: Victor Gollancz, 1935. New York: Macmillan Company, 1936. Reprints. Darby, Penn.: Arden Library, 1978; Darby, Penn.: Darby Books, 1980. Facsimile 1936 edition available from Salem, New Hampshire: Ayer Co. Publishers.

The Writings of E. M. Forster. London: Hogarth Press; New York: Harcourt, Brace, 1938. Folcroft, Penn.: Folcroft Library Editions, 1974.

HISTORY, TRAVEL (IN CHRONOLOGICAL ORDER)

Life Among the English. London: William Collins, 1942.

They Went to Portugal. London: Jonathan Cape, 1946.

Fabled Shore: from the Pyrenees to Portugal. London: Hamish Hamilton; *New York: Farrar, Straus, 1949.

Pleasure of Ruins. London: Weidenfeld and Nicolson, 1953. New York: Walker, 1966. Reprint. ppbk. New York: Thames Hudson/W. W. Norton, 1984. Portions of this book provide the text for *Roloff Beny Interprets in Photographs PLEASURE OF RUINS by Rose Macaulay,* ed. Constance Babington Smith (New York: Holt, Rinehart and Winston, 1964; rev. ed., 1977).

ANTHOLOGY

The Minor Pleasures of Life. London: Victor Gollancz, 1934. New York: Harper and
Brothers, 1935.

PUBLISHED LETTERS

Letters to a Friend: 1950–1952. ed. Constance Babington Smith. London: William
Collins, 1961. New York: Atheneum, 1962.
Last Letters to a Friend: 1952–1958. ed. Constance Babington Smith. London:
William Collins, 1962. New York: Atheneum, 1963.
Letters to a Sister from Rose Macaulay. ed. Constance Babington Smith. London:
Collins, 1964. *New York: Atheneum.

II. Unpublished Letters and Papers

Unpublished letters and papers of Rose Macaulay and Father Hamilton Johnson
used in this study are from archives at the Harry Ransom Humanities Research
Center at The University of Texas at Austin, and the Society of Saint John the
Evangelist, 980 Memorial Drive, Cambridge, Mass.

III. Selected Miscellaneous Writings by Rose Macaulay (in chronological order)

"Woman, The Eternal Topic." *Living Age* 310 (17 September 1921): 734–36. Re-
printed from *The Outlook,* 6 August 1921.
"Orphan Island." *London Mercury* 10 (August 1924): 350–59.
"Human Beauty." *Saturday Review* 145 (2 June 1928): 692–93.
"Christmas Problem." *New Statesman and Nation* 36 (6 December 1930): supp. ix–x.
"What I Believe." *Nation* 133 (16 December 1931): 666.
"Hatreds and Manners." *New Statesman and Nation* 2 (5 December 1931): supp. viii.
"Word on Family Life." *Spectator* 148 (20 February 1932): 245–46.
"Miss West, Mr. Eliot, and Mr. Parsons." *Spectator* 149 (22 October 1932): 534–35.
"Returning to Horridness in Literature." *Spectator* 150 (10 March 1933): 329.
"Stella Benson." *Spectator* 151 (15 December 1933): 892.
"Past and Present: Have We Improved?" *Spectator* 153 (23 November 1934): 792–93.
"On Linguistic Changes." *Essays and Studies by Members of the English Association,*
vol. 20, pp. 108–22. Oxford: Clarendon press, 1935.
"Freedom: Not Much So Far." *Spectator* 155 (22 November 1935): 862.
"Lyly and Sidney." *English Novelists: A Survey of the Novel by Twenty Contempo-
rary Novelists,* pp. 33–50. ed. Derek Verschoyle. New York: Harcourt, Brace and
Company, 1936.
"Full Fathom Five." [Macaulay's "Auto-Obituary"] *Listener* 16 (2 September 1936):
434.
"Christianity and Communism." *Spectator* 157 (4 December 1936): 992.
"Eccentric Englishwomen." *Spectator* 158 (7 May 1937): 855–56.
"Cambridge Men." *Spectator* 165 (22 November 1940): 520–21.

"Virginia Woolf." *Spectator* 166 (11 April 1941): 394.

"Virginia Woolf," *Horizon* 3 (May 1941): 316–18.

"Losing One's Books." *Spectator* 167 (7 November 1941): 444.

"Miss Anstruther's Letters." *London Calling.* ed. Storm Jameson. New York: Harper and Brothers, 1942. Reprinted in Constance Babington Smith, *Rose Macaulay,* pp. 161–70. London: Collins, 1972, 1973.

"Book-Building After a Blitz." *Saturday Review of Literature* 25 (6 June 1942): 15–16.

"Trying to Understand Russia." *Spectator* 173 (6 October 1944): 313.

"Luther and Hitler." *Spectator* 174 (1 June 1945): 500.

"Future of Fiction." *New Writing and Daylight: By Various Writers,* pp. 71–75. ed. John Lehmann. London: Longmans, Green, 1946.

"Parson and Princess Caroline." *Cornhill Magazine* 163 (Summer, 1948): 207–20.

"Free Run of the Shelves." *New Statesman and Nation* 36 (4 December 1948): 487.

"In the Ruins." *Spectator* 183 (18 November 1949): 660–61.

"Ruin-Pleasure." *Spectator* 184 (30 June 1950): 883.

"Virginia Woolf." *The Golden Horizon.* ed. Cyril Connolly. London: Weidenfeld and Nicolson Ltd., 1953.

"Coming to London." *Coming to London,* pp. 155–66. ed. John Lehmann. London: Phoenix House Ltd., 1957.

"In Spain and Portugal." *Spectator* 198 (22 February 1957): 239.

"What Christmas Means to Me." *Twentieth Century* 162 (December 1957): 515–18.

IV. Relevant Books and Articles

BIOGRAPHY

Smith, Constance Babington. *Rose Macaulay.* London: Collins, 1972, reprinted 1973.

BIBLIOGRAPHY

Loveman, Amy. "Clearing House: Books and Magazine Articles About Rose Macaulay." *Saturday Review of Literature* 12 (7 September 1935): 17.

Rizzo, Philip Louis. "Rose Macaulay: A Critical Survey." Unpublished diss. University of Pennsylvania, 1959. Pp. xviii–xxix.

PUBLISHED PH.D. DISSERTATIONS

Brussow, Margot. *Zeitbedingtes in den Werken Rose Macaulays.* Griefswald, 1934.

Wahl, Irmgard. *Gesellschaftskritik und Skeptizismus bei Rose Macaulay.* Tübingen, 1936.

UNPUBLISHED PH.D. DISSERTATIONS

Rizzo, Philip Louis. "Rose Macaulay: A Critical Survey," University of Pennsylvania, 1959.

Kuehn, Robert Earl. "The Pleasures of Rose Macaulay: An Introduction to Her Novels." University of Wisconsin, 1962.

Marrocco, Maria Jane. "The Novels of Rose Macaulay: A Literary Pilgrimage." University of Toronto, 1978.

Passty, Jeanette N. "Eros and Androgyny: The Writings of Rose Macaulay." University of Southern California, 1982 (Substantially revised and published as the present volume).

CRITICISM, HISTORY, OR BIOGRAPHY RELEVANT TO THIS STUDY

Alaya, Flavia. *William Sharp—"Fiona Macleod," 1855–1905.* Cambridge: Harvard University Press, 1970.

Alexander, Sidney. "Aunt Dot's White Camel." *Reporter* 16 (13 June 1957): 46–48.

Allen, Walter. Review of *Letters to a Friend: 1950–1952. The New York Times Book Review,* 21 January 1962, p. 2.

Bazin, Nancy Topping. *Virginia Woolf and the Androgynous Vision.* New Brunswick, N.J.: Rutgers University Press, 1973.

Beach, Joseph W. *The Twentieth Century Novel: Studies in Technique.* New York: Appleton-Century, 1947.

Beauman, Nicola. *A Very Great Profession: The Woman's Novel 1914–39.* London: Virago, 1983.

Bensen, Alice R. "The Skeptical Balance: A Study of Rose Macaulay's *Going Abroad,*" *Papers of the Michigan Academy of Science, Arts and Letters* 48 (1963): 675–83.

———. "The Ironic Aesthete and the Sponsoring of Causes: A Rhetorical Quandary in Novelistic Technique." *English Literature in Transition* 9 (1966): 39–43.

———. *Rose Macaulay.* Twayne English Authors Series, no. 85. New York: Twayne Publishers, Inc., 1969.

Bowen, Elizabeth. *Collected Impressions.* London: Longmans Green and Company, 1950.

Braybrooke, Patrick. *Some Goddesses of the Pen.* London: C. W. Daniel Company, 1927.

Brown, Sharon, ed. *Essays of Our Times.* New York: Scott-Foresman, 1928.

Burra, Peter. Review of *I Would be Private. Spectator,* 19 February 1937, p. 328.

Cadogan, Mary, and Patricia Craig. *Women and Children First: The Fiction of Two World Wars.* London: Victor Gollancz Ltd., 1978.

Church, Richard. *Growth of the English Novel.* London: Methuen and Company, Ltd., 1957.

Codaccioni, Marie-José. "L'échange dans *The Towers of Trebizond* et *The Mandelbaum Gate,*" in Société des Anglicistes de L'Enseignement Supérieur, Échanges: Actes du Congrès de Strasbourg. Paris: Didier, 1982.

Connolly, Cyril. Review of *Keeping Up Appearances. New Statesman* 30 (31 March 1928): 796.

———. *The Condemned Playground: Essays, 1927–1944.* New York: The Macmillan Company, 1946.

———. *Ideas and Places.* New York: Harper and Brothers, 1953.

Dalgliesh, Doris N. "Some Contemporary Women Novelists." *Contemporary Review* 127 (January 1925): 82.

Dangerfield, George. Review of *And No Man's Wit. Saturday Review of Literature* 23 (14 December 1940): 6.

Davenport, John. "Talk with Rose Macaulay." *New York Times Book Review,* 21 April 1957, p. 14.

Dobrée, Bonamy, general ed. *Introductions to English Literature.* London: The Cresset Press, 1958. vol. 5: *The Present Age from 1920,* by David Daiches.

Drew, Elizabeth. *The Modern Novel: Some Aspects of Contemporary Fiction.* New York: Harcourt, Brace, and Company, 1926.

Ellis, Geoffrey Uther. *Twilight on Parnassus: A Survey of Post-War Fiction.* London: M. Joseph, 1939.

Evans, B. Ifor. *English Literature Between the Wars.* London: Methuen, 1948.

Furbank, P. N. *E. M. Forster: A Life.* New York: Harcourt Brace Jovanovich, 1978.

Gilbert, Sandra M. "Costumes of the Mind: Transvestism as Metaphor in Modern Literature." *Critical Inquiry* 7, no. 2 (Winter 1980): 391–417.

———. "Soldier's Heart: Literary Men, Literary Women, and the Great War." *Signs: Journal of Women in Culture and Society* 8, no. 3 (Spring 1983): 422–50.

———. "Life's Empty Pack: Notes toward a Literary Daughteronomy." *Critical Inquiry,* 11, no. 3 (March 1985): 355–84.

Gould, Gerald. "Some of Our Humorists." *Bookman* 67 (October 1924): 3.

Hobson, Harold. Review of *The Towers of Trebizond. Christian Science Monitor,* 11 October 1956, p. 6.

Inglishman, John. "Rose Macaulay." *Bookman* 72 (May 1927): 107–10.

Irwin, W. R. "Permanence and Change in *The Edwardian* and *Told by an Idiot.*" *Modern Fiction Studies* 2 (May 1956): 63–67.

Johnson, Reginald Brimley. *Some Contemporary Novelists (Women).* London: Leonard Parsons Press, 1920; Reprint. Freeport, N.Y.: Books for Libraries Press, 1967.

Kluge, Margarete. "Die Stellung Rose Macaulays Zur Frau. (Nach ihren Romanen)." *Anglia* 52 (June 1928): 136–73.

Krutch, Joseph Wood. Review of *Told by an Idiot. Nation* 118 (12 March 1924): 288.

Lawrence, Margaret. *The School of Femininity.* New York: F. Stokes Company, 1936.

Lehmann, John, ed. *Coming to London.* London: Phoenix House, 1957.

Littell, Robert. Review of *Keeping Up Appearances. New Republic,* 9 May 1928, p. 358.

———. Review of *And No Man's Wit. Yale Review* 30 (Winter 1941): viii.

Lockwood, William J. "Rose Macaulay." *Minor British Novelists.* ed. Charles Alva Hoyt. Carbondale and Edwardsville: Southern Illinois University Press, 1967.

Lovett, Robert Morss. Review of *Told by an Idiot. The New Republic,* 16 April 1924, pp. 211–13.

———. Review of *Crewe Train. The New Republic,* 20 October 1926, p. 253.

Mansfield, Katherine. Review of *Potterism. The Atheneum,* 4 June 1920. Reprinted in her *Novels and Novelists,* pp. 208–9. ed. J. M. Murry. New York: Knopf and Company, 1930.

Marble, Annie R. *A Study of The Modern Novel.* New York: Appleton-Century, 1927.

Marder, Herbert. *Feminism & Art: A Study of Virginia Woolf.* Chicago: The University of Chicago Press, 1968.

Millett, Fred. "Feminine Fiction." *Cornhill Magazine* 155 (January 1937): 225–35.

"Miss Macaulay's Novels." *Times Literary Supplement,* 12 May 1950, p. 292.

Morley, Christopher. "Herrick's Buttered Ale." *Saturday Review of Literature* 9 (29 October 1932): 205.

Nicolson, Harold; Lehmann, Rosamund; Pryce-Jones, Alan; MacDonald, Dwight; Kinross, Patrick; Wedgwood, C. V.; Carter, Mark Bonham; Powell, Anthony; Plomer, William; Cooper, Diana. "The Pleasures of Knowing Rose Macaulay." *Encounter* 12 (March 1959): 23–31. Reprinted in Constance Babington Smith, *Rose Macaulay,* pp. 223–36. London: Collins, 1972, 1973.

Nicolson, Harold. "Spanish Journey." *Observer,* 6 May 1949, p. 291.

"Not for Burning [Review of] *Letters to a Friend*—Rose Macaulay." *Time* 79, no. 11 (16 March 1962): 88.

Novak, Jane. "Literary Life in London with Special Focus on the Work and Life of Rose Macaulay." Unpublished study. University of Queensland, Australia, 1978.

O'Brien, Kate. Review of *And No Man's Wit. Spectator,* 21 June 1940, p. 844.

"The Path to Home." Review of *Letters to a Friend. Times Literary Supplement,* 3 November 1961, p. 788.

Patterson, Isobel. Review of *Going Abroad.* New York *Herald Tribune,* 20 August 1934, p. 9.

Peterson, Virgilia. Review of *The World My Wilderness.* New York *Herald Tribune Book Review,* 29 October 1950, p. 7.

Plomer, William. Review of *Going Abroad. Spectator* 153 (6 July 1934): 26.

Prescott, Orville. Review of *The Towers of Trebizond.* New York *Times,* 10 April 1957, p. 9.

Priestly, J. B. Review of *Told by an Idiot. London Mercury,* December 1923, p. 205.

Pryce-Jones, Alan. Introduction to *Orphan Island.* London: Collins, 1960.

Quigley, Isabel. Review of *The Towers of Trebizond. Spectator,* 7 September 1956, pp. 331–32.

Raymond, John. Review of *The Towers of Trebizond. New Statesman and Nation* 52 (29 September 1956): 383.

Review of *And No Man's Wit.* London *Times Literary Supplement,* 22 June 1940, p. 301.

Review of *Daisy and Daphne. Dial* 85 (July 1928): 72.

Review of *Daisy and Daphne. Nation* 127 (4 July 1928): 22.

Review (in verse) of *The Furnace. Punch,* 11 December 1907, p. 432.

Review of *Keeping Up Appearances.* The London *Times Literary Supplement,* 29 March 1928, p. 241.

Review of *Personal Pleasures. Literary Digest* 121 (8 February 1936): 27.

Review of *The Towers of Trebizond.* London *Times Literary Supplement,* 7 September 1956, p. 521.

Review of *The Towers of Trebizond. Time* 69 (15 April 1957): 133.

Review of *The Towers of Trebizond. New Yorker* 33 (1 June 1957): 116.

Review of *They Were Defeated. New Statesman and Nation* 4 (22 October 1932): 492.

Review of *The World My Wilderness*. London *Times Literary Supplement*, 12 May 1950, p. 292.

Rolo, Charles. Review of *The Towers of Trebizond. Atlantic Monthly* 199 (June 1957): 91.

"Rose Macaulay: *Letters to a Priest*," [Excerpts from *Letters to a Friend*]. *The Observer*, 8 October 1961, pp. 21, 34.

Rosenback, E. "Rose Macaulay." *N. Sprachen* 33 (1925): 200–206.

Sandrock, Mary. Review of *The World My Wilderness. Catholic World* 172 (December 1950): 233.

Sherman, Stuart. *Critical Woodcuts*. New York: Charles Scribner's and Sons, 1926.

Smith, Constance Babington. "Rose Macaulay in Her Writings" (Marie Stopes Memorial Lecture, read 1 March 1973) in *Essays by Divers Hands: Being the Transactions of the Royal Society of Literature, New Series*, vol. 38, ed. John Guest. London: Oxford University Press, 1975, pp. 143–58.

Spender, Dale. *Time and Tide Wait for No Man*. London: Pandora Press, 1984.

Stallings, Sylvia. Review of *The Towers of Trebizond*. New York *Herald Tribune Book Review*, 14 April 1957, p. 3.

Stevens, George. Review of *Going Abroad. Saturday Review of Literature* 11 (25 August 1934): 69.

Stewart, Douglas G. *The Ark of God: Studies in Five Modern Novelists, James Joyce, Aldous Huxley, Graham Greene, Rose Macaulay, Joyce Cary*. London: Carey Kingsgate Press, 1961.

Strong, L. A. G. "A Tour of Time and Place," *Spectator* 149 (22 October 1932): 558.

Sturgeon, Mary C. *Studies of Contemporary Poets*. Enlarged and revised edition. London: G. G. Harrap and Company, 1920.

Swinnerton, Frank. *The Georgian Scene: A Literary Panorama*. New York: Farrar, Rinehart Company, 1934. London: William Heineman, 1935. (Revised edition, London: Hutchinson & Co., 1969).

———. "Rose Macaulay." *Spectator* 184 (12 May 1950): 653.

———. "Rose Macaulay." *Kenyon Review* 29 (November 1967): 591–608.

Taylor, Roehel. Review of *Keeping Up Appearances. Spectator* 140 (24 March 1928): 477.

Thomas, Sue. "Women's Novels of the First World War: Rose Macaulay's *Non-Combatants* and *What Not* and Rebecca West's *The Return of the Soldier*." Unpublished paper. University of Queensland, Australia, n.d. [prob. 1984 or 1985].

Tindall, William Y. *Forces in Modern British Literature: 1885–1946*. New York: Knopf Company, 1947.

Webster, Harvey Curtis. *After the Trauma: Representative British Novelists Since 1920* (Lexington: University Press of Kentucky, 1970).

Wedgwood, Cicely Veronica. Introduction to *They Were Defeated*. London: Collins, 1960.

West, Anthony. Review of *And No Man's Wit. New Statesman and Nation*, 13 July 1940, pp. 46–47.

West, Rebecca. "*Views and Vagabonds* by Rose Macaulay" from *The Freewoman*, 21 March 1912. Reprinted in Jane Marcus, ed. *The Young Rebecca: Writings of Rebecca West 1911–17*. New York: Viking/Virago, 1982, pp. 25–28.

Witherspoon, Alexander. "Milton is Still Timely." *Saturday Review of Literature* 11 (27 April 1935): 646.

Woods, Katherine. Review of *And No Man's Wit*. New York *Times*, 27 October 1940, p. 6.

Woolf, Virginia. *Orlando*. New York: Harcourt Brace Jovanovich, Inc., 1928, 1956.

———. *A Room of One's Own*. New York and London: Harcourt Brace Jovanovich, 1929, 1957, 1981.

———. *A Writer's Diary*. London: Hogarth Press, 1930.

BOOKS CONTAINING BRIEF BUT USEFUL RANDOM REFERENCES TO ROSE MACAULAY

Farrell, M. J. (Molly Keane). *Devoted Ladies*. New York: Penguin Books–Virago Press, 1985, pp. 92–93.

Glendinning, Victoria. *Vita: The Life of V. Sackville-West*. New York: Alfred A. Knopf, 1983.

Hassall, Christopher. *Rupert Brooke: A Biography*. New York: Harcourt, Brace & World, Inc., 1964.

Jameson, Storm. *Journey from the North: Autobiography of Storm Jameson*. New York: Harper & Row, 1970. (vol. 1 reprinted, London: Virago, 1984, 1986; vol. 2 reprinted Topsfield, Mass.: Merrimack Pubs. Circle, 1986. (There are references to Macaulay in both volumes.)

Woolf, Virginia. *The Letters of Virginia Woolf*, ed. Nigel Nicolson and Joanne Trautmann, 6 vols. New York and London: Harcourt Brace Jovanovich, 1980.

———. *The Diary of Virginia Woolf*, edited by Anne Olivier Bell, 5 vols. 1984.

General Index

Cross-references to Index of Fictional Characters are indicated by (*char.*).

Abbot Anastasius: hermit in "Concerning a Eunuch," 79; really Anastasia, 80. *See also* Anastasia; "Concerning a Eunuch"

Abbot Daniel, 21–24; Abbot Anastasius receives communion from, 79; Anastasia's transvestism commended by, 80; ascendancy of, lost in monastery of women, 22–23, 40; in Father Johnson's translation of "De Eunucho," 79–80; in Father Johnson's translation of "Eulogius," 170 n.8, 172 n.28; nameless Disciple of, 21–23; reception of, by Church fathers, 22; says the Drinking Woman is dear to God, 24; third story about, reprinted with commentary and notes, 149–58; third story about, summarized and discussed, 21–24, 40. *See also* "Concerning a Eunuch"; "Concerning the Abbot Daniel"; "Eulogius the stone-cutter"

Aberystwyth, Wales: R.M.'s rustication in, 47, 57

Adcock, Arthur St. John: R.M.'s letter to, 11

Addison, Joseph: misogyny of, 30; quoted in *M.P.L.*, 30

Adler, Irene: beats Sherlock Holmes, 109; transvestite adventuress, 109

Alcott, Louisa May: undermining of young women protested by, 205 n.18

Alger, Horatio: Dorothea like a hero of, 109

Altick, Richard D., 194 n.28

Anastasia: founded a monastery, 80; transvestism of, a means of salvation, 79–80. *See also* Abbot Anastasius; Abbot Daniel

Androgynous mind: Coleridge's statement about, 12, 37; Peter Margerison a manifestation of, 52; R.M.'s, 12, 17, 42, 52, 147–48; *Orlando* a manifestation of, 12; *T.T.* a manifestation of, 12; Woolf's theory of, 37–39. *See also* Macaulay, Rose; *Orlando*; *A Room of One's Own*; Singer, June; Woolf, Virginia

Anthony and Cleopatra: reference to, in *A Room of One's Own*, 211 n.4

Antigone: sisterly devotion in, 178 n.72

Armistead, Mrs. Elizabeth: union of, with Charles James Fox, q.v., 112

Arnold, Matthew: "Dover Beach" by, quoted in *T.T.*, 144, 210 n.73

Aspinall, Arthur, 112

Aubrey, John, 37

Augustine, Saint: *The City of God*, 211 n.88

Barnes, Djuna, 11

Baron Bonham-Carter. *See* Bonham Carter, Mark

Baym, Nina, 208 n.45

Bazin, Nancy Topping, 12, 166 n.7, 179 n.76

Beauman, Nicola, 167 n.15, 169 n.28

Bell, Vanessa, 212 n.8

Benjamin, Harry, M.D.: describes concepts used to determine gender, 181 n.2

Bensen, Alice R.: assessment of R.M.'s poetry by, 176 n.56; book-length study of R.M.'s total output by, 14; calls disguise of Miss Montana "a game element," 76; calls Katherine Varick ",the author's raisonneur, 120; gives evidence for R.M.'s "impas-

Index of Fictional Characters

Abbé Dinant (*W.W.*): religious ideals of, 110–11

Alvarez, Pilar (*A.N.M.W.*), 174 n.36; obese, immobile, and vitriolic, 188 n.13

Arthur, Mrs. (*D. & D.*); Daisy's shame at and love for, 185 n.56; illegitimate daughter of, 137

Ashe, Tommy (*N.-C.*): physical appeal of, for Alix, 136, 206 n.30

Aunt Dot (Dorothea ffoulkes-Corbett; *T.T.*): militant feminism of, 145

Axe, Francis (*W.B.P.*), 60–61; aesthetic preferences of, 60–61; Dorothea Dunster earns accolades of, 108; homosexuality of, 60–61, 63–64; misogyny of, 60–61, 108

Beechtree, Henry (*M.G.*), 75–80; exposed as former lady secretary, 76; gratuitous brother of, 140, 208 n.48; reporter for *British Bolshevist*, 76, 78–79; transvestism of, gives her mobility, 76. *See also* Montana, Miss

Bellairs, Molly (*M.B.*): described as "sunny," "tomboyish," 108; fear of damage to reputation of, 203 n.48; Sturm und Drang period of, 108

Bendish, Gerda (*D.A.*), 71–72, 74, 129, 131; adverse example of mother of, 135; advocates polygamy, 74; ambiguous age of, 190 n.37; compared to Phoebus Apollo, 191 n.41; duel of, with aunt, 74–75; earns accolade of "sportsman," 75; marries without attempting college, 135; prostitution pondered by, 203 n.44; Rosamond Thinkwell a stockier version of, 91; uncle describes as a "pretty thing," 204 n.13; wins Barry Briscoe's heart and marries him, 75, 206 n.26

Bendish, Kay (*D.A.*), 71–72, 74, 129, 131; Cambridge studies of, 205 n.15; faints, 191 n.39; successful father an example for, 135

Bendish, Neville (née Hilary; *D.A.*), 129–31, 133–35; ambition and envy felt by, 72, 131, 205 n.14; androgynous behavior and description of, 71–72; athletic ability of, 71–72, 133; avocations and vocation of, not traditionally feminine, 72; birthday presents of, include pocket knife and bicycle, 72; broods on free love, 87; celebrates like Michael Travis, 71, 190 n.25; "comes a cropper" in brother's practice exam, 134; conscientiously wifely and maternal, 72; could be mistaken for boy-hero, 71–72; desire of, to work, 206 n.25; falls prey to "the life force," 135; feels unfulfilled by marriage and children, 129–31, 133; had been cleverer than Kay, 205 n.15; handicapped by social, biological, and psychological factors, 72, 134, 204 n.12; husband and children of, 129; life crisis of, 205 n.21; lovely, intellectually gifted wife of British M.P., 71; Macaulayesque masculine name and characteristics of, 71-72, 133; medical aspirations of, 72–73, 131, 205 n.15; nervous breakdown of, 72, 131, 134, 206 n.25; oral gratifications of, 190 n.25; represents limitations of being a woman, 204 n.11; role models for, 133–34, 206 n.23; sacrificed ambition to become a doctor, 71, 130; successor of Jane Potter, 133; thoughts of, about husband's political work, 205 n.15

Bendish, Rodney (*D.A.*), 133, 205 nn. 14–15; Neville jealous of, 205 n.14;

aic, 43; serves as incitement to Platonic rapture, 43; sexual sharing of, by Michael and Jim, 44, 55

Chantry-Pigg, Fr. Hugh (*T.T.*): admonishes women to be careful, 146; highly bigoted, 145

Chapel, Arnold (*C.T.*): Denham trapped by love of, 205 n.17; feminine qualities of, 100; Audrey Gresham admired by, 98; marriage of, to Denham Dobie, 65, 100–102; streamside love scene with Denham precedes Orlando's and Sasha's, 101

Chester, Gerald (*W.N.*), 116; hopelessly retarded brother of Nicholas, 200 n.18

Chester, Joan (*W.N.*), 116–17, imbecilic twin sister of Nicholas, 116–17

Chester, Maggie (*W.N.*): normal sister of Nicholas, 116

Chester, Nicholas ("Nicky"; *W.N.*): abhorrence of feeblemindedness by, 116, 200 n.20; cathartic aspects of story about, 45–46, 200 n.18; derivation of name of, 183 n.22; desire of, for one person, 200 n.21; extremely able, 200 n.19; imbecilic twin sister of, 116–17; marriage of, to Kitty Grammont, 116–17; orignator of Ministry of Brains, 116; represents Gerald O'Donovan, 45; stick used by, is a phallic image, 197 n.61

Cleveland, John ("Jack" *T.S.F.*): Francis Conybeare's attempted assault on, 207 n.44; disparages Julian, 208 n.44; at gathering of Cambridge poets, 59; Giles is a foil and adversary to, 138; invents malicious story concerning John Milton, 59; seducer of Julian, 139–40; "sharing" of, by brother and sister, 140; tutor and protector of Christopher, 139–40; wronged Julian, 207 n.44

Conolly, Peter (christened "Nogood"; *O.I.*): boyfriend of Flora Smith, 93; Hindley half in love with, 57; symbolic castration of, rival by, 146 n.61

Conybeare, Christopher ("Kit"), 138–40; aspect of R.M.'s androgynous personality, 140; becomes an exile, 208 n.44; central role of, 138, 140; conversion of, to Catholicism, 207–8 n.44; encouraged by Mr. Cowley,

207 n.38; intrigue of, with church, 139; likenesses of, to sister, 139; pupil of Cleveland, 139

Conybeare, Francis (*T.S.F.*): accidentally kills sister, 207 n.44

Conybeare, Julian ("July"; *T.S.F.*), 58–59, 138–40, 174 n.36; accidental death of, 202 n.38, 207 n.44; acted the Lady in *Comus*, 58; aspect of R.M.'s androgynous personality, 140; envies men's opportunity for study, 139; erotic appeal of, in brother's clothes, 140; excels brother, 139; gifted poet and scholar, 58; has much in common with father, 195 n.46; heroine of *T.S.F.*, 139–40; object of tutor's carnal desire, 139–40; physical and temperamental likenesses of, to brother, 139; poetic genius of, disparaged, 208 n.45; use of, to point out limitations on women, 138

Cowley, Mr. (*T.S.F.*): allusive name of, 207 n.38; intervenes to encourage Kit, 207 n.38

Cradock, Belle (*S. Rel.*): marriage and stepchildren of, 197 n.65

Cradock, Benet (*S. Rel.*): Benet had more confidence than sister Claudia, 107

Cradock, Claudia (*S. Rel.*): Benet had more confidence than, 107; Catherine Grey in love with, 194 n.22; love affair of, with married man, 104; misrepresented as a virgin, 104; resemblance of, to R.M., 104; sheds light on Cary Folyot, 104

Cradock, Meg (*S. Rel.*): boyish preoccupations of, 107; contrasted with Dorothea Dunster, 107; physical and mental weakness of, 107; stress and exhaustion of, 108; sturdy body of, 107

Crevequer, Betty (*T.F., V. & V.*): and brother are "as two twin babes," 113; close linkage with brother precludes romantic attachment of, 199 n.5; heroine of *T.F.*, 113; in a gypsy cart, 184–85 n.52; in Italy, 135; life companionship of, with Tommy, 116; minor character in *V. & V.*, 114; physical and spiritual oneness of, with brother, 113–14, 199 n.13; pseudo-artistic ca-